DOSTOEVSKY
IN LOVE

DOSTOEVSKY IN LOVE

AN INTIMATE LIFE

ALEX CHRISTOFI

BLOOMSBURY CONTINUUM
LONDON · OXFORD · NEW YORK · NEW DELHI · SYDNEY

BLOOMSBURY CONTINUUM
Bloomsbury Publishing Plc
50 Bedford Square, London, WC1B 3DP, UK
29 Earlsfort Terrace, Dublin 2, Ireland

BLOOMSBURY, BLOOMSBURY CONTINUUM and the Diana logo are
trademarks of Bloomsbury Publishing Plc

First published in Great Britain 2021

A catalogue record for this book is available from the British Library

Library of Congress Cataloguing-in-Publication data has been applied for

ISBN: HB: 978-1-4729-6469-4; eBook: 978-1-4729-6470-0;
ePDF: 978-1-4729-6471-7

2 4 6 8 10 9 7 5 3 1

Typeset by Deanta Global Publishing Services, Chennai, India
Printed and bound in Great Britain by CPI Group (UK) Ltd, Croydon CR0 4YY

MIX
Paper from
responsible sources
FSC® C020471

To find out more about our authors and books visit www.bloomsbury.com
and sign up for our newsletters

Such an autobiography as yours might serve as material for a future work of art, for a future picture of a lawless bygone age. When the angry strife of the day has passed, and the future has come, then a future artist will discover beautiful forms for depicting past lawlessness and chaos . . . They will preserve at any rate some faithful traits by which one may guess what may have lain hidden in the heart of some raw youth of that troubled time.

The Adolescent

CONTENTS

KEY DATES

The dates in this book are in the Julian 'old style', which was 12 days behind the Gregorian 'new style' calendar used by western Europe at the time. I have indicated the Gregorian date in parentheses, in references to letters sent from Europe.

30 October 1821	Fyodor Mikhailovich Dostoevsky born, Moscow.[1]
27 February 1837	Fyodor's mother, Maria Fyodorovna Dostoevskaya (née Nechaeva), dies.
16 January 1838	Enters the Engineering Academy.
6 June 1839	Fyodor's father, Mikhail Andreevich Dostoevsky, dies.
October 1844	Resigns from the Engineering Academy.
15 January 1846	*Poor Folk* published in Nikolai Alexeevich Nekrasov's *Petersburg Miscellany* (*Petersburgsky Sbornik*).
1 February 1846	*The Double* published in *Notes of the Fatherland* (*Otechestvennie Zapiski*).
23 April 1849	Arrested for treason.
22 December 1849	Mock execution.
15 February 1854	Released from prison in Omsk.
6 February 1857	Marries Maria Dmitrievna Isaeva in Kuznetsk, Siberia.
December 1859	Moves to St Petersburg.
January 1860	First issue of the journal *Time* (*Vremya*), published in collaboration with his brother Mikhail Mikhailovich.

1860–1862	*Notes from the House of the Dead* published in *Russian World* (*Russky Mir*) and *Time* (*Vremya*).
1861	*The Insulted and Injured* published in *Time*.
24 May 1863	*Time* suppressed by government censors.
August–October 1863	Travels in Europe with Apollinaria ('Polina') Prokofievna Suslova.
24 January 1864	Receives permission to publish his journal under the name *Epoch* (*Epokha*).
1864	*Notes from the Underground* published in *Epoch*.
15 April 1864	Maria dies in Moscow.
10 July 1864	Mikhail dies in Pavlovsk.
Spring 1865	*Epoch* folds.
1866	*Crime and Punishment* is published serially in *The Russian Herald* (*Russky Vestnik*).
4 October 1866	Anna Grigorievna Snitkina begins work as Dostoevsky's stenographer.
15 February 1867	Marries Anna.
14 April 1867	Travels to Europe to escape creditors.
1868	*The Idiot* is published serially in *The Russian Herald*.
8 July 1871	Returns to St Petersburg.
1871–2	*Devils* is published serially in *The Russian Herald*.
1873	The first articles in *A Writer's Diary* are published in the magazine Dostoevsky is editing, *The Citizen* (*Grazhdanin*).
1875	*The Adolescent* is published serially in *Notes of the Fatherland* (*Otechestvennye Zapiski*).
1876	*A Writer's Diary* appears as its own publication.
1879–80	*The Brothers Karamazov* is published serially in *The Russian Herald*.
8 June 1880	Delivers memorial speech at the unveiling of the Pushkin monument in Moscow.
28 January 1881	Dies of emphysema.
1 February 1881	Funeral held in St Petersburg.

AUTHOR'S NOTE*

Why bother writing a book about Dostoevsky? In most portraits, he looks like a grumpy Saint Nicholas (and incidentally, he did spend one Christmas night riding across Russia in an open sleigh). He was such a contrarian that members of both the liberal left and the reactionary right were forever convinced that he was working for the enemy. Unlike many modern readers, he was a deeply committed Orthodox Christian, though he was famously eloquent about spiritual doubt. I know some people find the length of his four best-known novels imposing; perhaps others accept that he was a great philosopher, but don't have the patience for his insistent style, with its repetitions and digressions. He himself admitted, just as he was completing the first of his four great novels: 'I have been painfully aware for twenty years now that my literary vice is *prolixity*, but I can't seem to shake it off.'[2] All in all, he could be an exasperating man, and yet it seems to me that many of his ideas remain disconcertingly relevant today: the importance of understanding that autonomy and dignity are more precious to us than the rational self-interest of economists; that more people are killed by bad ideas than by honest feeling; that a society with no grand narrative is vulnerable to political extremism. He took great pains to understand the angry young men who were threatening to topple Russia and the rest of Europe in his lifetime, perhaps because he remembered what it was like to be one of them. More than anything else, Dostoevsky was a deeply moral writer, and he refused to turn a blind eye to the suffering he saw among the slaves

---

*I'll keep it short: as Dostoevsky says, 'Everyone knows what authors' prefaces are like . . .' (*Devils*, p. 499)

(for that is effectively what serfs were), the outcasts, the prostitutes, the humiliated, the sick and the silenced of his day. He was fiercely devoted to raising up the downtrodden and giving them a voice. And so, although I will be writing about Dostoevsky as a lover and a husband, I will also be writing about a broader, more inclusive kind of love, which he believed was the only possible answer to suffering in this world.

Aside from his writings, he had one of the most eventful lives of any novelist in history. He was a gambling addict and an epileptic, constantly on the brink of financial and physical ruin. As a young man, he was tried as a socialist revolutionary and narrowly survived a death sentence; yet by the end of his life he was being invited to dine with the Tsar's family and hailed as a national prophet. He was at different times an engineer, a soldier and a poet. He had an impressively turbulent love life. It wouldn't be a stretch to argue he was a foot fetishist (though Russia has a long tradition of symbolic foot-kissing). The way he proposed to his second wife is so quietly bashful that you can't help wanting to hug him. Sadly, many of those he was closest to, from friends to lovers to family members, died far too young.

Dostoevsky's autobiography would have been fascinating, and he had intended to write one. On Christmas Eve 1877, the twenty-eighth anniversary of his journey to Siberia, Dostoevsky wrote a four-point 'memo for the rest of my life', dividing his remaining years into four projects, the third of which was to write his memoirs. He estimated these would take him at least ten years, 'and I am already fifty-six'.[3] Sadly, his pessimism on this front was well founded, and he died before he could begin. However, the ghost of his autobiography is already present in his writings, and even his first biographer takes the trouble to note the biographical value 'in subjective passages scattered throughout his novels'.[4]

Undoubtedly his most powerful writing was drawn from his lived experience, whether recounting the quasi-mystical experience of an epileptic fit in *The Idiot* or hard labour in a Siberian prison in *Notes from the House of the Dead*. This book therefore cheerfully commits an academic fallacy, which is to elide Dostoevsky's autobiographical fiction with his fantastical life in the hope of creating the effect of a reconstructed memoir. *(The fact is, this is neither a story nor a memoir.)*[5] Indeed, I am not an academic, and if you are looking for a biography that never crosses such a line, there are already a number in print, not least Joseph Frank's wonderful five-volume intellectual biography, published between 1976 and 2002. At the other end of the spectrum, novelists such as Leonid Tsypkin and J. M. Coetzee have already written novels which vividly imagine the writer's inner life. My aim is to explore whether a synthesis is possible – a tale both novelistic and true to life, representing Dostoevsky in his own words. Because Dostoevsky's overarching project was to understand how people thought – the sometimes maddening ways we explain and deceive ourselves – and to represent that thought faithfully so that others might know themselves better.

To be clear, where I have used artistic licence, I have set some ground rules. Anything in quotation marks is a direct quote reported by Dostoevsky or one of his contemporaries and is cited in the notes. Similarly, the main narration is based on contemporaneous accounts and the work of trusted scholars, owing a particular debt to Anna Dostoevsky, Joseph Frank, Leonid Grossman, Kenneth Lantz and Peter Sekirin. Anything in italics – that is, anything written in the intimate first person and represented as his thought – might have been taken from his letters, notebooks, journalism or fiction. *At one point he talks to himself; then he seems to be addressing an invisible listener, a judge of some sort. But that's how it happens in real life.*[6] When writers conceive fiction, they often shear memories off from their context to use them as the building blocks of their new world. It is a kind of wilful source amnesia. By carefully parsing what is known of Dostoevsky's life, it is possible to re-attribute many of the memories and sense impressions that litter his fiction, and to give some insight into his habits of thought. *(There's a whole new approach waiting to be discovered. The psychological data alone are enough to point to the real trail. 'We've got facts!' they say. But facts aren't everything; knowing how to deal with the facts is at least half the battle.)*[7] Where I have ventured to attribute this inner life to a timeline, I have paraphrased, combined and abridged what

Dostoevsky wrote to fit the context, and cited the original for those who are interested. Where there are differing accounts of an event, I have generally opted for the version that Dostoevsky himself told. Because the self is only a story that we tell ourselves to make sense of our own actions, and that, in the end, is what I am determined to recover.

Well, that is the end of my introduction. I quite agree that it is superfluous, but since it is already written, let it stand.

And now to business.[8]

Prologue: Life is a Gift

1849

TODAY, 22ND OF DECEMBER, *after eight months of solitary confinement, I was taken with five others to the Semyonovsky Parade Ground.*[9]

Fyodor's friend, Sergei Durov, was standing next to him. There were three posts stuck in the ground.

'Surely we cannot be executed,' Fyodor whispered.[10] Durov indicated a cart nearby, on which there appeared to be several coffins covered with cloth.

Fyodor turned to his other companion, Nikolai Speshnev. 'We shall be with Christ,' he muttered in French.[11] But Speshnev only smiled and pointed at the ground.

'A handful of dust,' he replied.

The sentence of death was read to all of us, we were told to kiss the cross, our swords were broken over our heads, and we were put into white shirts.[12]

Then the first three – Petrashevsky, Mombelli and Grigoriev – were led up, tied to the pillar for execution, and caps were pulled over their eyes.[13] *A company of several soldiers was drawn up against each post. I was in the second batch and there was no more than a minute left for me to live.*[14] *I wanted to understand as quickly and clearly as possible how it was that I was living and in moments I would simply be a thing.*[15] *Not far off, there was a church, and the gilt roof was glittering in the bright sunshine. I stared persistently at the roof and the sunshine. I could not tear myself away from it.*

I had not expected that the execution would take place for at least a week yet – I had counted on all the formalities taking some time – but they got my papers ready quickly.[16]

At five in the morning I was asleep, and it was cold and dark. The governor came in and touched my shoulder gently, and I started.

'What is it?' I asked.

'The execution is fixed for ten o'clock,' he said.

I was only just awake, and couldn't believe it at first – I began to ask about my papers. But by the time I was really awake and saw the truth of the matter, I fell silent and stopped arguing, as I could see there was no point. The governor watched me. All I could say was, 'It's very hard to bear – it's so sudden.'

Those last three or four hours pass by in the preparations. You see the priest, have your breakfast – coffee, meat, even a little wine. The priest was there the whole time, talking. You get in the cart and the houses recede – but that's nothing.[17] *There is still the second turning. There is still a whole street, and however many houses have been passed, there are still many left. And so to the very end, to the very scaffold. At the most terrible moments of a man's life, he will forget anything but some roof that has flashed past him on the road, or a jackdaw on a cross.**

The most terrible part of the punishment is not the bodily pain, but the certain knowledge that in an hour, then in ten minutes, then in half a minute, your soul must quit your body and you will no longer be a man, and that this is certain – certain![18] *That's the real point: the certainty of it. A murder by sentence is far more dreadful than a murder committed by a criminal. If you are attacked at night, in a dark wood, you hope that you may escape until the very moment of your death. But in an execution, that last hope is taken away, and in its place there is only the terrible certainty that you cannot possibly escape death. It is the most dreadful anguish there is. Our Lord Christ spoke of this anguish. No one should be treated this way – no one.*

---

* *The Brothers Karamazov*, trans. Garnett, p. 810. Standing in the watching crowd was a seventeen-year-old in a tricorn hat named Alexander Egorovich Wrangel, with whom Dostoevsky would shake hands five years later, in a place known as the Devil's Sandbox.

The priest, who seemed a wise man, stopped talking when we reached the drill grounds, and only held the little silver cross for me to kiss. My legs felt feeble and helpless, and I felt a choking in my throat. I had that terrible feeling of being absolutely powerless to move, though I hadn't lost my wits. The priest pressed the cross to my lips, and I kissed it greedily, as if it might be useful to me afterwards. In that last minute, I remembered my brother; only then I realised how I love him![19]

Finally the retreat was sounded, and those tied to the pillar were led back, and it was announced to us that His Imperial Majesty had granted us our lives.

My life begins again today. I will receive four years' hard labour, and after that will serve as a private. I see that life is everywhere, life in ourselves. There will be people near me, and to be among people – that is the purpose of life, I have realised. The idea has entered my flesh and blood. Yes, it's true! I have beheaded my lofty, creative, spiritual self. There are many ideas I haven't yet written down. They will lacerate me, it is true! But I have my heart and flesh and blood which can also love, and suffer, and desire, and remember, and this, after all, is life.

When I look back and think how much time has been wasted in vain, how much time lost in delusions, in errors, in idleness, in ignorance of how to live, how I did not value time, how often I sinned against myself – my heart bleeds. Life is a gift, life is happiness, each minute might have been an age of it. Youth is wasted on the young! Now, I am being reborn into a new form.

But I have begun my story, I don't know why, in the middle. If it is all to be written, I must begin at the beginning.[20]

ONE

White Nights

1821–1845

T HERE ARE ONE OR *two things I can remember from childhood,*
but in a dreamlike fashion.[21]

Fyodor had been born in the Mariinsky Hospital for the Poor,
a large state hospital in Moscow, where his father was a doctor.
Originally from a line of clergy, Mikhail Andreevich Dostoevsky
had left his family in Ukraine some years earlier to study medicine
and worked with the single-minded purpose of establishing
himself and his family. Having risen through the ranks as a military
doctor, he had arranged to marry Maria Fyodorovna Nechaeva, the
daughter of a merchant, in 1819. A year later, their first son Mikhail
was born, and on 30 October 1821, their second son, Fyodor
Mikhailovich Dostoevsky.*

The couple had seven children in total,† all crammed into a tiny
apartment on the hospital grounds: Mikhail and Fyodor behind a
little partition; their oldest sister Varvara on the couch, and the little
ones strewn variously around their parents' bedroom as a traditional
prophylactic.

The young Fyodor was an energetic, curious child, constantly
talking to strangers and wandering off to explore, only to be gathered
up by his doting mother. *I remember huge trees near the house – lime*
trees I think they were – then sometimes the brilliant sunshine at the

---

*The second part of Russian names, the patronymic, is an indication of the father's
name. So all of Mikhail's boys were Mikhailovich, and the girls Mikhailovna.
† Their fifth child Vera also had a twin, who had suffered a cot death.

open windows, the little flower garden, the little paths, and you, mother. I remember clearly when I was taken to the church, and you held me up to receive the sacrament and kiss the chalice; it was in the summer, and a dove flew through the cupola, in one window and out the other.[22]

Dr Dostoevsky saved as much of his salary as he could, taking on private patients out of hours. When Fyodor was seven, his father was awarded the Order of St Anna for 'especially zealous service', which now officially put the Dostoevskys in the ranks of the hereditary nobility, albeit on the bottom rung. They hired staff – a coachman, cook, maid, and a nanny, who was quite tall and so fat that her stomach almost reached her knees. Once, the nanny caught a cough and claimed to have consumption; the young Fyodor found the idea of her wasting away extremely funny.

Apart from Sundays, when Maria would play guitar to her children, the early days blurred into one another. Their life in Moscow ran by clockwork. Wake at six; lessons at eight; lunch at one; two hours of silence while father took his nap, and one of the little ones shooed flies away from his face with a lime branch. Dinner; prayers; bed. The two older boys would sometimes play games with the children of patients or staff in the hospital gardens, and Fyodor would strike up conversations with adults even though he knew he wasn't allowed.*

When they were let out of the grounds at all, it was for a quick walk in the early evening, on the rare occasion that the weather was mild enough. More often than not, they would look out of the window at the poor, sick people drifting around the courtyard in their camel-coloured gowns, or beg the nanny to read them a story. She would whisper to them in the darkened room, so as not to disturb the parents: tales from *One Thousand and One Nights*, or Bluebeard. Fyodor was rapt. *I began reading avidly, and soon I was*

---

*A curious hearsay account of this period turned up later. According to the Soviet scholar Sergei Belov, Zinaida Trubetskaya overheard Dostoevsky recounting in the late 1870s how he used to play with a dainty nine-year-old girl who was the daughter of a cook or coachman, and who liked to show him flowers. One day, a drunk raped her, and she died of blood loss before Dr Dostoevsky could save her. *Woe to him who offends a child!* (*The Brothers Karamazov*, p. 353)

entirely absorbed in books. All my new cravings, my ambitions, the still vague impulses of adolescence, suddenly found a new outlet. Soon my heart and mind were so enchanted, and my imagination was developing so widely, that I seemed to forget the whole world which had surrounded me until then.[23] He read whatever he came across: at first it was a collection of stories from the Old and New Testament; later it would be Charles Dickens and Nikolai Gogol. Fyodor loved the contemporary poet Alexander Pushkin most of all, reading his poems over and over, poring over them with Mikhail and memorising whole chunks by heart.

Now that Dr Dostoevsky was one of the gentry, he was allowed to own land, and the family took on heavy debt to buy a small estate called Darovoe, a day's ride from Moscow, along with the small hamlet of Cheremoshnia next to it. The estate only numbered a hundred souls, and the land was not particularly fertile, so that most years the peasants barely harvested enough to feed the livestock,* but for a young boy whose whole world had consisted of an urban compound of poor, sick people, Darovoe was a paradise. Each spring, from the age of nine, Fyodor's mother and siblings would pile into the coach and he would take the coachman's seat, and they would leave Dr Dostoevsky behind for the calm and safety of the countryside, where the children could run around all day playing games, watched over by the peasants. One such game was 'horsies', which entailed the young masters of the house pulling together teams of peasant children, racing these 'horsies' along the road, and feeding them table scraps. In the evenings, the Dostoevsky children would help shell peas while the damp wood crackled in the hearth, and before bed, Fyodor would write out a note politely requesting that, if he died in the night, they wait a few days to bury him, in case he woke up.[24] *Everything, everything comes back so clearly. Thinking back, I could weep.*

The house stood on a hill, and beneath it, next to a grove of linden trees and birches, Maria created a large pond. From that

---

* At that time the size of estates was counted by the number of male serfs or 'souls' who were tied to the property.

first summer, Fyodor spent so much of his time here that it came to be known as Fedya's Grove. *How fresh it used to seem, yet how cold! Lights would be beginning to shine in the huts at the pond's edge, and the cattle would be wending their way home. Above, the sky would be a cold blue, save for a fringe of flame-coloured streaks on the horizon.*[25] There was nothing he loved more than this place full of mushrooms and wild berries, beetles, hedgehogs and squirrels, and the smell of damp wood. It was almost silent here, lending epic proportions to the slightest disturbance, whether the fluttering of a frightened bird, a bulrush rubbing against its neighbour in the breeze, or a fish nibbling at the surface of the pond. Across the water there would sometimes gather a thin mist, flattening shapes, the trees loitering in the depths like formless giants. But the point of a paradise is that it is lost, and this memory – of safety, security, exploration, games, a loving mother – was all the sweeter for its brevity.

One dry, bright, windy day at the end of that first summer, Fyodor's peace was shattered by a voice shouting: 'Wolf!'

Terrified, the little nine-year-old sped out of the copse towards the only adult he could find, a serf named Marko Efremov who had been ploughing the field thirty paces away. Fyodor grabbed at his sleeve and told him breathlessly about the wolf. The peasant scanned the field and the forest, then smiled at Fyodor indulgently.

'You're imagining things,' he said reassuringly.[26]

Poor Fyodor was deathly pale and trembling, and the peasant reached out to stroke his cheek. Although he was a burly man of fifty with grey hair salting his beard, he was as tender as a mother. It began to dawn on Fyodor that he must have been hearing things, even if he couldn't shake the impression it had made on him. The peasant made the sign of the cross over Fyodor, and then himself, and stood there watching over him while Fyodor walked back to the house, nodding encouragingly until he was out of sight. *If I had been his own son, he could not have looked at me with such love. What had prompted him to do that? He was our serf, and I his master's little boy.*[27]

That was the last time Fyodor saw the estate intact. On the third day of Easter week, 1832, the family was sitting around the table in Moscow, having tea, when one of the peasants from Darovoe burst in.

'What's wrong?' asked Dr Dostoevsky. 'What is it?'[28]

'The estate has burned down.'

In preparation for the festivities, a serf named Arkhip Saveliev had decided to do a hog roast on Good Friday. But it had been a windy day and the flames had blown against his hut, spreading onto the straw, and from there to the entire estate.

When they went to see the damage, the snow was falling in big wet flakes, melting as it touched the earth. The huts were blackened shells, half of them so badly burned that only the support beams were left standing. *As we drove in, there were peasant women drawn up along the road, a lot of women, a whole row, all thin and wan, with their faces a sort of brownish colour, especially one at the edge, a tall, bony woman who looked forty, but might have been only twenty, with a long thin face. And in her arms was a little baby crying. And her breasts seemed so dried up that there was not a drop of milk in them. And the child cried and cried, and held out its little bare arms, with its little fists blue from cold.*[29]

Both the doctor and his wife saw it as a punishment from God. Maria gave each of the peasants 50 roubles, sinking the family further in debt.* They rebuilt with difficulty. The barn and the granary had burned to the ground, so they didn't even have enough seed for sowing. In the lean years that followed, the peasants would remove the thatch from their roofs to feed the starving animals. Dr Dostoevsky's mood darkened. He worried aloud about Fyodor's mischievous side, telling him that if he wasn't careful he'd end up wearing the red hat of a Siberian convict. The doctor was particularly hard on his two eldest boys, who were now attending boarding school in preparation for their future careers as military engineers. *Every day he grew more morose and discontented and irritable; every*

---

* At the time, you could rent an expensive apartment in St Petersburg for a year for about 450 roubles, and there are 100 copecks in a rouble. In the second half of the nineteenth century, skilled artisans earned an average of 117 copecks a day; unskilled workers 71 copecks a day; and agricultural workers 30 copecks a day. See 'Wages and prices in Imperial Russia', *The Russian Review*, 69:1 (January 2010), pp. 47–72.

day his character kept changing for the worse.[30] On the weekends, when they returned from boarding school, he would stand them by the table to decline their Latin verbs and, if either of them made the slightest mistake, Dr Dostoevsky would explode with rage. *I could not bear the thought that one of the two people I so longed to love did love me and treated me kindly, while the other intimidated me.*[31] The boys were not allowed to go anywhere alone, they were not allowed to bring friends home, and they did not receive pocket money.

The doctor's bitterness and jealousy permeated the household. *Whenever I got home from school I would find everyone low-spirited, and my mother shedding silent tears, and my father raging.*[32] The doctor complained bitterly to his wife that Darovoe was being badly run, that he was being passed up for official recognition, that he was wasting so much money on the boys' education, that the peasants deserved flogging. When he discovered that Maria's brother was carrying on an affair with one of their maids, he slapped his brother-in-law in the face and banned him from ever setting foot in their apartment again. *How he could treat my poor mother so I cannot understand. It used to rend my heart to see how hollow her cheeks were becoming, how sunken her eyes.*[33]

Maria grew thinner and thinner, pained by coughing and yet desperate to cough. It soon became clear that she had tuberculosis, a disease which progressed slowly, but had no cure.* By late 1836, Maria's hair was cropped and her skin sallow. She was forever out of breath. *Ominous red spots burned on her cheeks, and her lips were parched from fever.*[34] Fyodor and the other children would keep her company, reciting her favourite poems to cheer her up.

Maria was confined to her room and soon there was no longer any hope of recovery. The doctor, who had been visiting every day, stopped attending. Maria called for the icon to be brought to her, and blessed the whole family while they wept. *I went to mother, lay down*

---

* The stately pace of deterioration and the comely pallor it brought on made tuberculosis the preferred coup de grâce among the Romantics: Lord Byron once said that 'I should like to die from consumption'. He later died from a fever made worse by doctors who insisted, against his pleas, on letting his blood with unsterilised instruments.

beside her, hugged her in my arms and said nothing. Mother hugged me, too, and asked no questions. I looked at her, but she seemed not to see me – she only held my hand tight in hers. I softly pulled away.[35] She died at seven o'clock on the morning of 27 February 1837, at the age of 37. *I closed my eyes, and saw her face with quivering lips. She crossed herself facing the church, and afterwards made the sign of the cross over me.*[36]

Dr Dostoevsky agonised over Maria's death. He locked himself in his room, talking aloud to his dead wife, headbutting the wall and moaning. Only alcohol temporarily quelled his despair. Not a man given to literary flourishes, he instructed Mikhail and Fyodor to find an epitaph for their mother's gravestone. They chose a line from the poet Nikolai Karamzin: 'Lie here, beloved dust, until the joyful dawn.'[37] In the midst of their grief, news reached Moscow that Alexander Pushkin, by now recognised as Russia's greatest poet, had been shot dead in a duel, and so, in the immediate aftermath of Maria's death, the whole nation was in mourning.

You will never know, mother, how I loved you then! Mother, where are you now? Do you hear me? Mother, mother, do you remember the dove in the church?[38]

There was nothing left for Fyodor and his older brother in Moscow. Two of their younger siblings were sent to live with their uncle and aunt, and the older boys were expected to go to the military academy to study as engineers in the hope that, one day soon, they might supplement the family's anaemic income. And so, little more than a month after his mother died, at fifteen years old Fyodor packed his belongings and they began the 700-verst journey to St Petersburg.* *I looked around for the last time, feeling sick at heart and full of misgivings about the harsh and hostile future that might be waiting on the road.*[39]

The weather was warm, that May. The three of them travelled at a leisurely pace, without changing horses, and would spend two or

* A verst is just over a kilometre.

three hours at each coach stop. *I recall how weary we finally became of the journey, as it dragged on for almost a week. My brother and I were eager to enter a new life and were prone to dreaming of 'the beautiful and the sublime' (the phrase was fresh then and spoken without irony). We had agreed that when we arrived in St Petersburg, our first stop would be the scene of Pushkin's duel, and we would look for his former apartment in the house on the Moika.*[40]

One afternoon, they stopped to rest the horses at a posting station in Tver. As Fyodor sat at the inn, looking out of the window at the station building, a troika pulled up and a government courier jumped down.* He was tall and well built, with a purplish face. He ran into the station to knock back a glass of vodka while the young driver threw his coat over his arm and got into another carriage with fresh horses. As he did so, the courier flew down the steps, jumped into the carriage and started punching the back of the driver's neck. The startled driver, in his turn, whipped the poor shaft horse with all his might. The horses started, but that did nothing to appease the courier: he raised his terrible fist over and over, punching the back of the driver's neck as hard as he could, and the driver in turn, barely clinging on, lashed out at the horses until they were out of sight. The government beat its servants, just as the servants beat the animals. *This disgusting scene stayed etched in my memory as a symbol of cause and effect. Every blow that rained down on the animal was the direct result of every blow that fell on the man. If I should ever found a philanthropic society I would make this courier's troika the society's seal, as an emblem and an admonition.*[41]

They soon arrived in St Petersburg. At its centre was the Palace Square, home of Tsar Nicholas I, from which power and influence rippled outwards concentrically. There, at the heart of the city, were the three seats of Russian Imperial power: the Admiralty; the Winter Palace; and a huge cathedral that was still under construction.

---

*The Russian carriage was traditionally harnessed in a troika formation with three horses abreast. They were driven so that the front horse would trot while the two side horses cantered, apocryphally to keep wolves at bay, and could reach speeds of 30 mph. The Russian horse whip (*nagaika*, нагáйка), a thick leather braid ending in a leather or even metal ball, also doubled as a defence against wolves.

In the middle of the square stood a column bearing the statue of Tsar Alexander I, a single 600-ton monolith that had been raised to celebrate victory over Napoleon. Nearby was a bronze equestrian statue of the city's namesake, Peter the Great, nicknamed 'The Bronze Horseman' after a famous narrative poem by Pushkin. If there were any lingering doubt that this statue stood in for the might of the Russian Empire, it had been raised on a granite pedestal known as the Thunder Stone: the largest single block of stone ever moved by humans, it weighed well over a thousand tons, and had been dragged six versts by 400 men over the course of nine months.

If the Palace Square was the heart of the city, the artery that supplied its lifeblood was Nevsky Prospect, running south-east towards the Alexander Nevsky Monastery. It was here that members of society would take their afternoon stroll, officers jostling with literati, shopkeepers and the endless green uniforms of civil servants. Towards the top of Nevsky Prospect were the accumulated delights of Europe, *parfumeries*, *Buchhändlerin* and *barbieri* jostling with signs in Cyrillic. In the morning, the street was filled with the smell of freshly baked bread as the old women came out in their rags to beg alms; but it remained quiet until midday, when the tutors and governesses would come out with their wards, correcting their posture. From two o'clock, the avenue blossomed into colour, as clerks finished up their business and couples walked arm in arm, the women in their finest gowns and the men sporting distinguished whiskers, some stopping for tea or to read a newspaper. The further you ventured away from the palace, the more the veneer of civilisation broke down until, eventually, you would find yourself among little huts and workshops, warehouses and sheds. In the dead of night, passers-by might be treated to the uncommon sight of prostitutes, in their silk dresses and jewellery, with feathers in their hats, being made to sweep the pavements by a detachment of police constables.

The great critic Vissarion Belinsky once observed that the court was a city within the city, a state within the state. But by the time Fyodor arrived, there were other ripples of influence originating elsewhere in the city: the literary circles formed around people like Belinsky, which would meet and discuss ideas that could never be committed to print. *It is indeed a well-known fact that the whole of Petersburg is nothing but a collection of an enormous number of small 'circles', each with its own constitution, laws, logic and oracle. It comes from our national character, which is a little shy of social life and prefers to stay at home.*[42] But it would be some years before Fyodor's spectacular entrance into the Belinsky circle, and his equally rapid fall from grace.

Having been built by decree, St Petersburg was a Europeanised and strangely artificial city, nothing like the Slavic Moscow that Fyodor knew. *It is the most theoretical and intentional town on the whole terrestrial globe.*[43] It was so new that in places it was still under construction; when he arrived, Russia's first railway was being completed, running from Semyonovsky Square to Tsarskoe Selo outside the city. It was an incredible time to be studying buildings, with the city changing all around him, including some of the most ambitious architecture in the world. The Winter Palace, recently restored after a major fire, boasted 1,057 rooms, 117 staircases, 1,945 windows and 1,786 doors. *I don't know if I am right, but I always imagined Petersburg as the spoiled younger son of a highly respectable father, a man belonging to a past age. His son gets a smattering of high life, acquires European airs and grows a moustache.* Papa is horrified, aware only of the moustache and of his son's helping himself freely to the money in his father's capacious pocket and observing, too, that his son is a bit of a freethinker and an egoist. But his son wants to live and he is in such a hurry that one can't help wondering where he gets all his energy from.*[44]

Mikhail was refused entry to the famous Engineering Academy at Mikhailovsky Castle on the grounds that he had tuberculosis, and so he went on to a less picky academy in Revel.† Fyodor had a hoarse voice from a chest infection he'd picked up before they set out, but was pronounced healthy and accepted in St Petersburg. He didn't receive a scholarship to cover his fees as his father had hoped – to get one of those, you had to offer lavish bribes.

---

* Fyodor could not yet grow a moustache.
† Now Tallinn.

Although there was an emphasis on academic excellence, the Academy still ran along the lines of a military school. Alongside their lectures, the students practised fencing, dancing, singing and, of course, endless marching. For his father's sake Fyodor applied himself to his studies, but in his spare time he read Hoffmann, Scott, de Quincey, Schiller, Hugo, Balzac and Pushkin (always Pushkin). When a new George Sand novel was published, he sat up all night reading it in a fever of excitement.

Very much a poet in engineer's clothing, Fyodor still understood how much appearance meant to his peers and how closely it would be read. He was barely considered a gentleman as it was. *I am afraid of one thing only: gossip. My enemies, all those wicked tongues, what will they say when they see me without a greatcoat? I mean, it's for other people that you go around in a greatcoat, and I suppose you wear boots for them too. I need boots to uphold my honour and my good name; whereas in boots full of holes both honour and name are lost.*[45] He had all the paranoia of an ambitious member of the lower-middle class, desperate to break into society but convinced that he would be outed by some invisible code. He took to buying tea to supplement his morning and evening ration, and often wrote to his father asking for money.

When he heard that Fyodor had not passed his first year (having been rude to his maths teacher), Dr Dostoevsky had a minor stroke. A few months later, one of Fyodor's letters requesting money received a strained response about the state of affairs in Darovoe: 'From the beginning of spring not a drop of water, not even dew. Heat and terrible winds have ruined everything. What threatens is not only ruin but total starvation. After this, can you really keep grumbling at your father for not sending you money?'[46] In the envelope was the money that he had asked for. It was the last letter he would ever receive from his father, who died a week later.

He was found one morning by some peasants in a ditch.[47] Dark rumours circulated among the family about the goings-on at Darovoe. Before his death, their father's drinking had got worse, and he had been prone to bouts of rage, whipping the peasants savagely. A peasant girl, Akulina, had been taken into the main house at the age of ten or eleven, and although she was still only fourteen, she had been assisting in Dr Dostoevsky's medical practice. The doctor had also made a mistress of the sixteen-year-old chambermaid, Katya, and she had given birth to a child, which had suffered a cot death.[48] It seemed macabre, but not unbelievable, that the doctor had been murdered by his peasants. A bottle of spirits down the throat and a cloth in the mouth. The body lying untended in the field for two days. *At first glance, the allegations looked serious.*[49] It was never proven – could never be proven – either way. But if he wasn't murdered, the alternative was that he had died as a consequence of stress, of drinking to put off the feeling of stress, of working to put off the ruin of the family, of working towards Fyodor's future as an engineer – a future that Fyodor himself was no longer working towards. Fyodor never explicitly acknowledged guilt, but as he built a new life in St Petersburg, far from the burned wreckage of his father's dreams, the first of his great archetypes was taking shape in his head: the drunken man, the dissolute man, the man marked for death.

I confess to you that Petersburg, I don't know why, has always been a mystery to me. Since my childhood, almost forsaken, abandoned in Petersburg, I was somehow always afraid of it.[50] Now orphaned, and with his beloved brother Mikhail 350 versts away in Revel, Fyodor spent most of his free time brooding on his bed or walking alone through the wide, flat streets, peering into the city as if willing it to give up its secrets. It never obliged, except for one especially cold January evening soon after his father's death. There was a particular moment, as Fyodor was crossing the Neva, when he perceived it all with perfect clarity. It happened just as the last of the sunset burned out on the horizon and the sky turned crimson over the city. The great expanse of the Neva, swollen with frozen snow, sparkled with needles of frost. Frozen steam poured from the noses of passing horses; columns of hot smoke, meanwhile, rose like giants from the roofs, rushing upward, intertwining and making it appear as if a whole new city was forming above the old one, in the air. It seemed, in that moment, as if the whole world, the real one down on the earth, with its inhabitants, strong and weak, its poor houses and gilded mansions, was only a fantastical vision, a dream that would one day rise up like steam into the sky and vanish. *I shuddered and at that moment my heart seemed to be flooded with a warm rush of blood, a powerful, unknown sensation. It was as if at that moment I came to understand something that until then had only been stirring vaguely within me, and had yet to be understood; it was as if my eyes were opened to something new, to a completely new world, unfamiliar to me and known only from dark rumours and mysterious signs. I believe it was at that very moment that my existence began.*[51]

Having graduated and received permission to live independently, Fyodor was employed in the drafting department, working on projective geometry and field cartography. *I made friends with no one and positively avoided talking, burrowed away in my little hole. Every day when I turned up at the office I tried to behave as independently as possible, and to assume a lofty expression, so that I might not be suspected of being abject.*[52] *As soon as I finished I would run home to my garret, put on my tatty dressing gown, leaf through my Schiller, and begin to dream, to suffer pains sweeter than pleasure, and to love.*[53]

Fyodor took a succession of rooms, some more salubrious than others. Although he drew a salary, Fyodor seemed to repel money. He couldn't afford real coffee, instead drinking a foul concoction made from barley. Still, he had just enough to sign up to the lending library at Smirdin's bookshop if he didn't buy boots (instead, he covered up the holes with ink). He often ran out of money entirely, living on bread and milk that he'd bought on credit with the shopkeeper. Occasionally he'd write to his younger brother Andrei for a few roubles so that he could buy kindling.

There was an old man in his quarters with the unusual nickname Mammal, who had a consumptive wife. Mammal's boots were worn thin and his five children often went hungry. There was also a young woman, Nadia, with whom Fyodor would read novels. *Even now I can't recall those evenings without trembling.* In return for reading to her, she darned his old stockings and starched his two shirt-fronts for him. Meeting her sometimes on the filthy staircase, with eggshell crunching like grit underfoot, she would blush. She was a dreamer too, pretty, kind and gentle. But she had a fiancé.

Eventually, he moved in, a petty official who wore a coat with a cat-fur collar, which presumably he hoped would be taken for marten. He was about forty-five, and had a wart on his nose. And then they moved away together. *I remember how I said goodbye. I kissed her pretty hand for the first time in my life. She kissed me on the forehead and smiled so oddly, so strangely, that it left a claw mark on my heart for the rest of my life. And she began laughing – why? It is all so painfully imprinted on my memory.*

Fyodor tried to console himself with literature. He thought he might turn his hand to writing plays. He started and quickly abandoned one called *Jew Yankel*. He tried translating George Sand and Balzac. At the Academy, he had met a few other students who were interested in literature, and sometimes they would meet up to talk about Gogol or play cards. *I spent most of my time at home, reading. I tried to stifle the seething within me by focusing on external impressions. Reading, of course, was a great help, but at times it bored me fearfully. One longed for movement in spite of everything. And so, furtively, timidly, in solitude, at night, I indulged in filthy vice, with a feeling of shame which never deserted me.*

Fyodor would sometimes write to his wealthy aunt for money, too. In the end he managed to beg 1,000 roubles and, feeling flush, went out for an evening's stroll. He stopped to watch a game of billiards at Dominic's Café, where someone offered to teach him how to play dominoes. It was a fascinating game – a mix of luck and logic. It must have taken him about 25 rounds, but eventually he lost all the money he had brought out with him, and trudged home.

Eventually, he found a lender who was willing to give him some money up front if he signed away his next four months' salary,

Notes from the Underground, p. 487. In a letter to Mikhail (22 December 1841), Dostoevsky complains about their younger brother, Andrei, staying with him: 'Impossible to work or to amuse oneself – you understand.' Later, he would write to Mikhail that 'the Minnas, Klaras, Mariannas etc. have become much more beautiful but they cost a frightful lot of money. And the other day Turgenev and Belinsky scolded me for my irregular life.' (16 November 1845)

which he did. It didn't help that he had also been giving people money to hear their life stories: there were the patients of his friend Dr Riesenkampf, and there was also a young German acquaintance who was a great raconteur but who sponged off him mercilessly. What could he do? He knew he was destined to be a writer, but you cannot speak before you have listened.

Although his financial future was by no means certain, Fyodor committed himself to the inevitable and tendered his resignation from the drafting department. *I resigned because I had to resign. I couldn't stand the service any longer. Life is bleak when one's time is wasted.*[54] He didn't have a copeck to buy clothes. He had written to his relatives offering to renounce his interest in the family estate for another 1,000 roubles up front, but they seemed not to trust him when he said he'd never ask for money again.

He moved in with Dmitri Vasilevich Grigorovich, a sullen young man whose French was better than his Russian, and who had been in the year above Fyodor at the engineering academy. Grigorovich had already published a couple of short stories in the manner of Gogol, and was working on an essay, 'The Organ Grinders of St Petersburg'. Crucially, for Fyodor, he had literary connections. Day and night, the two young men would read, and write, and talk about literature, above all Gogol, whose *Dead Souls* had just been published and was already one of the most famous works in the Russian language. *I read like a fiend, and reading had a strange effect on me. I re-read some book I'd read before, and it was as if new strength began to stir in me. I penetrated into everything, I understood with precision, and I drew from it the ability to create.*[55] He daydreamed of faces, a whole crowd of them, unable to see that their limbs were on strings, and unaware that behind them stood a laughing puppeteer. Gogol could write like that, but Fyodor wanted to give his characters more dignity. Fyodor imagined two poor neighbours: an old titular councillor, among the lowest ranks of the civil service, but honest, moral and devoted to his work, and a young woman, impoverished and sad. *Their story broke my heart.*[56]

After serving his notice, Fyodor spent all his time working on his new story, *a rather original novel* by his own estimation,[57] which he thought would be about the length of Balzac's *Eugénie Grandet*. He found himself totally caught up in the world of his characters and did nothing but write and rewrite. *If I was ever happy it was before I had ever read or shown anyone my manuscript; in those long nights spent in exalted hopes and dreams and passionate love of my work, when I was living with my characters, as though they were my family, as though they were real people; I loved them, I rejoiced and grieved with them, and sometimes shed genuine tears over my artless hero.*[58]

He recopied the manuscript of *Poor Folk* in the autumn and finished it in November 1844. In December he decided to go back through it again and rewrote it, and in February, again, he pruned, polished, interpolated and deleted. *It is almost twice as good now. But I'm through with it; I have promised myself not to touch it again. It is always the fate of first books to be corrected again and again, endlessly.*[59] It was spring by the time he was happy with it, the time of St Petersburg's famous White Nights, when the daylight stretches out through the evenings and it begins to seem as if it will never be dark again. His first novel sat on his desk, a thick notebook covered with small handwriting.

Fyodor wanted to send it to the popular radical journal *Notes of the Fatherland*, where Belinsky was chief critic, but he knew that there were heaps of manuscripts in their offices that never got read. *I had been reading Belinsky with great interest for some years, but he seemed to me to be severe and menacing, and I had thought to myself: 'He would only laugh at my Poor Folk'. But only sometimes.*[60] When he considered his options (self-publish it, throw himself into the Neva, etc.), he found himself at a loss. Then, one day, he spoke about the manuscript to Grigorovich, who mentioned that his friend Nikolai Nekrasov was starting a new magazine, and asked if he might show it to him. Nekrasov was the same age as Fyodor, but he already had an impressive career behind him. Having refused to join the army, his father had cut him off, and he had lived in abject poverty for years, building a reputation for himself as a poet and a talented critic for *Notes of the Fatherland*. Nekrasov was friends with the budding short-story writer Ivan Turgenev and even knew Belinsky himself.

Fyodor went with Grigorovich to hand Nekrasov his manuscript, but he was so crippled with nerves that he made his excuses and bolted almost immediately. He went for a long walk through St Petersburg and, not wanting to go home just yet, called on an old college friend. They stayed up late, and so did the sun, dipping only reluctantly as the new day approached. *When I came home it was already four o'clock, as bright as day. The weather was fine and warm, and when I got in I didn't go to bed, but sat looking out of the open window. Suddenly the bell rang and startled me.*[61]

Nekrasov and Grigorovich rushed into Fyodor's room and embraced him in raptures, on the brink of tears. While Fyodor had been out, they had taken *Poor Folk* back to Nekrasov's place, intending to read the first ten pages and make a decision. After ten pages they decided to read another ten, and they had carried on like that all night, taking turns to read the manuscript aloud. The moment they had finished it, they had come to see him.

They spent about half an hour with me then, and in that time we talked of God knows how many things, catching each other's meaning before we had finished a word, speaking hastily of poetry and of truth and of the state of things – and of Gogol too, of course. But mainly we spoke of Belinsky.[62]

'I intend to take Belinsky your manuscript today,' said Nekrasov triumphantly, shaking Fyodor by the shoulders. 'Let's see what happens. What a man you are! You and he must meet one another, for he is a splendid fellow. Now, I must be off – go to bed, and then come and see me later.' They left, but of course he couldn't sleep.

When Nekrasov did come back, he delivered the good news that Belinsky loved *Poor Folk* too. It was almost unbelievable – Fyodor had become a literary sensation, literally overnight. Nekrasov suggested going to meet Belinsky, but Fyodor was so nervous that he refused to leave the house. *All my life up to now, in all my dreams of how I would behave with people, I always imagined myself being very clever. It was very different in reality – I was always very stupid; and I confess sincerely, I always got terribly flustered.*[63]

'What am I to him?' Fyodor asked, cringing.[64] 'What would I do there? What do we have in common? He is a scholar, a well-known writer, a famous critic. What am I?'

'Fyodor Mikhailovich! What humility! And for whose sake? Haven't I read *Poor Folk*? Hasn't Belinsky read it?'

'So, what of it?' Fyodor asked slyly, suppressing a smile. His crippling self-consciousness wrestled with his vanity until, at last, Nekrasov managed to bundle him out of the door.

Belinsky lived in a big house on the corner of Nevsky Prospect and the Fontanka Canal, where people sold apples and gingerbread. He had a courtyard apartment with windows facing onto the stables. Fyodor got as far as the doorbell before retreating back down the stairs, and Nekrasov had to warn him that he was going to annoy Belinsky more by his absence before Fyodor would agree to go back up and announce himself.

They were shown into a neat office with houseplants, polished floors, a tidy desk, and the faces of literary giants everywhere: portraits and busts of Voltaire and Rousseau, Pushkin and Gogol. Belinsky appeared among them, a short man with blond hair and such a hard stare that it was difficult for anyone to meet his eyes, let alone Fyodor, who, at moments like this, had a habit of squeezing himself together as if he was trying to gently and quietly fade from the room.*

When they were all seated, Belinsky shrieked in excitement: 'Do you, you yourself, realise what you have written?'[65]

Fyodor sat there, failing to disappear.

'You, as an artist, could have written this only guided by your God-given instinct. But have you understood all the terrible truth you have shown us? It cannot be that you, with all your twenty years, have understood that.' Belinsky fell into raptures over the old clerk,

---

* Dostoevsky credited himself with inventing a word for this: стушева́ться or *stushevatsya*. It means to be wiped off the face of the earth, 'delicately, so to say, gradually, sinking imperceptibly into nothingness. It's like a shadow on a pen-and-ink drawing that gradually shades from black ever more lightly until it's reduced to whiteness.' (*A Writer's Diary*, November 1877, cf. *The Unpublished Dostoevsky*, Volume 2, p. 28)

the way he had pinpointed the whole tragedy of these characters so vividly, through such significant little moments. It was precisely the sort of social novel that Russian literature had been crying out for, and that Belinsky had demanded to see from the new generation. 'To you, an artist, the truth has been revealed and proclaimed; it has come to you as a gift. So cherish your gift, remain faithful to it, and be a great writer!'

Fyodor left in a state of ecstasy. He stopped at the street corner, looked up at the luminous day, at the passers-by, and felt that something quite decisive had just occurred, something he had not anticipated in his wildest dreams. *I recall the moment with complete clarity, and I could never forget it after. It was the most wonderful moment of my life.*[66]

Circles within Circles

1846–1849

I DON'T THINK MY *glory will ever be greater. Everywhere there is a passionate curiosity about me. Everyone considers me a prodigy. Belinsky couldn't love me more. The other day, the poet Ivan Turgenev returned from Paris and immediately became attached to me with such devotion that Belinsky reckons he has fallen in love with me. I have practically fallen in love with him myself. A poet, a talent, an aristocrat, handsome, rich, intelligent, educated, twenty-five years old.*[67] A head taller than Fyodor with sky-blue eyes, and fluent in French and German, Turgenev already had the air of a man of the world. He had spent time abroad, studying at the University of Berlin at the same time as Karl Marx and meeting George Sand, who was infamous in literary Russia as one of the only radical voices from the continent that had slipped through the net of censorship. Turgenev was not yet making much of a living from his writing, but his mother had an estate numbering 5,000 serfs, so he could afford to take his time.* He was everything, in short, that Fyodor wished to be.

In the evening Turgenev read my work to our entire circle, that is, to twenty people at least, and it caused a furore.[68] *Belinsky said that he has complete faith in me, because I am so versatile. I have a deep well of ideas, but I can't talk about any of them to Turgenev for fear that*

---

*Or so Fyodor thought. In reality, Turgenev's mother was miserly and refused him an allowance, so he borrowed money to pay for his tailoring and always contrived to leave dinner before the bill appeared.

tomorrow, all of Petersburg will know about it. If I began to recount all my successes for you, I would run out of paper.[69]

Fyodor was soon invited into the circle of Ivan Panaev, another of St Petersburg's taste-makers. The first night he went along with Nekrasov and Grigorovich, his face was contorted into a rictus of social anxiety, but the others encouraged him, and he began to come out of his shell. Panaev was great fun – funny and childish. *I think I fell in love with his wife. She is not only intelligent and pretty, but very nice and straightforward.* Avdotya was about the same age as Fyodor, and was quietly at work on her own short stories. He took to her immediately. She went out of her way to be welcoming and kind to him, seeing that he was so nervous. He watched her move around her salon like a dancer, every movement keeping time with some silent music. She was beautiful, too, with silken black hair, a perfectly straight nose and olive skin. *But it is not enough to grow fond of people – one must possess the art of making people fond of you.*[70] Fyodor later found out that Madame Panaeva was already ensconced in a ménage à trois with Nekrasov.

As he grew in confidence, Fyodor began to speak more freely (and loudly) at the meetings of their circle. It didn't take long before he found himself arguing about both literary and political matters, even with Belinsky, whose flippant attitude to Christianity wounded Fyodor deeply. At the same time Fyodor was working hard to finish *The Double*, the story of a low-ranking civil servant called Golyadkin who is haunted by a doppelgänger, a man just like him, and yet suave, attractive, somehow imperceptibly better at being himself. In the crucial scene before he meets his double, Golyadkin inveigles himself into a party, where he stands awkwardly in front of his boss's daughter, the beautiful Klara, stammering and floundering and blushing, before retreating to the corner of the room and fantasising about saving her from a falling chandelier. Golyadkin lurches forward to grab Klara's hand for a dance and she shrieks; he is detached from her by the other guests and directed quite firmly towards the stairway at the entrance, where he stumbles and falls down the stairs into the courtyard. Shortly after that, he is confronted by his second self, and the impostor begins to take his life from him, piece by piece. It ends in the only way possible: he is driven off to the asylum.

The Double was published by *Notes of the Fatherland* in February 1846, just weeks after *Poor Folk* was published in Nekrasov's *Petersburg Miscellany*. Belinsky praised Dostoevsky's talent and depth of thought in general terms, but he also stuck the knife in: 'It is obvious that the author ... has not yet acquired the tact of measure and harmony, and, as a result, many criticise even *Poor Folk* not without reason for prolixity, though this criticism is less applicable there than to *The Double*.' Fyodor had been right that his fame had peaked in the autumn, but he could not have foreseen how quickly it would desert him. This new development revealed the terrible paradox at the heart of paranoia: yes, perhaps it is unreasonable to believe that people are insulting you behind your back, but that doesn't mean they are not. Grigorovich, for reasons best known to himself, began reporting to Fyodor that the others were having great fun at his expense. Turgenev and Nekrasov had been passing around *a strange poem about a poor knight, a fragment without a beginning or an end,*[71] in which they pretended to be Belinsky addressing Fyodor, 'The Knight of the Doleful Countenance':

Upon the nose of lit
You blossom like a zit[72]

They take a malicious delight in spotting every one of my mistakes.[73] They even teased Fyodor for the sudden illness that had overtaken him at the party of a local Count, Mikhail Yurevich Vielgorsky. While there, he had been introduced to an attractive young blonde named Senyavina, who had been keen to meet him, but Fyodor had sadly failed to capitalise on this opportunity for a flirtation by losing consciousness and falling to the floor.

Soon Belinsky, Nekrasov and Panaev abandoned *Notes of the Fatherland* for a rival magazine, *The Contemporary*. Now openly hostile to the direction Fyodor's writing was taking, Belinsky wrote that his new story, 'Mr Prokharchin', was 'affected, *maniéré*, and incomprehensible'.* Fyodor's only defender was the new chief critic of *Notes of the Fatherland*, Valerian Maikov, a literary prodigy even compared to Dostoevsky. Two years younger than Fyodor, he had already made a name for himself as a formidable critic, and he saw that, whereas Gogol was a social poet, Dostoevsky's talent was for psychology. 'In *The Double*,' he wrote, 'he penetrates so deeply into the human soul, he looks so fearlessly and passionately into the secret machinations of human feeling, thought and action, that the impression created by *The Double* may be compared only with that of an inquisitive person penetrating into the chemical composition of matter.'[74]

The two young men quickly became close friends, their sympathies instinctively aligned. Maikov began preparing a long article about Dostoevsky's impressive output: *Poor Folk*, *The Double*, 'A Novel in Nine Letters', 'Mr Prokharchin' and now *The Landlady*. As soon as Maikov had finished it, the article would rehabilitate Dostoevsky as one of the most significant writers of his generation. Maikov was still working on it when, one summer's day, he went out into the countryside near St Petersburg for a long walk and a swim, caught sunstroke, and died.

This did not help with Fyodor's hypochondria. He now became morbidly fascinated by reading medical textbooks, particularly those on phrenology, mental illness and the nervous system, reading lists of symptoms in the hope of naming what it felt like to be him. Some nights he couldn't sleep. He suffered from subtle hallucinations; he wrote fervently, almost manically.† He began to mistrust his own senses and on one night convinced himself that he was going to die. *As it got darker my room seemed to grow larger and larger, as though the*

---

* Yes, he did actually switch to French in order to accuse Dostoevsky of being mannered. (Frank, p. 97)

† Had he been born in our time, he may have found what he was looking for: some patients with temporal lobe epilepsy have what is known as Geschwind Syndrome, characterised by hypergraphia (manic writing), hyperreligiosity, atypical sexuality, circumstantiality (an inability to explain oneself without giving excessive, irrelevant details), and an intensified mental life. Although, as Ivan Karamazov would later discover, naming your devil doesn't make him disappear.

walls were retreating, and at dusk I gradually began to sink into a sort of mystic terror. It is a most oppressive, agonising state which I don't know how to define, something unnatural, passing all understanding, even as it takes shape and stands before me as a hideous and undeniable fact. It seems to me something like the anguish of people who are afraid of the dead.[75]

It was around this time that Fyodor's doctor, Stepan Yanovsky, bumped into him in St Isaac's Square, being propped up by a soldier, his collar undone. He was delirious, and all he would say as Yanovsky led him home was, 'I am saved!' The doctor let some blood, which came out black – a worrying sign. Even when the patient had settled down, it was clear that he was anxious and unhappy. He seemed to have been suffering from some sort of nervous breakdown. *When a man is dissatisfied, when he hasn't the means to show what is best in him, to express himself fully (not out of vanity, but because of the urgent necessity of realising himself), he at once gets involved in some quite incredible situation; he takes to the bottle, or becomes a gambler, or a rabid duellist.*[76] Or, he might have added, a revolutionary.

I loved to recall and visit at certain dates the places where I was once happy in my own way. I loved to build up my present in harmony with the irrevocable past, and often wandered like a shade, aimless, sad and dejected, down the streets and alleyways of St Petersburg, and although the past was no better I felt as though somehow it had been.[77] It was on one of these strolls that Fyodor met the man who would lead him to the firing squad.

He had been making his way down Nevsky Prospect when he was approached by a rather short, theatrical figure in a cloak. The man's black eyes glowed between his thick beard and his broad-brimmed hat.

'May I ask what the idea of your next story is?' the stranger enquired.[78]

He introduced himself as Mikhail Vasilievich Butashevich-Petrashevsky. Born two days after Fyodor, Petrashevsky now worked as a translator in the Foreign Office. He didn't work for the income since he was independently wealthy, but the Foreign Office gave him access to banned books, a number of which had made it into his personal library.

Petrashevsky was a strange combination of frivolous and committed, a utopian socialist in the mould of Fourier.* On the one hand, Petrashevsky had tried to put his principles into practice and start a commune for his peasants. (They had gone along with the idea until building work on the 'phalanstery' was completed, at which point they burned it to the ground.) On the other hand, he sometimes seemed little more than a prankster – once, when his boss ordered him to cut his hair short, he had turned up to work wearing a long wig. He hosted his own circle, this one more overtly political than Belinsky's. If you were being ungenerous, you might say that the common denominator in all these pursuits was that he liked being the centre of attention.

Petrashevsky may have been rich, but his house on Pokrovsky Square was small and sparsely furnished (though he did have a piano). Fyodor found it a welcome change from the Belinsky circle. The guests would often stay talking until two or three o'clock in the morning, possibly enticed by the free food and drink. *If we had drunk a great deal – and that did happen sometimes – we flew into raptures, and even on one occasion sang the 'Marseillaise' in chorus.*[79] Fyodor recognised Valerian Maikov's younger brother, Apollon, who was starting out as a poet, and although he didn't quite have his brother's genius, they talked easily, drinking tea and smoking cigarettes together. Sometimes Fyodor would browse Petrashevsky's extraordinary library, borrowing books on socialism, whether Europhile or Slavophile, Christian or atheist. But mostly, he would stand among the chattering guests as they set the world to rights. *We talked of the abolition of censorship, of phonetic spelling, of the substitution of the Latin alphabet for the Russian, of someone's having been sent into exile the day before, of some scandal, of the advantage of splitting Russia into nationalities united in a free federation, of the abolition of the army and the navy, of the restoration of Poland as far as the Dnieper, of serfdom, of manifestos, of women's rights, and so on.*[80]

---

* That is, Charles Fourier, who coined the word 'feminism', not his exact contemporary Joseph Fourier, who discovered greenhouse gases.

One item of serious interest was the speech that Tsar Nicholas had given to a group of nobles about finding ways to free the serfs by turning them into tenants. It wasn't clear how that would work in practice, but the fact that the Tsar was even considering it was a huge step. Of all the issues they discussed, it was the liberation of the serfs that Fyodor believed in most passionately. He may technically have been a landowner, but some of his fondest childhood memories were of wandering around Darovoe, chatting to the labourers and playing with their children. He had once run two versts to get a glass of water for a peasant woman's baby while she was out in the field. The idea of owning people as property seemed immoral to Fyodor.

The possibility of emancipating the serfs had been floating around liberal society for some time, a perennial favourite when conversation ran dry. But one morning in the early spring of 1848 socialist ideas took on a new urgency. On Nevsky Prospect, people were snatching newspapers out of each other's hands, a current of shock running down the street: Italy was in revolt. It seemed that the reforms of Pius IX had provoked uprisings in Milan, Venice and Naples. Soon after, there came reports of revolutions in Berlin and Vienna. On the question of the serfs, the Tsar suddenly fell silent.

In the feverish atmosphere, Petrashevsky's meetings began to attract a number of new people. Fyodor brought along his twenty-year-old friend Golovinsky. Petrashevsky invited along a colleague from the Foreign Office, Antonelli. He was a typical liberal, the son of a painter like Maikov, and immediately threw himself into any conversation criticising the government or the church.

Then there was Nikolai Alexandrovich Speshnev, who had just returned from Europe. Rumour had it that he had seen action as a volunteer for the liberals against the Catholics in Switzerland. *He was not very talkative, he was elegant without exaggeration, surprisingly modest, and at the same time bold and self-reliant. Our dandies gazed at him with envy, and were completely eclipsed by him. His face, too, made a great impression on me*[81] *– it was a strange sort of face, not unlike a mask. His eyes were a little too blue somehow, their gaze a little too fixed. There was something terribly unpleasant about it.*[82] Speshnev spent a lot of his time in Petrashevsky's library, reading, and wouldn't often take part in the conversations going on in the next room – but where the others flirted with ideas, Speshnev really appeared capable of anything. Once, when the group was happily sitting around complaining about censorship, he interjected: 'Since only the spoken word remains to us, I intend to use it without any shame or conscience, with no sense of dishonour, in order to propagandise for socialism, atheism, everything, everything that is good in the world. And I advise you to do the same.'[83] Fyodor had hardly expected to get on with a militant atheist, but there was something about his passion and conviction that distinguished him as an exceptional man. Here, among the champagne socialists, was a true revolutionary.

One last colourful addition to the circle is worth mentioning. Rafael Chernosvitov was a little older than most, an ex-army officer turned Siberian gold prospector with a wooden leg. His colourful language reminded Fyodor a little of Gogol, but there was also something disconcerting in his sudden appearance in the group, especially since he seemed not to be anyone's friend in particular. Chernosvitov was also remarkably candid about the potential for a peasant uprising. *Can there possibly be an informer among us here?*[84] Quietly, Fyodor warned Speshnev that he might be a spy, but Speshnev's curiosity got the better of him, and he and Petrashevsky took Chernosvitov off for a tête-à-tête. At this private meeting, Chernosvitov assured the other two that, if they really wanted to know, all the free Siberian peasants had weapons already. Speshnev allowed himself to speculate that, if the army were to be drawn east across the Urals, Moscow and St Petersburg would be left undefended and vulnerable. Petrashevsky, meanwhile, had turned white, and abruptly ended the conversation. It was one thing to talk of reform over a glass of wine, quite another to plot a violent uprising. For all his gleeful provocation, Petrashevsky did not, after all, want to overthrow the Tsar.

The extent to which Petrashevsky had lost control of his own circle became increasingly clear as a few of them began to talk in more concrete terms about what should be done. One evening at dinner, Fyodor read out Belinsky's famous open letter to Gogol, in tribute to his lost friend and mentor – Belinsky had recently died, and now the two would never have an opportunity to reconcile. The letter decries serfdom and calls for the government to follow the rule of law: 'This is a country where people sell other people, where there is no guarantee for the individual, for honour, for private property. There is no police order, but instead a huge network of thieves and robbers. The most urgent questions of national importance for Russia at present are the abolition of serfdom; the abolition of physical punishment; and the enforcement of laws that already exist. Russia is sleeping in apathy!'[85] There was a roar of approval in the room, but Petrashevsky tried to quell his audience: yes, reform was necessary, but there was no reason it might not be done through the proper channels. Change the laws and the rest would surely follow.

Speshnev had already given up on Petrashevsky. It was no longer necessary to argue with such people. Instead, he had begun to cultivate his own circle, by invitation only, at the house of the poet Sergei Durov. Among their number was Fyodor Dostoevsky.

They still talked of art and music and poetry, and indeed most of them were writers. Here, among a handful of like-minded friends, they were free to discuss their ideas, even their most dangerous ideas, with an implicit trust that there were certain matters that could not be broached among the loose tongues of the Petrashevsky circle. The bond was strong enough that, when he heard Dostoevsky was short of money, Speshnev lent him 500 roubles, enough to keep most people going for several months. *I'll never be able to pay back such a sum, and he won't take the money back; that's the kind of man he is. From now on, he is my Mephistopheles.*[86] Instead, at their next meeting Speshnev suggested that Fyodor write a seditious paper which they might smuggle out to be published in Europe. Someone else suggested getting hold of their own printing press. They were thrilled by their own audacity, each egging the other on. Speshnev began working on a written oath that they might sign, to bind their fates together: 'I, the undersigned, do hereby undertake to pledge myself unreservedly to a full and complete participation in the rebellion and the subsequent fighting at such time as the Committee decides to come out in open rebellion, and I further undertake to provide myself with firearms and other weapons ...'[87] *It was as if, during those final days, I was trying to run away from a clear and full understanding of my situation.*[88]

Soon after that, Fyodor went to stay the night at Apollon Maikov's house, hoping that, in the intimacy of late-night conversation, he might convince him to join in the conspiracy. As Fyodor pulled on his red nightshirt, they began to talk about the two circles, Petrashevsky's and Durov's. That Maikov was sympathetic, he knew, but what remained to be seen was whether he was prepared to put his ideals into practice.

'Of course, you understand that Petrashevsky is a gossip. He is not a serious person and nothing can possibly come of his undertakings,' Fyodor said.[89] 'And for that reason several serious people from his circle have decided, without telling the others, to form their own secret society with a secret printing press in order to print various books and even magazines. We had our doubts about you – for one thing, you are too proud.'*

'What do you mean?' Maikov asked.

'Well, you don't recognise authority. For instance, you do not agree with Speshnev.'

'I am not particularly interested in political economy. And it does seem to me that Speshnev talks nonsense. But what of it?'

'For the good of the common cause you must exercise self-control. There are seven of us now: Speshnev, Mordvinov, Mombelli, Pavel Filippov, Grigoriev, Vladimir Miliutin and myself. We have chosen you to be the eighth. Do you want to join our society?'

'But what is the purpose?'

'Its purpose is to organise a coup in Russia, naturally. We already had a printing press designed by Mordvinov. It was ordered bit by bit, in different places. It is all ready.'

If Fyodor had expected Maikov to be honoured, he was mistaken.

'Not only do I not wish to join the society, but I advise you to get out of it. What sort of political leaders would we make? We are

* A bit rich, coming from Dostoevsky.

poets and artists, not practical men, and we haven't a copeck. Surely, you don't think we are suited to be revolutionaries, do you?'

They argued for some time before bed, and it was the first thing Fyodor brought up when they woke in the morning. But Maikov held firm.

'I woke up before you did and thought about it. I won't join, and you should get out too, if you still can.'

'Well, that's my own affair,' Fyodor replied irritably. 'And, listen, only seven people know what I told you. You are the eighth – there must not be a ninth.'

'As far as that is concerned, here is my hand. I won't say a word.'

Fyodor trusted Maikov more than most. But it was not Maikov who would betray them.

At 4 a.m. on 23 April 1849, Fyodor returned home from seeing Grigoriev and fell asleep. *Less than an hour later, as if in a dream, I saw several peculiar and suspicious people enter my room. I heard the sound of a sword hitting something in the room, as if by accident. What was that? I struggled to open my eyes, and I heard a pleasant and sympathetic voice: 'Please get up.' I saw a handsome District Police Officer with delicate whiskers. It was not he who spoke, however, but a man dressed in a blue uniform with colonel's insignia.* There was another soldier in a blue uniform – the uniform of the Third Section[†] – standing at the door.

'What's happened?' Fyodor asked, getting out of bed.

'Pursuant to the order . . .' It seemed that they had a warrant for his arrest. The situation was a little absurd, they dressed in full regalia, he in his bedclothes.

'Please would you let me . . .' Fyodor began.

'Please don't worry. Get dressed, we'll wait,' said the colonel in an even nicer voice. Fyodor dressed, and they asked to have his books. All his papers and letters were neatly bound in string.

They didn't find much, but made a lot of mess not finding it. One of the police officers wanted to show off his detective skills, so he

---

[*] Sekirin, pp. 86–7. A neighbour remembers the police violently breaking down the door and Dostoevsky attempting unsuccessfully to break the window and climb out; see Sekirin p. 133.
[†] i.e. the secret police.

went to the fireplace and stirred the ashes. Another stood on a chair next to the fireplace to see whether anything was hidden in the wall, and he fell off it with a terrible racket. The first officer picked up an old coin and examined it attentively, perhaps considering it a bonus.

'What do you think, is it counterfeit?' Fyodor asked.

'Well, we will have to investigate,' the officer stammered and added it to the confiscated materials.

They all went out into the frigid air, where there was a carriage waiting. The landlady and her husband had come out to see them off – they must have been awoken by the officer's fall. The old man looked at Fyodor in a dull, official way. The officers sat inside the carriage with Fyodor and they went down to the Fontanka, across the chain bridge and along the edge of the Summer Garden.

When we arrived, I saw that there were many people inside, some of whom I recognised. Someone must have informed on them. Durov had been arrested, and Petrashevsky. *All of them were silent and sleepy. One of the high-ranking officers conducted the reception of the newcomers. Men in blue uniforms were constantly coming in, bringing with them new victims . . .* One of the people they brought in was Fyodor's younger brother, Andrei, which was baffling until the two of them worked out that Andrei had been mistaken for Mikhail. He hadn't done anything that was likely to result in a long sentence, but Fyodor begged Andrei not to give the game away immediately, to buy Mikhail some time to get his affairs in order and say goodbye to his wife and their newborn child.

Having been given almost no information, the group of haggard and enervated poets gathered around the ranking officer, who was holding a list of names. In front of Antonelli's name was written: 'The police agent in this case.'

So, it was Antonelli.

————

At around midnight Fyodor was taken to Peter and Paul Fortress, where Peter the Great had his son tortured. The sharp spike of the cathedral spire didn't so much reach up towards God as impale the sky. Fyodor was shown into a small, dark room in the Alexeevsky cells. It had three by two metres of stale air, but with a very high ceiling. The windows and doors were covered in iron bars, the bed in grey cloth. Was this the cell in which the Decembrist Colonel Bulatov had killed himself by repeatedly head-butting the wall?*

They took from Fyodor 60 copecks, a short, shabby winter coat, a shirt, a vest, underwear, boots, stockings, a scarf, a handkerchief and a comb. He was given a thick grey prison robe and stockings and the door was shut. He would spend the rest of the year there, leaving only to be interrogated. Before his arrest, Fyodor had begun publishing an audacious novel, one of the first Russian novels with a complex, female protagonist, the eponymous *Netochka Nezvanova*. He'd already covered her tragic early life and infatuation with a young princess named Katya, and the plan had been to follow her into early adulthood. No one was publishing anything remotely like it; but now it would have to be abandoned.

Oh, how happy I would have been if I could have blamed myself! I could have borne anything then, even shame and disgrace. But I judged myself severely, and my exasperated conscience found no particularly terrible fault in my past, except a simple blunder which might happen to anyone.[90] Fyodor sat for months in his cell, not knowing what was likely to happen, reliving the past. He suffered from haemorrhoids, and nervous throat spasms. He managed to sleep only about five hours out of twenty-four, lying awake in the darkness for four or five hours a night, and could eat only castor oil. His nerves began to fray, and at night the floor would seem to heave under his bed as if he were sloshing around in a ship's cabin. Still, after a few months the guards gave him permission to take brief walks in the

---

*The Decembrist Revolt was a failed military coup in the last month of 1825, intended to force liberal reforms such as a written constitution and the abolition of serfdom. The Decembrists originally planned to assassinate Alexander I in May 1826, but the Tsar disobligingly died of natural causes in December 1825, leaving the throne to his younger brother, Nicholas. When 3,000 rebels massed in Senate Square on the first day of Nicholas's reign, he ordered them to be routed with 36 cannon. The five leaders were hanged and 100 more exiled to Siberia. Tsar Nicholas I was subsequently not very fond of liberals.

garden, in which he counted 17 trees, and later they even allowed him a candle.

After the endless interrogations came the death sentence and the subsequent ordeal of the mock execution.* The whole thing was awful, as bad as he could ever have imagined, and yet also, if he allowed himself the thought, which he always did, thrillingly *literary*. He felt like the protagonist in Victor Hugo's *The Last Day of a Condemned Man.*

Mikhail had been released and came to visit on Christmas Eve, a few hours before Fyodor began his journey to Siberia. He was very distressed, lip trembling, tears in his eyes, and by the way that Fyodor ended up trying to console him, an observer might have assumed it was the older brother who was going off to hard labour.

'Stop, brother,' Fyodor said. 'You know me. I'm not going to my grave, this isn't my burial – and they aren't wild animals out there. They are people, perhaps better and worthier than I am.'[91] They would not exchange another word for over four years. Fyodor had heavy iron shackles put on him as the bell struck midnight: Christmas Day. He got into the open sleigh, and they drove on past the festive lights of the city. He felt sad riding past Mikhail's apartment but it was only later, stuck in a snowdrift crossing the Urals, that he would break down in tears at the thought of leaving Europe behind. It was a punishing journey of 3,000 versts, riding in temperatures as low as 40 degrees below zero.† Or to put it another way, it was a month with nothing to do but stare at the back of an official as he lashed out at the horses.

---

*The Commission of Inquiry that convicted him was headed up by the novelist Vladimir Nabokov's great-great-uncle, General Ivan Alexandrovich Nabokov.
† Minus 40 is the only temperature where Celsius and Fahrenheit are equivalent. Dostoevsky could have been using the now obsolete Réaumur scale, which would mean it was $-47°C$, but that seems unlikely as the lowest recorded temperature in Omsk is $-41.1°C$. René Antoine Ferchault de Réaumur was a remarkable polymath who also devised a new formula for porcelain, observed that crayfish can regrow their limbs, and proved that rope is stronger than the sum of its strands.

THREE

The Dead House

1850–1854

FYODOR DOSTOEVSKY, 28 YEARS.[92]
Description: White skin, clear face, grey eyes, regular nose, blond hair, small scar on the forehead over the left brow.*

Build: Strong.

Why sentenced: Distribution of printed works directed against the government.

Who made the decision: His Majesty – His personal decision with his General-Adjutant.

Punishment: Deprived of all civil rights.

Behaviour: Good conduct.

Term: Four years of hard labour in prison with consecutive service as private in the army.

Religion: Christian Orthodox.

Height: 2 arshins, 6 vershoks.†

Family status: Single.

What is hell? I maintain that it is the suffering of being unable to love.[93]

---

* Others describe him as having a grey pallor, grey-blue eyes, little dark red or 'scrofulous' spots, and being covered with moles.
† Five feet, six and a half inches. His contemporary Baron Wrangel described him as 'a bit taller than average', though others described him as shorter than average, possibly owing to his posture. According to Max Roser, the average height for a Russian male in 1850 was five feet, five inches (165 cm).

On 23 January 1850, when finally they arrived in Omsk, Fyodor was taken to the prison in his fetters. Durov was there, too, but Fyodor had decided to avoid him at all costs. They had barely spoken to each other during the past four weeks, except at a stop in Tobolsk, where they had an opportunity to meet the wives of the Decembrists (one of whom gave Fyodor a Bible). At times on the journey, the cold had been so severe as to be almost unendurable, but he might as well get used to suffering, since there was nothing he could do about it now.

My first impression on entering the prison was one of disgust, and yet – strange to say – it seemed to me that it would be easier to live here than I imagined on the journey. The prisoners walked freely around, though they were in fetters, talking and smoking.[94] It was already dark and the men were returning from their work to be lined up for the evening roll call. It was there that Fyodor had his first encounter with the angry (or perhaps drunk) Major Krivtsov. *His spiteful, purple, pimply face made a very depressing impression, as though a malicious spider had run out to pounce on some poor fly that had landed in its web.*[95] The Major ordered Fyodor's head to be shaved (or half of it, in fact, from ear to ear) and his clothing and property were to be taken, except for his Bible, which he was allowed to keep, and which had ten roubles slotted down the spine. He was given his prison clothes: a grey and black cap, a coat of the same colour, with a yellow diamond on the back, and a sheepskin with a high collar to protect the ears. Turning to him, the Major warned: 'Mind you behave yourself. I don't want to hear of you, or there will be corporal punishment. If you put one foot out of line – the lash!'[96]

Shortly afterwards, Fyodor was taken straight to his barrack, a low, stuffy room, the gloom punctuated by weak tallow candles (there were small windows, but the ice on them was an inch thick). He was given a low shelf to sleep on, by the door. The boards were rotten. In one corner was a proper bedstead where an old soldier would be locked in with them to keep the peace. On the ground, the filth lay thick and slippery. At the far end was a wooden trough which stank unmistakably of stale shit, to say nothing of the prisoners themselves. He could not see, or if he saw, could not identify, anywhere that a person could bathe.

When our prison room was shut up, it suddenly assumed a new aspect, and it was only now that I could see my fellow prisoners completely at home.[97] *They all quietly settled down in their places and lit their own candles. One sat down to stitch his boot, another took up sewing. The stove took six logs at once, but the ice in the room barely thawed, and it produced horrid fumes.*[98] A group squatted on their heels around a rug to play cards. They took out their loose change and persuaded one destitute soul to keep watch at the door all night for a paltry five copecks. He seemed happy enough, listening out in the passage by the door in the frost, but probably he was a pauper by nature. *Everywhere in Russia there have always been, and always will be certain strange individuals who, while humble and by no means lazy, are destined to be broke for ever.*[99]

As he lay on his plank, Fyodor was conspicuous by his idleness. Looking around the room, there were not more than five people who weren't up to something, and their work wasn't restricted to light sewing: one of his more ambitious neighbours was making a multi-coloured Chinese lantern, which had apparently been ordered in the town at a fairly good price. The prisoner introduced himself as Efim Belykh, and it transpired that, far from being a peasant, he used to be an army ensign, before murdering a Caucasian prince. He worked methodically without stopping until he was finished, put the lantern neatly away, said his prayers, and went to sleep. *I lay down on the bare boards, put my clothes under my head (I had no pillow), and covered myself with my sheepskin. But for a long time I could not get to sleep, though I felt exhausted and broken by the monstrous strangeness of my first impressions. There was much ahead of me that I had never dreamed of.*[100]

Before it had grown light, someone was beating out a tattoo on a loud drum. *By the dim candlelight, the prisoners began to get up, shivering with the cold. Most were silent and sullen. They yawned, stretched and wrinkled their branded foreheads.*[101] Ten minutes later the duty sergeant unlocked the doors. As their door opened, the fresh winter air rushed in, and Fyodor watched it turn to swirling cloud as it met the stuffy air of the barrack. Someone brought in a pail of water and the prisoners began to quarrel over the single ladle, filling their mouths and washing their hands and faces, while others crossed themselves.

They all wandered sleepily over to the kitchen, where the cooks (also convicts) were cutting up bread, sharing the prized regulation knife. The others kept calling them 'kitchen maids', which they didn't seem to mind. The rest of the prisoners stood round in their caps and sheepskin coats, crumbling their bread into cups of kvass.* An old man sat at one of the benches, scowling as he gummed his bit of bread, and bickered familiarly with a young man who came to sit next to him. By the time they were all belted up and ready for roll call, the kitchen had become incredibly noisy. *And what masters of swearing they are! Such elaborate oaths, artistic, even. They turned bad language into a science of abuse.*[102]

On that first morning, he was not sent out to work with the others, who had to clear snow around government buildings or bake alabaster for pounding. He was allowed three days to rest from the journey. Left to his own devices for the short daylight hours, he familiarised himself with the grounds. The prison yard was an irregular hexagon, perhaps 200 paces long and 150 wide, surrounded by a high fence or stockade with 1,500 posts (one of the prisoners had counted them). One for every day of his sentence, near enough. Along the sides there were two long, wooden barracks, the kitchen and a storage hut. If you glimpsed through the gaps in the fence, you could see only a muddy rampart guarded by sentries and a thin strip of sky – a free, open sky, hardly the same as the one which gave a ceiling to the prison yard. *But man is a creature that can get used to anything; indeed, that's the best definition of him.*[103] Which was just as well because, when they returned to the kitchen for dinner, the great cauldron of cabbage soup had been thickened not only with grain, but with an immense number of cockroaches.

The next day, he was taken to the engineers' workshop to have his fetters changed. It was a low stone building in a large courtyard,

---

* Kvass is a small beer made from fermented rye bread and considered non-alcoholic in most Slavic countries. Russians had been drinking it for about a thousand years as an alternative to water.

comprising a smithy, locksmith, carpentry and painter's workshop. Belykh had come along too, to mix paints, and Fyodor mentioned the grim looks he had been attracting.

'Yes,' Belykh replied, 'they don't like gentlemen, especially the political ones. They'd ideally like to kill them. But what can you expect? They've all been serfs or soldiers.'[104] It was nauseating to think that he might be killed by a group of peasants, like his father before him, not least because he had been arrested for plotting their emancipation.

In the smithy, they took off his first fetters, which he couldn't work in as they were made up of rings and sat outside the clothes. He had a brief moment without them – ten pounds lifted off his body! – before the new ones went on. He had to take off his trousers, put on the fetters, which attached to a belt around his waist, then put his trousers back on over them. Strange to think that he would not take them off again until he was thirty-three.

Some peasant girls from the town came round selling white rolls – some of the girls quite little. One of the convicts began flirting with one of the older girls quite unashamedly, and Fyodor turned back to Belykh incredulously.

'Are they really . . .?'[105]

'It does happen,' Belykh replied, lowering his eyes.

Apparently, their mothers baked the rolls and the girls brought them in to sell to the prisoners. When they grew up, they kept coming to the prison, only they stopped bringing the bread. Of course, a rendezvous was a complicated business. It meant arranging a time and a secluded spot, not to mention coming to an understanding with the guards, all of which involved considerable expense. And so instead, smuggled vodka was considered the most economical of the available vices.

During those first days I loitered miserably around the prison, tormented by a terrible devouring melancholy.[106] *'A dead house,' I thought to myself, standing on the prison steps at twilight and looking at the convicts who had returned from work, loafing about the yard.*[107] *But it's my world now, which I must live in whether I like it or not.* It was almost a relief when, on the fourth morning, he was sent out to work.

Out in the yard, an officer stood with a few other soldiers. The roll was called and the tailors were sent off first. Then there were those in the workshops, followed by the unskilled workers. Fyodor was assigned to help break up old government barges on the River Irtysh behind the fortress.*

Two or three men went off to get tools. The day was cloudy but warm, almost thawing, as they set off with a rhythmic, metallic clinking. Fyodor was eager to find out what sort of work it was, this hard labour, and how he would acquit himself, doing manual work for the first time. On the way, they met a bearded man who stopped and put his hand in his pocket, and a convict rushed forward to receive his loose change. Some of the group were sullen, others listless, though one was inexplicably merry, singing a jaunty tune, which drew heckles. *He was evidently one of those volunteer entertainers, or rather buffoons, who make it their duty to amuse their gloomy companions, and who get nothing but abuse for their trouble.*[108]

Presently they reached the riverbank, where the barge lay trapped in the ice. On the other bank the steppe stretched into the blue distance. From up on this side the broad landscape opened up and he could just see the black specks of nomads' tents. There, men were living free, utterly unlike the men here; there time itself seemed to stand still, as if they and their flock were still in the time of Abraham.

I expected that everyone would get straight to work, but they had no intention.[109] Some of the party sat down on the nearest log; people started taking little pouches of tobacco and short, home-made willow pipes out of their boots. The soldiers had formed a half-hearted cordon around them. They lit their pipes, watching peasants trudge down the road to work. A brisk, lively woman came selling rolls, and the communal 5 copecks was handed over, the rolls shared out.

Eventually the sergeant came to chivvy them along, and they slouched down to the river. They bickered about how best to

---

*This is the 4,000-km-long river in which Ermak Timofeevich, Cossack conqueror of Siberia, was killed and washed away in a Tatar ambush in 1585.

preserve the barge's beams and ribs. One silent lad went over and grabbed a beam, but no one came to help him.

'Shall I pickle you for the winter?' shouted the sergeant. 'Get on with it!'

They began unwillingly and incompetently. *It was quite irritating to see a crowd of sturdy workmen who seemed determined to be puzzled about how to go about the work.*[110] They started to remove the smallest beam, but it began to break, and they stopped again for a lengthy discussion about what was to be done. In the end, it seemed that axes weren't enough, and other tools were needed. Two people were dispatched with a convoy to the fortress to get them. The others serenely sat down on the barge, pulled out their pipes, and began smoking again at their leisure. The sergeant gave up and stormed off to the fortress.

An hour or so later, the officer in charge appeared. He heard the convicts out and then announced that they were to get four beams out without splitting them and break up a good chunk of the rest before they could pause for their meal. Suddenly axes started swinging, bolts were unscrewed. Others thrust thick poles into the ground and 20 of them levered out the beams. *Wherever I tried to help, I was superfluous, in the way, pushed aside.*[111]

Finally one of them turned and said, 'Why do you keep sticking your nose in where you're not wanted?'

'You're out of your depth,' chimed in another.

Fyodor went and stood on his own at the other end of the barge.

'Look at the workmen they send us,' said another. 'He can't do anything.'

The others seemed to find that very amusing.

The barge was by now seething with activity. It was a lot of work, but half an hour before the drum beat, it was done, and they started back to the fortress, tired but content. It seemed they would work as hard as necessary for that bare half hour of relative freedom.

On the way back, Fyodor fell into a reverie. *The labour itself did not seem so very hard, so penal, but after a while I realised that the penal character of the work lay not so much in its being difficult and unremitting as its being forced.*[112] The work itself was barely worth doing – most of the salvage was only good for firewood, and would sell for a pittance in the town. *It occurred to me that if one wanted to crush, to annihilate a man utterly, to inflict on him the worst possible punishment, so that the most ferocious murderer would shudder at the thought, one need only give him work that was absolutely useless and nonsensical. If he had to pour water from one vessel to the other and back, over and over again, or move a heap of earth from one place to another and back, I believe the convict would hang himself in a few days or commit a thousand new crimes, preferring to die rather than endure such humiliation, shame and suffering.*[113]

Fyodor returned to the fortress that evening worn out and miserable. He paced up and down along the fence as dusk came on, counting the fence posts, thinking how many days he had ahead of him, all exactly alike. As he walked, a big mongrel came wagging up, black with white markings. No one else had taken any notice of him. Fyodor bent to stroke him. The dog stood quietly, wagging his bushy tail. *I don't know what came over me, but I fell to kissing him, I put my arms around his head; he put his front paws on my shoulders and licked my face. From that day, when I returned from work during that hard and gloomy period, I would hurry behind the prison buildings to find the dog leaping and whining with joy. And I remember I even took pleasure, as though I were gloating to myself of my own misery, in thinking that this dog was the only creature who loved me, who was devoted to me, my only friend in the world.*[114]

———

As it turned out, there was nowhere to bathe at all within the fortress. There were two public bath houses in the town, one for the rich and the other for the poor, and it was the latter to which they were taken one frosty, sunny morning. Everyone was delighted to escape the grounds of the fortress, and to see the town. The guards weren't taking any chances, and an entire platoon of soldiers accompanied them with loaded rifles. Next to Fyodor walked Petrov, a short, well-built man of forty, never without a lump of tobacco resting on his gum, who was in the 'special class' reserved for the worst criminals. For reasons that Fyodor couldn't discern, Petrov had begun to seek him out most days, and would stop by to exchange a word or two with him. *He seemed to look on me as a sort of child, almost a baby, who didn't understand the simplest things of the world.*[115]

It was almost as cold inside as it had been outdoors. In one corner, someone was selling hot spiced tea and rolls. Petrov helped Fyodor to undress, which was not as easy as you might assume, in fetters. First you had to unlace the leather bands that went underneath the ankle irons to prevent the iron from rubbing off the skin. Then, you had to get your underclothes off from under the fetters. There was a real art to it: first you pulled one side down underneath the fetters, pulled your foot out, and then drew the leg of it back up through the ring, then you had to repeat the action on the other side. He had had to do it once before, on the way here, when they stopped in Tobolsk – he'd been shown the ropes by a robber who had been chained to a wall for the past five years.

Fyodor gave Petrov a few copecks to get soap, and he duly returned with a little coin of it, no deeper than a slice of cheese. Each of them was allowed a single bucketful of hot water. Petrov led him by the arm towards the bathing room, as Fyodor stumbled in his loose fetters.

'Pull them up, around your calves,' Petrov repeated, holding Fyodor up like a nurse, 'and now be careful – here's a step.' *I wanted to assure Petrov that I could walk alone, but he wouldn't have believed me. And yet he was not servile in the least; if I had offended him, he would have known how to deal with me. I had not promised him money for his services, and he himself had not asked me for any. Why, then, did he look after me?*[116]

They opened the door to the bathroom itself. Imagine: a square room 12 paces across, in which were packed at least 80 men. Steam blinded the eyes and there was nowhere to put a foot down. Fyodor tried to turn back, but Petrov egged him on. They squeezed through the slippery bodies to the benches at the end, over the heads of men squatting on the floor, who stooped to one side as they passed. Every place on the benches was taken. Petrov began negotiating with a convict for a place on the bench with a copeck that he'd had the foresight to bring with him, and the convict immediately ducked underneath the bench, where others still were swarming, and where it was hot and dirty, the slime on the floor accumulating to the depth of almost half a finger. *There was not a spot on the floor as big as the palm of your hand where there was not a convict squatting, splashing from his bucket. Some washed themselves standing, and the dirty water trickled off them onto the shaven heads of the convicts sitting below them. Further up on the top bench, others huddled in the steam. Men of the peasant class don't wash much with soap and water; they only steam themselves terribly and then splash themselves with cold water – that's their idea of a bath.*[117]

Petrov had sat down at Fyodor's feet and declared himself very comfortable. He helped Fyodor to soap himself, and washed his 'little feet', as he called them. Around them, fifty birches rose and fell in unison as the peasants thrashed themselves stupid among the steam, the shouting and the clanking of chains. As prisoners passed each other, some of their chains got tangled up and they would fall into the liquid filth, cursing. As they grew hotter, the steaming backs of the convicts began to reveal every lash they had received in the past, so that they all began to look freshly wounded. *A shiver ran through me at the sight of them. It occurred to me that if one day we should all be in hell together it would be very much like this place. I could not help expressing this thought to Petrov; he looked around and said nothing.*[118]

Time passed, and little by little I got used to it. Every day, I was less bewildered by my new life. My eyes grew accustomed to my surroundings. To be reconciled to this life was impossible, but it was high time to accept it as a stubborn fact. I no longer drew the same intense curiosity from the other convicts. I walked around as if I were at home and kept to my place on the planks. Regularly once a week I went to have my head shaved. I felt that work would prove my salvation: let me be out in the open air, make myself tired, grow used to carrying heavy weights. At first my love of work provoked the other convicts, who jeered and mocked me. But I took no notice.[119] Once, he woke up around two in the morning to the sound of stifled sobs. A little grey old man of sixty, a schismatic who had been imprisoned for burning down an Orthodox church, was sitting up on the stove, reading prayers aloud from a little book. From time to time he muttered, 'Lord, do not forsake me! Lord, give me strength! My little ones, my darling little ones, I shall never see you again!' *I was filled with an indescribable sorrow.*[120]

The first real break from routine came with Easter, when the prisoners had complex arrangements in place to secure their contraband vodka. First, they had to find an agent, whether soldier or prostitute, who would acquire a quantity of vodka (and, inevitably, water it down). The smuggler on the inside would then turn up to the handover with a clean ox-gut, fill it with the vodka, and try to fasten it somewhere inconspicuous, though he might bring a few copecks with him just in case a guard required further assurance. It was a risky business, and so naturally the smuggler was prone to decant a little for his troubles and water the rest down further. The prisoners had to save up for months for the pleasure of drinking this weak vodka on the traditional holiday binge. *This day has been the object of the convict's dreams, night and day, and has kept up his spirits through the weary routine of life. A cup of vodka costs five or six times as much as in a tavern; you can imagine what they will have cost by the time he is drunk.*[121]

By the second day of Easter, the sky was blue, the sun warm and bright (*but there was only gloom in my heart*).[122] The prisoners didn't have to work today and the prison staff had left the convicts to their own devices. Many were already drunk and fights were breaking out across the prison. People sang hideous songs and played cards. On one or two occasions, knives were drawn. A huge Tatar named Gazin lay out cold under his sheepskin, having been beaten senseless by six of the others. He barely showed any sign of life. *All this had worn me out to the point of illness. I made my way to my place and lay down on my back, my hands behind my head, and closed my eyes. I liked to lie like that: a sleeping man was left alone.*[123] Still, he was exposed, lying on his back: the Major sometimes burst into the barracks at night and, if he found anyone sleeping on their right side or their back, he'd punish them the next day. (He had taken up a notion that Christ only slept on his left side.)[124] Lying there with the peasants shouting all around him, Fyodor suddenly remembered the day that he had heard someone cry, 'Wolf!', in the copse in Darovoe, and he remembered how the kindly serf Marko had comforted him. He remembered every detail, down to the motherly way that Marko had touched his cheek. *People talk to you a great deal about your education, but some good, sacred memory preserved from childhood is perhaps the best education. If you have only one good memory left in your heart, even that may prove your salvation.*[125]

Fyodor felt progressively more ill over the next few days. He had terrible diarrhoea from the holiday food – a thin porridge with an imperceptible amount of fat in it – and the joints in his legs became inflamed. One morning, he was too sick to work, and stayed lying on his plank while the others went out for the morning shift. Just then, the Major turned up for a spot inspection, and was incensed to discover Fyodor lying down in the barracks. He flew into a rage and ordered Fyodor lashed. The duty officer tried to explain that he was ill, but the Major was having none of it: he declared that Fyodor was being protected, and must be flogged immediately. Soldiers were dispatched to gather switches and preparations were already underway when the commandant himself, General de Grave, arrived, and called the whole thing off. He even gave the Major a dressing down for trying to flog a sick prisoner.

Soon after the holidays I was taken ill and went to our military hospital.[126] What 'taken ill' meant he struggled to verbalise, so violent was the seizure, the convulsions, the foaming mouth and ragged pulse. It began with an aura, an unpleasant confusion of thought and sensation, as if time itself was being crumpled by a great force. But that was only a foretaste of the disturbance to come. The next moment, the Devil shot into his spine, but Fyodor was gone by then. He went rigid and fell to the ground, landing on his back and head, his muscles spasming rhythmically and painfully. He flapped about on the barrack floor like a galvanised frog. He woke up in a puddle of filth, some of it his own.

The hospital was a long, narrow, one-storey wooden building about half a verst from the fortress, painted a yellow ochre. The doctors there were kind, and efforts were made to clean all the surfaces, though the beds still had bugs. The other patients noticed that Fyodor had brought his own tea – his only real extravagance in prison, other than the occasional bit of meat when he was sick of cabbage soup. Someone offered to get hold of a pot for Fyodor, and one of their neighbours accused the man of being a flunkey. *But I did always prefer to do everything for myself, and indeed I wanted to avoid looking like a soft-handed, womanish little gentleman.*[127]

One of the other patients sneezed into a checked cotton handkerchief that was full of brown snuff. He sneezed again, wrinkling his nose to reveal ancient, blackened teeth in his dribbling red mouth. Then he opened his handkerchief, examined the phlegm, and smeared it on his brown hospital dressing gown. *I began an involuntary inspection of the dressing gown I had on. By now, it had begun to warm on me and smelt more and more strongly of medicines, plasters and some kind of pus, which was not to be wondered at, since it had been on the backs of patients for innumerable years.*[128]

It was while in hospital that Fyodor began to understand what it was to get the lash in Siberia. Two lines of soldiers in uniform were drawn up, each with a thick stick in their hand, to form the formidable 'green street'. The prisoner was stripped and his arms bound to rifle stocks by two officers, whose job it was to drag him the entire length (since he would inevitably stumble after the first few blows landed). As a rule, 500, 1,000, or even 1,500 strokes could be endured, but if the sentence was any more than that, it would be divided into halves by the doctors, and after the first half the prisoner would be taken to the military hospital for a break to improve their chances of living through the second half. Fyodor met one man who had been subjected to 4,000 strokes, and he himself seemed a little surprised he had survived. *Men leaving the hospital for the second half of their punishment were usually gloomy and disinclined to talk. The convicts never talk to the man, and do not attempt to speak of what is in store for him. No unnecessary talk, no attempt at consolation.*[129] *I asked many questions about the pain – I wanted to find out how bad it was, or*

what it could be compared with. But I could not get a satisfactory answer.
They all gave the same answer: it burns; it scorches like fire; it is as though
your back were being roasted.[130] The prisoners all said that the birch
was worse than the rods – it bit the skin more, somehow, and with
a birch a man might be beaten to death in as little as 500 strokes.

The hospital was the only place where Fyodor could take notes, in
a minor conspiracy of smuggled paper arranged with a sympathetic
doctor. He made notes on some of the prisoners he had met: as
well as Petrov there was Aristov, a well-educated, good-looking
man who chillingly refused to make a distinction between good
and evil; there was also Ilinsky, a young man convicted of killing
his father, though he maintained his innocence and didn't seem the
type. Either of them would make fascinating characters when he
started up writing fiction again. Fyodor also had countless hours
to reflect on his own life up to now. *Lying alone on the hospital bed,*
abandoned by those I loved so fondly and intensely, some trivial incident
of the past, often unnoticed at the time and soon forgotten, came back all
at once to my mind and suddenly took on a new significance, completing
and explaining to me what I had failed to understand before.[131] But
the doctor couldn't protect him for ever, and as soon as he had
recovered, Fyodor was sent back to prison.

One of the prisoners, a Pole called Rozhnovsky, seemed surprised
to see him alive. It turned out there had been a mistake in the
hospital registers and Fyodor had been marked as dead. Despite
the ongoing evidence, Rozhnovsky and a few of the others called
him 'dead man' from that point on.

I did at last become accustomed to my life in prison. But it took me almost
a year, and it was the hardest year of my life. It is imprinted on my
memory for ever. I believe I remember every successive hour of it.[132]

More than the physical hardship, it was difficult not to have
any news from Mikhail or from friends in St Petersburg. With
every season that passed, new works were being published, new
genres developing, new themes, new types of characters. It was not

entirely true that he couldn't read or write, but both activities were severely restricted. He had the New Testament that he had been given by one of the Decembrist wives, and one of the officers was kind enough to smuggle him in a couple of books by Dickens. He could only write when there was a free bed in the hospital, where one of the doctors sometimes let him rest. He managed to write a letter to Mikhail once, through the official channels, but he never received a reply. *I feel like a limb that has been lopped off.*[133] Other political prisoners had received letters – why not him? Could Mikhail really not be bothered to write, if only to tell him that he was well? Had he been put off by a surly clerk, and accepted the first answer he was given? Was he even alive? What had happened to his children?

Should I describe all my years in prison? I don't think so. Those long, wearisome days were as monotonous as drops of water falling from a roof after rain. I remember that all that time, though I had hundreds of companions, I was terribly lonely, and at last I grew fond of that loneliness. In my isolation I reviewed all my past life, down to the smallest detail, pondered over my past, and even at times blessed fate for sending me this solitude. I swore to myself that the mistakes and lapses of the past would never happen again.[134]

One season replaced another. In the summer, the convicts would go out to work making bricks three or four versts from the fortress, then carrying them a few hundred paces to the new barracks that were being built. They would spend the short nights scratching at fleas and would be woken at five in the morning, just as the itching finally eased up. The prisoners would travel to work with their mascot Vaska, a beautiful white goat that had turned up one day, at the head of the column. They twisted flowers around his horns and hung garlands over him; there was even talk of gilding his horns in the workshop. At the camp they let him jump up on the tables or butt people for laughs. But one day the Major stopped them on the way to work and ordered the goat to be killed, cooked and put in the prisoners' soup.

I think men pine more bitterly for freedom in the bright sunshine than in the grey days of autumn and winter.[135] Sunshine made everyone impatient and quarrels more frequent. People would stare out at the steppe, stretched out for a thousand versts before them, and sigh deeply. It seemed as if anyone could simply run off and live in the forest somewhere, sleeping under the canopy of the stars. On those days, Fyodor would stare hungrily through the gaps in the stockade on their return to the fortress.

When winter came around, the days grew shorter and they would be locked up in the draughty barracks for hours on end, with ice on the windows and the nauseous smell of animal fat coming off the candles. But at least there was Christmas Day, one of the three days of the year when the prisoners were not sent off to work. Everyone approached the day with great solemnity. Efim Belykh took out the pristine clothes he had been saving and brushed them down; straw was laid down on the floor; everyone went to bed much earlier than usual. In the morning, the guard wished them his best, as the stars began to dim and the frost to sparkle, smoke curling up from the kitchen chimneys. In the kitchen the wives of Omsk left them gifts of pastries and fine bread. The priest came to give them a blessing in front of the icon. One year they even staged a play. But every year a number of them would get surreptitiously drunk, and begin to quarrel, and the next day they would inevitably be sent back out to work again in the deep snow.

In the last year of his sentence, Fyodor managed to get hold of one of the St Petersburg journals. *It was as though news had come to me from another world: my former life rose up before me full of light and colour, and I tried from what I read to guess how far I had dropped behind.*[136] It seemed that so much had happened while he had been away. He pored over every line for hidden meanings and allusions, looking for traces of conversations that he recognised. He leapt at any article signed by a name he knew, though there were many he had never seen before. *How sad it was for me to realise how remote I was from this new life, how cut off from it all.*[137] And yet in some ways, this enforced solitude had also been a kind of salvation. With only a New Testament for company, Fyodor had spent the past four years thinking deeply about God and religion. *At such a time one thirsts for faith as withered grass thirsts for water. I am a child of this century, a child of doubt and disbelief, I always have been and always will be (I know that), until they close the lid of my coffin. But despite all that, there is nothing more beautiful, more profound, more sympathetic, more reasonable, more courageous, more perfect than Christ. Moreover, if someone succeeded in proving to me that Christ wasn't real, I would rather stay with Christ than with the truth.*[138]

On the day of his release, Fyodor went around the barracks to say his goodbyes. Strong, calloused hands reached out to him. Others held back, eyeing him with undiminished hatred. Then the drum beat, and they went off to work, leaving him behind. Ten minutes later, he was taken to the smithy. One of the prisoners who worked there turned Fyodor around and lifted his foot onto the anvil. The prisoner struck at the iron and the fetters simply fell away. He stared at them. It already seemed hard to believe that they had been on his legs moments ago.

'Well, God be with you!'[139] said the prisoners, gruff but pleased.

Yes, God was with us! Freedom, new life, resurrection from the dead . . . What a glorious moment![140]

FOUR

The Devil's Sandbox

1854–1859

J OHN 11:44: AND THE dead man came out.[141]
They let him out in Omsk – *a nasty little town with hardly any trees.** Fyodor hadn't seen or spoken to his brother since Christmas Eve, 1849, and Mikhail was the first person he wrote to, regaling him with the gory details of his imprisonment. In the letter Fyodor asked for money, and a copy of *Notes of the Fatherland*, and books, and he also wanted to know whether there was any way to arrange a transfer to the Caucasus. But most of all he needed money and books. *Why, they are sure to allow me to publish in six years or so, and possibly even before that. Books mean life – they are my food and my future!*[142]

He was soon posted to the 7th Line Battalion of the Siberian Regiment in Semipalatinsk.† *To cheer me up, people tell me, 'You'll meet nothing but simple folk there.' Yes, but I'm more wary of a simple man than of a complicated one.*[143] He didn't relish being a private again – it wasn't much better than being a prisoner, and on the odd occasion it was worse (once, when he was cleaning out the barracks, a sergeant kicked him in the face). He stood guard at the windows of the local prison or at the army grocery shop, dreaming of life

---

* Letter to Mikhail, 22 February 1854. Perhaps the most representative thing you can say about modern-day Omsk is that it has a metro system with only one station.
† Now Semey in Kazakhstan, it was founded as a fort town near a ruined Buddhist monastery. The surrounding steppe is so remote and featureless that it was used as a nuclear testing ground by the Soviets.

55

elsewhere. But he soon became acquainted with town society through the commander of the barracks, Belikhov – a friendly, tipsy man who would later shoot himself after embezzling government funds – and his life became a little easier after that.

Whenever he had time off, he explored the town, a bleak settlement not far from the Eurasian Pole of Inaccessibility, which consisted of unpainted wooden buildings scattered around the River Irtysh, with seven mosques and a solitary Orthodox church. The place was so dusty that locals called it the Devil's Sandbox. To the north was a Cossack settlement, to the south a sad desert of Tatars, and in the middle, the fortress. There were about five or six thousand inhabitants including the garrison, and out of those, perhaps ten or fifteen who subscribed even to a single journal. The town shared a piano. The women gossiped; the men drank vodka and played cards. The idea that the same country was at war in the Crimea seemed hopelessly abstract here – they might as well ask what was going on in Hong Kong.

Fyodor soon received special permission to live in his own quarters, close to the barracks. *In the first place I wanted a separate tenement, not a room in other people's lodgings; secondly, though I could make do with one room, it must be a large one, and, of course, it had at the same time to be as cheap as possible. In a confined space, even thought is cramped.*[144] He found himself an isolated log house in the middle of a heath. In order to protect it from bandits, there were no windows at the front of the building, only two at the back, facing onto a tall fence. The main room was dim, with a low ceiling and clay walls, but it was big and, crucially, he was alone. *It is now almost five years that I have been under guard among a crowd of people, and I never had a single hour alone. To be alone is a normal need, like eating and drinking – otherwise, this forced communism becomes an unbearable torture. It was this that made me suffer most during those four years.*[145]

In fact, he was not wholly alone – the place was host to a number of cockroaches already. He had rented it from an old widow for five roubles a month, for which he would get cabbage soup sans cockroaches, black bread and porridge; she would do the laundry, and the eldest of her two daughters, a widow at twenty-two, would come around to clean what could be cleaned. Sometimes she would stay after she'd finished the cleaning, sometimes even slip into her negligé, a red sash around her waist. (He had, after all, been in prison a long time.) Out in the town, Fyodor also met a seventeen-year-old girl he became extremely fond of, Elizaveta Nevrotova. He would see her in the marketplace, selling white loaves like the girls who had visited the prison to support their families. He was bound to his service as a private, of course, and she had no education, but he wrote her letters all the same. 'My beloved Elizaveta – Yesterday, I wanted to see you.'[146]

One day in autumn, he received the ominous message that the Public Prosecutor for Civil and Criminal Affairs wanted to see him. Fyodor dressed in his red stand-up collar and grey army greatcoat and went to bite the bullet. He arrived to find a young man of twenty-one who immediately set about apologising for not having called on him in person, and began handing over letters and parcels for him. There was a letter from Maikov, and another from Mikhail, with 50 roubles enclosed, and the prosecutor had underwear and books for him, too. It transpired that this young man, Baron Alexander Wrangel, had been in the crowd at Fyodor's mock execution and knew all about his situation. While Fyodor was standing there looking through the parcels, the Baron received a letter of his own. Opening it there and then, the Baron read a little, burst into tears, and threw his arms around the surprised private. Fyodor could not resist this sort of emotional honesty, and they became friends then and there.

The two men would meet often. Fyodor found Wrangel kind, a little proud – *but only on the surface and I rather like that*[147] – impressionable, studious, moderately cultured. What would anger most men only saddened him – *the sign of a great heart.*[148] This was a man who could be trusted, a man with whom one could discuss ideas. (Wrangel was also generous enough to loan him 125 roubles, which didn't go amiss.) The two men soon took a cottage together and would stay up late into the night, Fyodor drinking tea and pinching a little of Wrangel's tobacco for his pipe, or going out to swim together in the river. Fyodor would help Wrangel in the garden, wearing a faded rose-coloured jacket, his silver watch chain dangling around his neck. They went out into the steppe on horseback, too, but Fyodor never wrote about the landscape. He felt nothing for the yawning sky, whole clouds roaming across it like a ghostly caravan, the endless carpet of flowers, the double horizon of the earth and the birch trees – he was interested only in people.

Sometimes the landlady's daughters would join them for a spot of gardening and he would find himself reciting Pushkin, even singing opera. But these were distractions. He needed to get permission to return to European Russia and he had to begin writing again. That was the most important thing. Life could not continue until he was allowed to publish. *I have the strong impression that very soon, any moment now, something decisive is going to happen to me, that I am approaching the critical point in my life, that I have ripened and that something is about to happen, something quiet and bright, perhaps dreadful, certainly inevitable.*[149]

On 18 February 1855, Tsar Nicholas I died in the Winter Palace, officially of pneumonia, although there were rumours that he had poisoned himself after the humiliating turn of the war in Crimea. When the news reached Semipalatinsk on 12 March, it raised the possibility of an amnesty for Fyodor, particularly since Nicholas's son, Alexander, was rumoured to be more liberal. Fyodor immediately penned a sycophantic poem dedicated to his dead tormentor, and another to the new Tsar Alexander – the Tsar is dead, long live the Tsar – hoping that these prostrations might set a precedent. But this was not the decisive event.

One day, his commanding officer, Belikhov, invited him to dinner, where he met Alexander Isaev, a local excise officer who had been struck off a few months earlier for drunkenness. He had depended on his salary for an income, and his young family was now slipping into poverty as local society looked disinterestedly on. He was a curious fellow, passionate and stubborn, honourable and unseemly, civilised in his conversation and yet almost never sober. *But it wasn't him who attracted me, it was his wife.*[150]

Madame Isaeva had the same Christian name as his mother: Maria. *She was terribly thin, quite tall, with a delicate and elegant figure.*[151] At twenty-eight years old she was pretty, intelligent and cultured, a rare combination in this part of the world. He found her at times playful, and at others extremely volatile. She had that scornful kind of cynicism that is the last refuge of an idealist who has been disappointed too many times by the realities of the world, *sick, irritated and embittered by being under-appreciated and misunderstood.*[152] She was physically frail and given to coughing, like the heroine of a good romantic fable. Fyodor found himself spellbound, as if he were looking in on some warped memory of his own past: Maria the consumptive, put-upon mother, her husband the sometimes violent drunkard, and their son, the seven-year-old Pasha, the awkward little boy looking awkwardly on.

Fyodor offered himself as a tutor to Pasha, a smart but distracted young boy who took no interest in his studies, and befriended husband and wife as if he were a well-wisher, taking any opportunity to lecture Isaev while he got to know Maria better. The better he knew her, the more convinced he was that he loved her, and that she loved him in return. He finally had an answer to the inscription on his mother's locket: 'The feeling of love fills up my heart; when will you feel it, for your part?'* What might his mother have thought of her second son if she had known that he would first fall in love in his mid-thirties, as an army private in Siberia, and with a married woman?

Against the expectations of everyone who knew him, Isaev actually managed to find another job. It was a humiliating demotion to assessor, but it was work all the same. The snag was that the job was in Kuznetsk,† more than 700 versts deeper into Siberia, which meant that Fyodor would have to say goodbye to Maria, possibly for ever. 'You see, she has agreed to go, she didn't protest. That is what is so galling,'[153] Fyodor explained to Wrangel.

On the day the Isaevs were due to leave, Fyodor invited them over to say farewell before seeing them off. Wrangel dutifully topped

---

* My translation from the French: 'J'ai le cœur tout plein d'amour; quand l'aurais-vous à votre tour?'
† Now Novokuznetsk.

up Isaev's champagne glass until he was insensible, whereupon they lumped him in Wrangel's carriage; Fyodor got into a second carriage with Maria so that they might have some privacy. It was a clear, moonlit night. They stopped at the forest on the outskirts of town, where the lovers wept and embraced. Then Fyodor and Wrangel picked up Isaev, transferred him to Maria's carriage, said their goodbyes, and the horses started up.

Fyodor stood rooted to the spot, tears rolling down his cheeks. He could see the carriage disappearing down the forest path; next he could only hear it; then it was gone. Gently, Wrangel took his hand and he came to, as if waking from a long sleep, and got in the carriage without a word. Back at his lodgings, he paced silently back and forth in his soft shoes, as was his habit, while the sun came up. *Suffering and pain are always mandatory for broad minds and deep hearts. Truly great people, it seems to me, should feel great sadness on this earth.*[154]

For two weeks now, I've been so sad that I don't know what to do with myself.[155] He moped around the town like a lovesick teenager, waiting for the coachman to come from Kuznetsk in the hope of receiving a letter. He went over to the Isaevs' old apartment and took their potted ivy into his care; the dog greeted him enthusiastically but wouldn't leave the house. He wrote to Maria, but the letter only reminded him of the distance between them. Come twilight, when he would normally have paid a visit to the Isaevs, he was desolate. *My heart has always been that way – it latches onto the things that are dear to it, and when the time comes for me to tear it away, it bleeds.*[156]

When he had nothing else to do, he wrote reminiscences about his time in prison. He had been composing in his head during the whole of his incarceration, seething with ideas. He had been aching to get it all down on paper, but then he had met Maria, and – *I couldn't write. Something long overdue had finally happened, carried me away and absorbed me. I was happy, I couldn't work.*[157] Now that she had left, he was miserable, but at least he could write again. He was even working on a comic novel, *The Village of Stepanchikovo*, about a passive-aggressive middle-aged pseudo-intellectual who begins meddling in an unsuspecting family's affairs. He was also catching up on a five-year reading backlog. Turgenev had collected his first batch of stories together in 1852, *A Sportsman's Sketches*, which had propelled him to fame. *I like Turgenev best. It is a shame, however, that with all his immense talent he is so uneven. I like Lev Tolstoy very much, too, although I don't think he will write much. (Still, I may be wrong.)*[*]

Try as he might to distract himself, he was desperate to see Maria. He hatched a plan to meet her in Zmiev, 150 versts from Semipalatinsk. He would claim to his superiors that he was sick, and Maria would have to come up with her own excuse to get away from Isaev. Fyodor arranged a sick note from a sympathetic doctor and set out with borrowed horses for Zmiev, a day's ride away. When he got there he didn't find Maria. Instead, she had sent a note saying that she could not be there as her circumstances had changed. Wearily, he got back into his carriage and rode all day home again. Then, in August 1855, she wrote to inform him that her husband had died. *So she was left with a child in a far-flung, savage district in hopeless beggary.*[†] Fyodor had wanted to be with Maria before, but now what he wanted might also be seen, given her circumstances, as chivalrous. He sent her his last 25 roubles, along with a proposal of marriage, and waited for the coachman to ride hundreds of versts to Kuznetsk

ply to be ridden back again through the snow a week and for her re
ply, she declined; she could not marry a private. later. In her re

the distance between them keenly, and his attempt to Fyodor felt
aria didn't forget him had all the subtlety of a debutant. make sure Ma
ell her about all the parties he had been attending for He wrote to t
rowing in mention of the local ladies he had been Shrovetide, t

ov, 18 January 1856. Unusually, the name Lev (meaning Lion) was
stoy's authorised translators, first in French as Léon, and then in
by Constance Garnett, with whom the writer was friendly. Why
ave been dubbed Leo when Dostoevsky was never Theodore may
accident, but it seems telling that Fyodor remained stubbornly

ishment, p. 21. Maria was actually in contact with her father, who
roubles from Astrakhan.

Letter to Maiko
localised by Tols
English as Leo
Tolstoy should h
be a historical a
Russian.
† Crime and Pun
had sent her 300

61

dancing with. It backfired spectacularly. Maria replied that she felt tortured by the thought that her only friend was already forgetting her. Worse still, before he could formulate a reply she wrote again, asking for his advice as a friend: what if a nice old man in a secure position wanted to marry her instead?

Fyodor wept all night. *I barely understand how I go on living. The joy of love is great, but its sufferings are so intense that it would be much better never to love at all.*[158] He became fixated by the idea that he was now living out the exact plot of his own novel, *Poor Folk*. The beautiful, abandoned young woman and the poor, devoted older man who loved her as dearly as his own life, but who could not provide for her; the young woman whisked away from him by a richer man she didn't even love. Fyodor replied to the letter threatening to kill himself and begging her not to commit herself yet. *I have never lived through such despair – a deadly anguish is tugging at my heart; at night I have horrible dreams; I cry out in my sleep; I am choked by spasms in my throat; and my tears are either stubbornly dammed up or gush out . . . Come what may, I just cannot give her up. At my age, love is no whim.*[159]

This was his first true love and, having no basis for comparison, he held nothing back, but pinned his self-esteem to the relationship. There was no apparent alternative, no possibility of criticism. The first person to truly see someone in this way holds over them the possibility of taking away their mirror; the lover is scared to lose the object of their love, yes, but more scared that if they leave, they will lose sight of themselves. The fact that such a relationship has never come before raises the horrifying possibility that it might never come again, that this might be the only love, the one true love spoken of so often in art. So the artistically inclined are prone to falling for the narrative convenience of a single, predestined love, and to chasing it in terror. The pleasure and the suffering are inextricable. *In despair there are the most intense enjoyments, especially when one is acutely conscious of the hopelessness of one's position.*[160]

Maria wouldn't marry Fyodor until he had money – but he couldn't get money without first obtaining permission to publish his work, or at the very least, a promotion to the rank of officer.

Meanwhile, the townspeople of Kuznetsk were plotting against him, flinging marriage proposals at Maria, wearing her down, tormenting her with her own hopelessness. She wrote that she loved him more than anything, but here she was entertaining a proposal from another. Worst of all, Mikhail, who had always been Fyodor's closest confidant, had barely written to him at all since he had been released. He wrote Mikhail another long letter telling him everything, but without much hope of a reply. 'My brother, can it be that you have changed towards me? How cold you are, you don't want to write, once in seven months you send some money and a letter of three lines. Just like charity. I don't want charity without a brother! Don't insult me! My friend! I'm so unhappy!'

In her next reply, Maria appeared comforted by Fyodor's misery. This was the answer she had been looking for: he hadn't forgotten her. And yet she also wrote, 'We have suffered too much, have been too unfortunate, to dream of marriage.' Her instinct for melodrama chimed perfectly with Fyodor's desire to live one out. He hatched a more audacious plan than the trip to Zmiev: he would go all the way to see her. With Belikhov's help, he was assigned to guard the delivery of a wagonload of ropes to Barnaul, which would take him most of the way. From there, he continued on without permission to Kuznetsk.

When he arrived, Maria began to cry. *Her lips faintly quivered, as though she wanted to utter something, some greeting to me, but she said nothing. My heart ached as I looked at those pale, hollow cheeks, feverishly parted lips, and eyes that gleamed under long, dark lashes with feverish fire. But my God, how lovely she was!*[161] He quickly learned that Maria had met a twenty-four-year-old schoolteacher named Nikolai Borisovich Vergunov and planned to marry him, despite his income being as pitiful as Fyodor's. That struck Fyodor as a very bad idea, and he told her all the reasons why – well, *about a tenth of it.*[162] He stayed for two days, swallowing the feeling that he had been humiliated and insulted, and meeting with both Maria and Vergunov himself. *He had fair hair, large, soft, dreamy blue eyes, in which there were occasional flashes of the most spontaneous, childish gaiety. He was weak, confiding and faint-hearted; he had no will whatever. He had at most one virtue, a good heart, positively a dangerous possession with his other failings.*˙ Fyodor tried instead to dissuade the two of them from entering into such an unequal marriage, pointing out in a brotherly way that Vergunov didn't have any money and was going to ruin her for the sake of his own happiness (*imagine, he was offended*).[163] When he realised that haranguing them was only pushing her and Vergunov closer together, he changed tack. Fyodor talked to Vergunov on his own, and in the end they even became close. *He cried, but that's all he knows how to do.*[164] Maria responded well to Fyodor's more dignified bearing towards the end of the trip and, before he took his leave, she told him, 'Don't cry, don't be sad – not everything is decided yet.'[165]

Knowing that his rival would be right beside her and he far away, and seeing that she might marry Vergunov anyway, Fyodor swallowed his pride. *I felt that I might be mistaken in my conclusions about him if only from the fact that he was my enemy.*[166] Deciding to live up to his own high ideals and perform a true act of love, Fyodor wrote to Wrangel asking him to pull a few strings to see if he could get Vergunov promoted, so that the newlyweds might have a better life. *This is all for her, for her alone, if only so that she won't be impoverished.*[167] A cynic might judge that, having noted how his selfishness had repelled her, Fyodor had decided to risk everything on a grand gesture. Whatever the motivation for helping his rival, it impressed Maria greatly, and Fyodor held out hope that she might put off the marriage to Vergunov until he could obtain his own promotion.

On 30 October 1856 – not a moment too soon – he received his commission as a second lieutenant. He obtained permission for fifteen days off from Belikhov and rushed to see Maria. *She is all that matters in my life. I think of nothing else. All I want is to see her, to hear her voice. I am an unhappy madman. This kind of love is a disease.*[168] On his arrival, he was struck by how ill she looked.

˙ *The Insulted and Injured*, pp. 39–40, 95. In general, Fyodor believed that a good heart was all that anyone needed – 'one may err in ideas, but the heart cannot err' (Letter to Maikov, 16 January 1856) – but he was willing to make an exception for his rival.

Her hair was still beautiful, but her cheeks were red and blotchy. *Her lips were crusted, her breathing uneven and broken. Her eyes had a feverish gleam, but their gaze was sharp and still, and her consumptive, distressed face made a painful impression.*[169] He explained everything about his situation to her, honestly and frankly, his new position as an officer and his hopes to be allowed to publish imminently, and asked whether she would be his wife. This time she said yes.

Fyodor borrowed 650 roubles from a local captain of engineers attached to one of the nearby mining operations, and another 600 from his uncle to set them up. The ceremony was held on 6 February 1857, with the local police chief and his wife acting as the bride's parents. In a Russian wedding, it was traditional for the bride to be washed while her party sang, for her maiden's braid to be taken out, and plaited again as two braids, but perhaps Maria decided to forego this ritual for her second marriage. At the wedding itself, Nikolai Vergunov was in attendance – he was by all accounts a simpleton, but still one whose unfeigned kindness extended to celebrating the wedding of his erstwhile fiancée to his rival. At thirty-five years old, it might finally have seemed that Fyodor was starting a new life in which he could approach happiness. But he made a lot of predictions, and not all of them came true.

As they stopped in Barnaul that night, Fyodor had his first full epileptic fit. He'd had fits before, but had been reluctant to call his condition by its name, and in the past his doctors had assured him that they were simply nervous fits. This one was of a different order.

It began as a flash of light. Suddenly he felt his whole body seized with tension. *The sense of life, the consciousness of self, were multiplied ten times during that lightning strike. My mind and heart were flooded with extraordinary light; all my unease, my doubts, my anxieties were submerged in a lofty calm, full of serene harmony, joy and hope. But this moment, this flash, was only a prelude to that final second when the fit began. That second was, of course, unendurable.*[170]

Thinking of that flash of beauty later, as he nursed his crumpled body, he would try to tell himself that it was nothing but a disease, an interruption of health. And yet, in spite of himself, he felt the opposite. Up to then he hadn't suspected such a feeling could exist, a feeling of completeness, of proportion, of reconciliation – an ecstasy, even. *It is not earthly – I don't mean that it's heavenly, but that an earthly creature cannot endure it. He must be physically changed or die.*[171] Language was too weak to express it. It was not as though the experience had made him hallucinate, or even distort his reason, as you might expect from hashish, opium or wine. It was rather an extraordinary quickening of consciousness – not merely understanding that he was alive, but feeling the life course through the tips of him like electricity. *At that second, that is at the very last conscious moment before the fit, I had time to say to myself clearly and consciously, 'Yes, for this moment one might give one's whole life!'*[172] He thought it was, perhaps, the same moment that existed for the epileptic Mohammed, when Allah showed him all the heavens and returned him to earth in the time it took for a drop of water to fall from his pitcher. And yet Maria only saw her husband fall to the ground, gnashing his teeth, his body pulsing to an imperceptible rhythm, wracked into unholy forms.

It scared my wife to death and filled me with sadness and depression.[173] The learned doctor told him that, in spite of the other advice he'd been given, Fyodor had real epilepsy and could expect to suffocate during any one of the fits as a result of his throat closing. Given that he might have a fit at any time, sometimes several in a month, and that there was no known cure or prevention, it seemed likely that this was how he would die. It could happen in a month or in a year, or in ten – there was no way of knowing. *I begged him to tell me the whole truth, on his honour. He advised me to beware of the new moon.*[174]

———

The marriage never really recovered after that first night. *The black cat has run between us.*˙ Maria, by some accounts, felt she had

---

˙ *The Insulted and Injured*, p. 184. Or to put it more cynically: *such a wild, outrageous love is like a fit, like a deadly noose, like an illness, and as soon as it is gratified, the scales fall from the eyes, and the opposite feeling comes – loathing and hatred, the desire to strangle, to crush.* (*The Adolescent*, p. 336)

been duped into marrying an invalid (she must have whispered it hoarsely from her own sickbed). *Although her soul overflows with the noblest sentiments, she is fiery and irritable, and quick to slap you down. It's her eyes that scare me . . . Yes, her eyes. The red blotches on her cheeks scare me too, not to mention her breathing. Have you seen how people breathe with this sickness, when they're all worked up?*[175] Almost as soon as they were married, Fyodor had stopped mentioning her in his letters, or if he did, it was as an afterthought, a single sentence tacked onto pages of entreaties for money or news about a change in his situation.

Say you've come to cherish a certain dream: you've been enchanted by an idea, a theory, a conviction, or, well, a woman. You rush off in pursuit of love with all the intensity your soul can muster. But no matter how well your heart bribes you, if it is founded on a delusion, something you exaggerated and distorted because of your initial rush of feeling – solely to have an idol you can bow down to – then, of course, you know it deep down; doubt weighs on your mind and prevents you from living peaceably.[176] It was a miserable time for Fyodor, having finally grasped what he had been chasing for three years, only to find that it didn't make him happy. *It seems to me that I've already experienced everything on earth and there is nothing left to strive for.*[177] After all, Christopher Columbus was happiest not when he reached America, but when he was still discovering it; life was what mattered, not the discovery itself but the process of discovering.[178] Perhaps, when it came to it, he had valued the chase more than the object. *We shall have to work out our future happiness by suffering; pay for it somehow by fresh miseries. Everything is purified by suffering.*[179]

He finally received permission to publish again and scrabbled to complete the various ideas that had been bubbling away for years. *I'm trying to write a novel but it's difficult – I can't get on. I daresay I could knock it off somehow, and it might turn out interesting, but it's a pity to spoil a good idea. I've even thought of ditching the novel and knocking off a short story, something light and graceful without a trace of pessimism.*[180] And so first he turned his hand to two comic tales, *Uncle's Dream* and *The Village of Stepanchikovo*, parts of which had been gestating even in prison.* He continued making notes on his time in Omsk, as well, and was considering writing the first great prison novel. But what excited him most was *The Insulted and Injured*, a novel inspired partly by the desperate love triangle that he had been caught up in with Maria and Vergunov. The story concerned a good man, a novelist, who was hopelessly in love with a destitute but beautiful young woman who had fallen into a doomed relationship with a kind imbecile (the imbecile was in love with someone else, too, which technically made it a love quadrangle). *The mere mechanical exercise of writing counts for something. It will soothe me, cool me, arouse anew in me my old literary habits, will turn my memories and sick dreams into work, into occupation.*[181]

Fyodor had almost given up on hearing from his brother when he received a letter containing a very interesting proposal. Mikhail had been in industry for some time and now owned a cigarette factory, but what he really wanted to do was to start a new literary journal. With Tsar Alexander having declared an intention to ease censorship, and the expectation of liberal reforms to come, it was now almost the explicit job of the intelligentsia to suggest ways that society could be improved. Suddenly everyone was publishing articles about politics, about different models of society, and especially about the emancipation of the serfs. If they had their own journal, the brothers Dostoevsky could publish exactly what they wanted, within reason – political articles, stories, serial novels. To flag their intention for the journal to address the zeitgeist, they would call it *Time*.† It might even turn a neat profit if they could attract a healthy number of subscribers.

The whole year of 1859 was spent in anticipation. In March, Fyodor was formally discharged from the army on account of his haemorrhoids and his epilepsy. It was the outcome he had been hoping for, but it also meant that he now relied entirely on his

---

* When Nekrasov read *The Village of Stepanchikovo*, his response was that 'Dostoevsky is finished. He will no longer write anything important.'

† *Vremya* (Врéмя) in Russian. They beat the American *Time* magazine to the punch by sixty-three years. *Vremya* is now the name of the main evening newscast in Russia.

writing income and on new loans to pay back his old ones. *Uncle's Dream* was published in the journal *Russian Word*, where he read an intriguing article 'From the Notes of a Gambler', which recounted the exploits of a young man who had won and lost huge sums at the roulette table in Europe. It described a certain class of more discerning gamblers who, by keeping cool under pressure, were able to earn a good living at roulette. How different life would be if Fyodor had a large sum of money to hand – perhaps, one day, he would be allowed a passport.

Although he received a copy of the journal issue containing *Uncle's Dream*, he heard no word from Mikhail about the critical reception. Instead, his brother wrote to him that he had fallen ill. *I visualised so graphically that he might suddenly die and that I should never see him again.*[182] Luckily, Fyodor was finally given permission to live anywhere except in the two capitals of Moscow and St Petersburg. Of all places, he chose Tver, the small town where he had watched the government courier lashing out at the horses. There, at least, he would be close enough for Mikhail to visit him. Better still, Fyodor, Maria and her son Pasha would finally have escaped Siberia, where they had suffered so much.

Fyodor had two fits on the journey, and the prices in some of the stopping places were literally extortionate since travellers had no option but to pay. Still, considering that it was a journey of 3,500 versts, it passed without incident. The weather was wonderful, and there weren't any problems with the carriage or the horses the whole way. One evening at around five o'clock, as they wound between the foothills of the Urals, through the woods, they came upon the boundary between Asia and Europe. They decided to stop for a moment to mark the occasion. There was a little hut there, and an army pensioner came out to greet them. Fyodor stepped out of the carriage and crossed himself. They took out a flask covered in woven straw, and drank a toast of orange-blossom brandy with the old man, then went to pick wild strawberries. The world was coming back to life.

They passed through the forests of Perm and Vyatka. On they went, through Kazan, Nizhny, Vladimir. When they arrived at last in Tver, they found a furnished apartment of three small rooms and began to get acquainted with a town they both hoped to leave quickly. *I keep up our friendships myself; Maria doesn't want to do so, since we have no place to entertain.*[183] She wasn't a pessimist at heart, but a disappointed optimist; having lived a sheltered life, she had the habit of thinking everyone better than they really were, and it was hard on her now to see the world as it was. But she could be spiteful, too: during one argument, she shouted at him, 'There isn't a woman living who can love an ex-convict!'* To all who met her, when she agreed to see anyone at all, she appeared as a woman living on without knowing why.

Tver made no better an impression on Fyodor now than it had when he was a teenager. *Bleak, cold houses of stone, no activity, nothing of interest, not even a decent library. A real prison!*[184] But Mikhail was soon well enough to travel and, on the night of his arrival, Fyodor went to pick his brother up at the station three versts away. The train arrived at three in the morning. Almost ten years after embracing on a snowy Christmas Eve in Peter and Paul Fortress, the brothers Dostoevsky were reunited again. But too soon, it was time for Mikhail to return to St Petersburg, and Fyodor wasn't permitted to follow him there.

Now free to roam anywhere in the Russian Empire except where he wanted to go, Fyodor decided to take matters into his own hands and write to the Tsar himself:

Your Majesty,
Please allow me to come to St Petersburg to consult with doctors who live in the capital. Please, resurrect me, allow me the possibility of improving my health, so that I can be useful to my family and maybe, to some extent, to my fatherland.[185]

---

*Slonim, p. 162. Fyodor's daughter Lyubov wrote about Maria in her memoirs, but with such extraneous and easily disproven detail that the account is considered unreliable. Lyubov suggests that Maria never gave up Vergunov but spent the night before the wedding with him, and that he followed them to Europe, holding midnight trysts with Maria along the way.

Ironically, this delayed his permission. The Third Section had already made the internal decision to grant permission for Dostoevsky to live in the capital, but when he wrote to the Tsar, the bureaucracy waited to make their decision official in case it was countermanded by the Tsar himself. Still, in November 1859, the former convict and retired officer Fyodor Dostoevsky finally received permission to return to St Petersburg and to resume his literary career in earnest.

One life is over and another is begun, then that one is over – and another begins, and so on, endlessly. All the ends are snipped off as if with scissors.[186]

FIVE

Young Russia

1860–1862

S T PETERSBURG HAD CHANGED since Fyodor had last seen it. Down at the bottom of Nevsky Prospect was the new Nevsky Bridge – the first proper bridge to span the Neva, which also made it the longest bridge in Europe. Near the other end of Nevsky Prospect was the largest cathedral that Fyodor had ever seen. They had been building St Isaac's Cathedral since before he was born, and now that it was finally complete, it towered over the city.* Facing it, only a hundred paces from the apartment where he had been arrested, stood a newly erected bronze statue of Tsar Nicholas I, his tormentor, who had personally orchestrated his mock execution.

Fyodor walked on to the river. There wasn't a cloud in the sky and the water was almost blue, a great rarity on the normally black Neva. *The cathedral's dome stood out better here, on the bridge, than in any other spot. Through the pure air, its every decoration was discernible.*[187] This was the precise spot where he had once stood, looking out at the magnificent panorama, and his life as an artist had begun. *It seemed outlandish and bizarre, as if I really imagined that now I might think the same old thoughts as before, take an interest in the same old subjects. It was almost funny, yet my chest felt so tight it hurt.*[188]

It was imperative that he re-establish himself on the literary scene. Since censorship had eased up, there had been a great flowering

---

* None of the civic buildings were allowed to be taller than the cornice of the Winter Palace (30 metres), meaning that, at over 100 metres, the cathedral was over three times as tall as any of the surrounding buildings.

of political writing. At the reactionary end, there was Mikhail Nikiforovich Katkov's *Russian Herald*, which was conservative and Slavophile – that is, it rejected the idea that Russia had anything much to learn from Europeans. At the radical, Westernising end was Nekrasov's journal *The Contemporary*, the chief critic of which, Nikolai Gavrilovich Chernyshevsky, had recently emerged as the de facto leader of a new generation of socialists, publishing earnest articles on such burning questions as 'Are Women Human?' Chernyshevsky and his band of so-called 'rational egoists' were emerging as the most popular new intellectual movement of the decade, particularly among the youth. Fyodor was happy to argue with all of them at length. *I'm extremely ill-tempered, but not always, just at times. That's what consoles me.*[189]

The brothers Dostoevsky staked out their own place amid the cacophony by plotting a middle way, as they saw it, between the radicals and the reactionaries – progressive, but also proudly Russian. They called their new movement 'back to the soil',* and their journal, *Time*, was to be its lodestar. In one of the first editorials, Fyodor wrote about the importance of bridging the gulf between the common people and the educated classes. 'We foresee the Russian idea perhaps becoming the synthesis of all those ideas which Europe is developing with such persistence and such courage within its separate nationalities, and everything that is hostile to those ideas, perhaps, becoming reconciled and receiving further development in the Russian national spirit.'[190]

Guided by his brother's connections, Fyodor began to go to the poet Alexander Miliukov's house on Tuesday evenings, where they scouted for sympathetic collaborators. The first of their editorial staff, Apollon Alexandrovich Grigoriev, had unkempt hair and a fluffy goatee. He was handsome but unusual looking, too, his grey eyes set unusually far apart like a prey animal. At social occasions, he might sometimes be found in a red silk peasant's smock, strumming a guitar. He had a Romantic disposition, which gave him the sort of intense grandeur that Fyodor never quite pulled off. A sympathetic

---

*The word in Russian is *Pochvennichestvo* (Почвенничество).

sort of Slavophile, he had already written about the importance of the soil in the decade that Fyodor had been in exile, converging out of conviction on the same conclusions Fyodor had only formed in uncomfortably intimate contact with the Russian people.

The second major contributor to *Time* was more head than heart. Nikolai Nikolaevich Strakhov was a philosopher and scientist, a teacher of mathematics, physics and natural history, who would go on to defend a thesis 'on the bones of the wrist of mammals' (though a professorship would elude him). A little younger than Grigoriev, he had recently been arguing against the ethical dangers of materialism.* He and Fyodor held a magnetic intellectual rapport – Strakhov's political views were already very similar to Fyodor's, and the two of them could talk for hours. They would sit next to each other to work, go on excursions, and made plans to travel abroad together. Fyodor did not even mind seeing Strakhov in the immediate aftermath of a seizure, when he usually refused all company.

Time's offices were at Mikhail's apartment on the Ekaterininsky Canal (known to locals as The Ditch), where washerwomen would do their best to scrub clothes in the fetid water. It was a poor, dilapidated area of the city close to Haymarket Square. Gloomy, three-storey houses had squatted there since the eighteenth century with thick walls and gratings on the little ground-floor windows. *Inside and out, the houses are somehow inhospitable and frigid – they seem to be keeping something dark and hidden – and why it seems so merely from the look would be hard to explain.*[191] In Fyodor's own little hovel nearby, he established an anti-social routine, calculated to avoid interruptions from Maria or his stepson Pasha. *I don't yet know what will come of it, but I'm determined to work ceaselessly without taking time out to look up from my work.*[192] It would begin at midnight, when the rest of the city had gone to bed. Fyodor would sit up with his samovar, drinking tea and writing through the night. Then he would sleep through the morning and wake up in time for the magazine's editorial meeting at three in the afternoon. After business was concluded, the brothers

---

* A remarkably insightful critic, Strakhov would be the first to understand the huge significance of Tolstoy's *War and Peace*.

Dostoevsky might have dinner or go along for tea with Strakhov and his friends. When he saw Maria at all, it was to discuss practical matters; she kept up no pretence of being in love. *I reckon there's no love in the world in which two people love each other as equals.*[193]

Having published the first part of his prison memoir, *Notes from the House of the Dead*, in *Russian World* to immediate acclaim, he brought the remainder of the book over to *Time* with the aim of luring the many readers who were waiting for the next exclusive instalment. There simply wasn't anything like it in Russian literature, and *Time* needed the subscribers. Simultaneously, he finished *The Insulted and Injured*, which he knew would complete his rehabilitation as a great writer. *I could barely stand upright, but my heart was filled with joy, infinite joy. My novel was finished. Freedom and money!*[194] But the stress of the work also made him ill, and he couldn't keep up with the pace. In the spring he had a serious epileptic fit, after which he was unconscious for three days. As he recovered, Fyodor saw enemies everywhere he looked. He had alienated his old friend and doctor, Stepan Yanovsky, by writing long, intimate letters to his wife suggesting that they separate.* Nekrasov was up to his old tricks, writing mocking couplets about him in *The Whistle*. When the printing press broke down as they were preparing to go to press with their next issue, Fyodor was sure it was an act of sabotage by Nekrasov, Chernyshevsky and the others. *Such things happen, but not just as a new issue is about to be published! Just before we renew our annual subscriptions! This is somehow connected with* The Contemporary – *I am sure it is!*[195]

Although they were making a loss for now, the brothers Dostoevsky were building subscribers. In 1861 the magazine published salacious stories of French murders, highlighting the dark side of the human soul, and three stories by a new American writer named Edgar Allen Poe: 'The Tell-Tale Heart', 'The Devil in the Belfry' and 'The Black Cat'. (The slightly unhinged air of

---

* At one meeting, Yanovsky had to turn her portrait around to stop his patient staring at her. Dostoevsky found the gesture so amusing that he wrote to tell her about it and later fictionalised it in *The Idiot*.

Poe's narrators must have appealed to Fyodor.) The next year, the brothers would toe their way up to the line of censorship by publishing a work on minor social protest movements in Russia, as well as a translation of another American work called *The White Slave* by Richard Hildreth – but by that time, the Tsar had made his long-anticipated declaration that serfdom was to be abolished.

———

The Emancipation Manifesto was finalised and signed by the Tsar on 19 February 1861 but, sensing that it might go down better at a time when the supply of alcohol was restricted, the authorities put off the announcement until after Lent had begun – specifically 5 March, Forgiveness Sunday. Ironically, emancipation was the very issue over which Dostoevsky had spent a third of his life suffering. Almost immediately on his return from Siberia, it was being declared that agitating for the liberation of the serfs was not a crime, but simply good sense. *Well then, the legislators of humanity were criminals to a man, if for no other reason than that, by introducing a new law, they violated the old one.*[196]

In practice, the young Tsar had hardly emancipated the serfs from their former owners, and the declaration did not settle the issue. The serfs might technically be freed, but they would have to buy land off the aristocracy, who set the prices unilaterally. Not only that, but they had to pay 'redemptive dues' to the state treasury for the next 49 years, at an annual interest rate of 5.5 per cent. Most of the peasants couldn't read the wordy declaration themselves, and rumours circulated that the real liberation was being thwarted by the local gentry. There was unrest in several districts culminating in a massacre of peasants in Kazan province, which even the government might have conceded was not the intended outcome.

Meanwhile, as intellectuals acclimatised to the young Tsar's *glasnost*, seditious pamphlets began to circulate in St Petersburg. First there was *The Great Russian*, which argued for a national assembly to help bring the Tsar into contact with his people – an incremental change. But it was followed by a much angrier, more radical pamphlet, *To the Young Generation*, which had all the hallmarks of Chernyshevsky's gang. The pamphlet argued that the Tsar had created a new order in which he was surplus to requirements, and demanded an elected, salaried leader! This added to a growing instinct at the Winter Palace that any further move towards liberalisation would be taken taken as a sign of weakness.

Sensing danger, the government began to clamp down. They started in the universities, which had become much more relaxed in recent years, permitting anyone to attend lectures and even allowing students to set up libraries or publish their own newspapers. The government reimposed fees and imposed other restrictions on the students' activities that would come into effect in the autumn term. The students were furious at this curtailment of their freedoms. They organised a protest march through the streets, which drew a huge crowd of onlookers, as well as police and soldiers. Although the march remained peaceful, a number of students were arrested and taken to Peter and Paul Fortress. The university, in the meantime, was shut down for a year. As a sign of their good faith, the Dostoevskys cooked up a generous side of beef at Mikhail's apartment and sent it to the imprisoned students, along with bottles of cognac and red wine, compliments of the editorial board of *Time*.

Fyodor was becoming quite a hero to the now idle students, male and female, who had devoured his memoirs of prison life and revered him as a symbol of authentic socialist resistance. Fyodor, for his part, wanted to keep them on the straight and narrow. *If I can attract them all and group them round myself I shall be saving them from perdition by guiding them into a new outlet for their ambitions.*[197] One of the students who had made use of her clear schedule to submit to *Time* was a twenty-one-year-old student called Apollinaria Prokofievna Suslova. Her story, 'For the Time Being', was about a young woman who escapes a loveless marriage and gets by on tutoring work. It was a perfect expression of the nascent women's movement, which fitted nicely into the tenth issue in October 1861. *She was very, very good looking, with that Russian beauty so passionately loved by men. She had a full figure, with soft, as it were noiseless movements, softened to a peculiar over-sweetness, like her voice. She was very white in the face, with a pale pink tint on her cheeks. The modelling of her face might be said to be too broad, and the lower jaw was set a trifle forward. But her magnificent, abundant hair and charming grey-blue eyes with their long lashes would have made the most indifferent person, seeing her in the street, stop at the sight of her face and remember it long after.*[198] Fyodor found himself rather taken with her, particularly as he was trapped in an unfulfilling marriage, which he delicately referred to as 'my domestic circumstances'. Proud and ambitious, she cultivated the friendship of the great novelist, and before long Fyodor was calling her Polina.

Fyodor gave readings whenever he was invited by various student groups, the largest of which was a fundraiser organised by the Literary Fund. This particular 'literary-musical evening' managed to attract some big names: the pianist Anton Rubinstein was going to play Beethoven's *The Ruins of Athens* in honour of the Greek revolt against the Turks, and there would be readings by the usual suspects, Nekrasov and Chernyshevsky, as well as an eccentric professor called Pavel Pavlov. On stage, Fyodor recounted the death of a soldier in the prison hospital, revelling in the gory detail. But to the surprise of all present, the unmistakable star of the evening was Professor Pavlov. His lecture, 'A Thousand Years of Russian History', had passed the censorship, as it was ostensibly a celebration of the millennium of the Russian nation, but it was not what the professor said so much as the way he said it: trembling and shrieking like the prophet Jeremiah, the history lesson was transformed into a condemnation. *I must confess I could not believe my ears.*[199] As Pavlov worked himself up to fever pitch, the audience rattled their chairs and banged their feet on the floor. *The last words could not be heard in the roar of the crowd. One could only see him raise his arm and bring it down again triumphantly.*[200] He climaxed to uproarious applause and a spontaneous outbreak of the 'Marseillaise'. (And he was taken away to prison the next day.)

Not long after the fundraiser, Fyodor and Strakhov decided to take advantage of the hot, dry weather to take a steamer out along the Neva into the surrounding countryside for the day. Looking back at St Petersburg receding in their wake, however, they noticed huge clouds of black smoke rising into the air in three or four different places. They soon arrived at a park, where a group of gypsies were singing and playing music, but the fire in the city was clearly catastrophic and any thought of lazing about on the grass seemed absurd in the circumstances, so they got back on the boat. Over the next week, the fire spread across a large part of the city, turning houses and shops into smoke.

A great fire at night is always thrilling. That is what explains the attraction of fireworks. But with those, the artistic regularity and the complete lack of danger give them the playful fizz of champagne. A real conflagration is something else. The horror and the sense of personal danger, together with the exhilaration of the fire, produce in the spectator (though of course not in the person whose things are being burnt) a certain disturbance of the brain and, as it were, a challenge to those destructive instincts which, alas, lie hidden in every heart, even that of the tamest little clerk ... Of course, the very man who enjoys the spectacle will rush into the fire to save a child or an old woman; but that is another matter.[201]

There was a grand tradition of arson in Russia. Peasants called it the Red Rooster, and it had always been one of the few effective weapons they had against landowners.* But this was an indiscriminate fire in the middle of the city, burning down second-hand markets and the housing of the poor. People began blaming it on 'the professors'. This was not helping to restore the connection between Russia's intelligentsia and the people – it was turning them against each other.

To make matters worse, Fyodor then discovered an offensive leaflet attached to his doorknob titled *Young Russia*. The author called for a march on the Winter Palace, for revolution, for the founding of a federated and democratic republic, political franchise for women, the sacking of monasteries and the abolition of marriage. Invoking the 'great terrorists' of the French Revolution, the leaflet proclaimed that anyone who was not with them was against them. One line in particular must have struck Fyodor: 'We shall give one call – "take up axes" – and then we will kill the imperial party

---

*We have to take Andrei Dostoevsky's word for it that the fire at Darovoe in their childhood was the result of a hog roast on a windy day.

without mercy.' *Its contents were quite outrageous, and it was couched in the most ridiculous terms. Their level of education, their mentality, and their utter lack of understanding of reality oppressed me terribly.*[202]

Furious, Fyodor decided to pay his first ever visit to Chernyshevsky's house that afternoon and to beg him, if necessary, to make the young generation see reason. When Fyodor knocked on the door, it was opened not by the servant but by Chernyshevsky himself, who welcomed him cordially and showed him into his study. Fyodor came straight to the point.

'Nikolai Gavrilovich, what on earth is this?'[203] He handed the proclamation to Chernyshevsky, who read it through, reacting as if he had never seen it before. When he had finished, Chernyshevsky replied with a faint smile, 'Well, what about it?'

'Are they really so stupid and ridiculous? Is there really no way of stopping them and putting an end to this abomination?'

'Do you really think I support them? Or that I could have had a part in writing this wretched leaflet?'

'Of course not. And I hardly think it necessary to assure you of it. But in any case they must be stopped somehow. Your word means something to them, and of course they're afraid of what you might say.'

'But I don't know any of them,' Chernyshevsky protested.

'I'm sure you don't. But you certainly don't need to know them or speak to them personally. You only have to declare your condemnation somewhere and they'll hear about it.'

Chernyshevsky wavered. 'It may not have any effect. Besides, irrelevancies like this are unavoidable.'

'But they do harm to everybody and everything.'

Just then, the doorbell rang. Fyodor had said his piece and took this as his cue to leave.˙

˙Chernyshevsky recalled the same meeting differently, claiming that Dostoevsky asked him to do something about the fires, and that he had agreed so as not to upset a man who was mentally deranged. See 'My meetings with Dostoevsky' by N. G. Chernyshevsky, quoted in Sekirin, pp. 161–2.

It had begun to seem as if a gulf had opened up between the socialists of Fyodor's generation and the youth of the time. The socialists of the 1840s had been idealists and reformers, some of them champagne socialists, it was true, but also sensible, progressive men. Polina's generation were of a different sort. Perhaps the only writer who really understood what was going on was Turgenev, whose novel *Fathers and Sons* had been published in the same month as the fundraiser.* The novel staged the new generational conflict that had opened up between an older generation of sophisticated but essentially hand-wringing liberal intellectuals whose activism extended to a barbed remark – already immortalised as 'superfluous men' – and a young generation who claimed to recognise only science, action, material good. The novel's hero, if there is one, is really a tragic figure: Bazarov is desperate to believe only in social utility, to be an unfeeling rationalist who discards art and feeling as pointless – a Nihilist, in a word. But he feels deeply in spite of himself. And although Bazarov has lofty thoughts about the Russian people in the abstract, he actively dislikes the actual peasants he meets. This emerging conflict between the rational and the humane, between abstract ideas and lived experience, was to cast a long shadow.

Turgenev certainly got into trouble over his Bazarov, who was restless and troubled (the sign of a great heart) despite all his nihilism.[204] Predictably, *The Contemporary* leapt to the young generation's defence and tore the book to pieces in their review, claiming that Bazarov was a monstrous caricature and Turgenev no true liberal. Perhaps more worryingly, *The Russian Word*'s radical chief critic, Dmitri Pisarev, thought Bazarov was an excellent role model, a Satanic anti-hero who was separated from the dumb masses by his ability to step outside the law: 'Nothing except personal taste prevents him from murdering and robbing',[205] the reviewer wrote

---

* Literally translated, the original title is *Fathers and Children*, but the novel contains no significant daughters and *Fathers and Sons* has a better cadence. You could not have the same semantic mirroring in Russian without unbalancing the sound – it would be *Otsy y synovya* instead of *Otsy y deti* – and Turgenev is too elegant for that.

with disconcerting relish. Worst of all, the book was taken up enthusiastically by the fusty old reactionaries, who were pleased to see Turgenev complaining about the youth of today. Only *Time* understood the significance of what Turgenev was trying to say. Fyodor read the book as soon as it came out in Katkov's *Russian Herald* and assigned Strakhov to write a glowing review about it. It was a beautiful review – perhaps the only one that really penetrated to the heart of the matter – and when it came out, Turgenev took Strakhov and the brothers Dostoevsky out for dinner at the Hotel Clea to thank them. (On the way there, they bumped into an acquaintance of Turgenev's, who shouted at him, 'See what your Nihilists are doing! They're burning down Petersburg', as if naming them had suddenly made him responsible for their behaviour.)[206] Charting a path between the radical left and the reactionary right was not going to be easy, and Turgenev was grateful to have at least a handful of fellow travellers.

That said, the *Time* editors were struggling themselves to steer clear of censorship without being derided as weak or even conservative. They wrote an editorial about the fires, pointing out that there was no actual evidence to link them to the *Young Russia* leaflet, which they dismissed as a schoolboy prank. The censors rejected it. The editors submitted a second article on the topic, which was also rejected. Mikhail, as the editor-in-chief, was then called in for questioning, though it turned out the authorities only wanted to know the names of these schoolboys who had written the leaflet, and Mikhail had to explain that the part about the schoolboys had unfortunately been poetic licence. But the authorities were on the defensive now. On 15 June they suspended publication of *The Contemporary* and *Russian Word* until the following spring. Three weeks later, they arrested Chernyshevsky. *It's a foul time now, a time of wearisome and melancholy waiting. But after all, a journal is a terribly important thing; one must not risk losing it, because no matter what happens, journals expressing all shades of contemporary opinion must remain.*[207]

By this time, though, Fyodor's mind was drifting to thoughts of Europe. St Petersburg's climate wasn't good for Maria, so he had shipped her off to an aunt in Vladimir, 180 versts east of Moscow. Now that the journal was beginning to gain a little momentum, Fyodor was determined to go and see a doctor in Paris, Trousseau, who might be able to shed some light on his epilepsy. While he was there, he might as well travel around – he had, after all, never been to Europe. It was only a short journey from Paris to London, and he'd always wanted to see Italy. *I've dreamed since I was a child of going to Italy!*[208] Perhaps Strakhov could come too. *We'll see Naples, stroll around Rome, for all I know, caress a young Venetian woman in a gondola.*

However, Fyodor was not nearly as impressed by Europe as he had hoped to be. *Paris is an exceedingly boring city, and if it didn't have a number of quite remarkable things, one could really die from boredom. The French, honest to God, are the kind of people who make one sick. The Frenchman is quiet, honest, polite, but insincere, and money for him is everything. He has no ideals. Don't ask him for his thoughts, let alone his convictions.*[209] He went on to London, where he visited the exiled socialist Alexander Herzen, a short, rather stocky man with an enviably thick beard. (At forty, Fyodor's was only just beginning to grow out.) He was a marvellous conversationalist but although they found common ground they arrived at it from completely different outlooks. Herzen was a born emigré, a gentleman who had no roots in Russian soil, a consummate European, a citizen of the world, you could say, who nevertheless lay claim to patriotic feeling when the mood was right. The conversation was cordial but they were not destined to become close friends.†

---

* Letter to Strakhov, 26 June (8 July) 1862. Strakhov, a confirmed bachelor, later recalled the Dostoevsky brothers' attitudes to flings with a little less fondness: they 'regarded with utter calm all irregularities of that sort, spoke of them as of amusing trivialities, to yield to which at a leisure moment was fully permissible. Physical indecency was considered nothing at all. This strange emancipation of the flesh acted as a temptation and in certain cases led to consequences it is painful to recall.' (Slonim, p. 114)
† If Fyodor noticed the officers of the Third Section watching him as he left, he never told anyone.

It was interesting to see the city of Charles Dickens, but not exactly relaxing.* On Saturday nights, men, women and children would go out until five in the morning, with the gas jets of the street lamps casting an infernal glow over proceedings. *Everyone is in a hurry to get blind drunk.*[210] He wandered among the prostitutes and the drunks around Haymarket and poked his nose into a casino, where there was music and dancing, *but the English never shake off the gloom even in the midst of gaiety; even when they dance they look sullen.*[211] Back out in the cold, he gave sixpence to a little girl covered in bruises. She could only have been six, perhaps younger. *What struck me most was the look of distress, such hopeless despair on her face ... She kept shaking her tousled head as if arguing about something, gesticulated and spread her little hands and then suddenly clasped them together and then pressed them to her little bare breast.*[212]

Strakhov joined him in Geneva and they travelled down through Turin and Livorno, talking day and night. On one of their walks through Florence, they had their first major falling out over whether two plus two always equals four. Strakhov was an insightful critic and understood literature, but his scientific training sometimes made him infuriatingly logical. While talking about the problem of the radicals, Strakhov insisted that people must be responsible for the consequences of their ideas. It didn't matter whether they understood the implications or not – if you insist on adding two to two, you get four. But for Dostoevsky, intention mattered greatly. These radicals did not want everything to end badly, they wanted to do good, even if there were mistakes in their working, or some hidden motivation prevented them from coming to the logical conclusion. Fyodor believed as a Christian that even the gravest sinner knew goodness and might be redeemed; Strakhov claimed to believe as

---

*Incidentally, a recent suggestion that Dostoevsky and Dickens met during this week turned out to be a hoax by Arnold Harvey (aka Stephanie Harvey aka Graham Headley aka Trevor McGovern aka John Schellenberger aka Leo Bellingham aka Michael Lindsay aka Ludovico Parra), a melancholy independent historian who had never secured academic tenure. ('When Dickens Met Dostoevsky', *TLS*, 10 April 2013; cf. 'The Man behind the Great Dickens and Dostoevsky Hoax', *Guardian*, 10 July 2013)

a Christian that people on earth were, in some essential way, rotten to the core. Fyodor explained that this was a tendency in Strakhov's thought that he truly despised and would persecute until his dying day. There wasn't much left to say after that, so they shook hands and went their separate ways for the remainder of their travels.

On his return to St Petersburg, Fyodor started seeing the student Polina regularly. It turned out that she was the daughter of a serf who had bought his freedom before becoming a merchant, making Polina a living link between the intelligentsia and the soil. It must have seemed an extraordinary stroke of luck that the living embodiment of Fyodor's ideals happened to be a beautiful and impetuous twenty-two-year-old woman. They started an affair, and before long Polina was working on a new story, 'Before the Wedding'. She asked Fyodor to divorce Maria, but that was out of the question. He might be desperately unhappy in the relationship, but he would not give up his obligations to her, or to her stepson. The weather was better in Vladimir, but the fact of the matter was that Maria was dying of consumption, and might not even live out the next year. Fyodor was falling in love with Polina, but he could not abandon his wife in such circumstances.

Fyodor published an account of his travels through Europe under the title *Winter Notes on Summer Impressions*, and the lovers talked about going there together. Polina had always wanted to see Paris. Perhaps they could go to Baden-Baden and have a flutter at roulette. And Italy, too – how nice it would be to wander around the old piazze hand in hand with a lover rather than bickering with a friend. He would send on money for Maria's doctor and Pasha's tutor, whenever another payment came through from sales of *Time*. Polina went ahead to Paris in late spring and Fyodor began to tie up a few loose ends that were keeping him in St Petersburg. But just as he was preparing to leave, on 24 May 1863, the dreadful news came through that *Time* had been suppressed by the censors.

SIX

Polina

1863

I T WAS AUGUST BY the time Fyodor left for Paris, two months later than he had intended. The train station in St Petersburg was pandemonium: apart from the usual customs officers, police, hotel touts and cab men, there were soldiers everywhere, and even some of the travellers were carrying pistols in case things got out of hand. As he settled into his cabin and the train passed through Poland on the way to the border with Germany, everything appeared calm, though soldiers were on duty at every station. There were insurgents at large, hiding in the villages and woodlands.

The recent nationalist uprising in Poland had been the very subject of Strakhov's article, 'The Fateful Question', which had been intended as a patriotic defence of Russian interests but which was written in such a roundabout way that he'd got the journal banned.˙ Mikhail was now on the brink of ruin. Having taken on debts in order to put out advertisements and build a subscriber base, the brothers were now unable to print the magazine that would earn their money back. Fyodor had already written to Turgenev to politely beg that he hold off publishing a new story until they could sort everything out with the authorities. In the meantime, he had

---

˙One of the prominent Polish nationalists was Apollo Korzeniowski, a magazine publisher, campaigner against serfdom, and translator of both Victor Hugo and Charles Dickens, who had just been sentenced to exile in Vologda, northeast of Moscow. He brought with him his wife and their five-year-old son, Józef Teodor Konrad Korzeniowski, who would later write in English as Joseph Conrad.

set about rustling up the money to make the trip to join Polina in Paris. Eventually he obtained a loan of 1,500 roubles from the Society for Aid to Needy Writers and Scholars, possibly helped along by the fact that he was on its Executive Committee, with a gentleman's agreement to hand over his copyrights if he hadn't repaid the loan by the following February (but of course no one ever enforced those sorts of terms).

Fyodor mislaid another 12 days on the train between St Petersburg and Wiesbaden, since the rest of Europe had now adopted the Gregorian calendar.* Stopping at Wiesbaden for the night, he went out to the casino for a flutter. Amazingly, he made good money, and kept going, and held his nerve, and by the end of the night he had won 10,400 francs. He took them back to the hotel, locked them in his suitcase and decided to leave the next morning. But on further consideration, it did seem a peculiar idea to stop while he was doing so well. If he could win 100,000 roubles, he would cure his money troubles for ever. He quietly believed that he had worked out a foolproof system for winning, and this success seemed to have borne it out. (*I really do know the secret: it is terribly silly and simple and consists of restraining oneself at every moment, at every phase of the game, and of not losing one's head.*)† The real issue, as he saw it, was that everyone lost control and abandoned the system – watching the little white ball race around the wheel and begin to lose pace and veer off its course, over and over, even a cold fish like Strakhov would crack eventually.

---

* Passengers had to change at some point anyway, because Russian trains ran on a wider gauge of track than German trains. Apocryphally this was either intended to forestall an invasion, or because the Tsar simply wanted his trains to be bigger.
† Letter to Varvara Constant, 20 August (1 September) 1863. There actually exists a strategy, known as 'martingale', which is mathematically infallible but requires high stakes for low wins. The method consists of betting the table minimum on either red or black; if you lose, you double your bet, which will cover the previous loss, and so on until you regain your initial loss(es). You stand a 48.65 per cent chance of winning the table minimum at European roulette, but the cost of covering consecutive losses mounts exponentially, so a prudent casino will take the low probability of your catastrophic loss (when you run out of money) over the high probability of your making meagre gains. In this light, even writing begins to look like a reliable way to earn a living.

Four days later, Fyodor was still in Wiesbaden. He had lost half his money, but he was still up by 5,000 francs. He sent money home, some for his brother, and some for Maria for her doctor's bills. After that, he really did have to leave: Polina was waiting for him and he was now months late for their rendezvous. He packed his things and took the next train bound for Paris. What a marvellous thing, to be on the way to see one's lover with a suitcase full of money. And he really did feel that the doctors were better in Europe.

———

He arrived in a warm, rainy city on Tuesday 26 August. *I like Paris this time because of its exterior, that is, its architecture. The Louvre is a superb thing, and all that embankment, right up to Notre Dame, is amazing.*[213] There was a coffee house he liked where they had Russian newspapers, but first he wanted to see Polina.

She had told him to write to her before visiting – an oddly formal request considering that they were lovers – so he dashed off a quick message to her. But he was too impatient to wait for the reply, so he set off on the heels of the courier.

When he arrived at her lodgings, he was shown into the reception room. She took a long time coming down, and Fyodor's excitement gave way to tension. When Polina did finally appear, she looked pale and anxious.*

'How are you?' she asked nervously.[214]

This was not quite the hero's welcome Fyodor had anticipated.

'What's the matter?' he asked uneasily.

'I thought you weren't going to come. I wrote you a letter.'

'What letter?' he asked.

'To stop you coming here.'

---

* Later, Polina would write a highly autobiographical and self-regarding story about their meetings, 'The Stranger and her Lover'. Before she opens her mouth at this first meeting, the heroine exudes beauty, anxiety, mental suffering, embarrassment, shyness, unconquerable strength and passion, gentleness and kindness, giving 'an impression of fanaticism which distinguishes the faces of madonnas and Christian martyrs'.

'Why?'

'Because it is too late.'

Fyodor hung his head. Too late. *Everything always goes right for some people, while with others nothing ever comes off.*[215]

'I must know everything,' he began after a long, heavy silence. She suggested they go to his lodgings, where they might speak in private. She took up her hat and mantilla, and they got into the carriage that was waiting for Fyodor outside. They sat in silence as the carriage rattled through the streets. Neither of them looked at the other.

'*Vite, vite!*' Fyodor shouted at the driver, who appeared puzzled by the request.

Fyodor held her hand and pressed it hard, his body convulsing with sudden and unexpected grief.

'Calm down – I am with you,' she said.

Coming into the hotel, Fyodor gave her his arm. The doorman started to grin when he saw Polina, but quickly changed his mind when he saw their faces.

In the room, Fyodor fell at her feet crying, clasping her knees.

'I have lost you. I knew it!'

She managed to coax him onto the sofa, where she explained that, while she had been waiting for him, she had met a Spanish medical student named Salvador, and had fallen in love. Fyodor really did want to know everything: when they had met, whether she had slept with him yet, whether she was happy. As he had learned, intelligence gathering was the first step towards shifting the power dynamic in a love triangle. It sounded like it could be worse: this Salvador didn't seem like a serious person, though he couldn't possibly be as wet as Nikolai Vergunov. Not only that, but Salvador did not reciprocate her love, so in a way, she and Fyodor were in the same boat, siblings in misery.

The thought came to him now, as it always did when he was on the verge of despair, that an experience like this would make wonderful material for a story. Ever since he had been sent to Siberia, storytelling had been his last refuge, the skin that kept distance between his tender heart and the cruelties of the world. He urged Polina to write him letters, particularly when she was especially happy or unhappy, and suggested that they might still go to Italy together, not as lovers but as brother and sister. Before she left, she promised to see him again the next day. Polina had presented him with the end of a story, but Fyodor could see that only a few judicious edits were required to turn it into the beginning of another.

After she had left, he picked up the reply she had sent him, which had crossed paths with him earlier that day. It began abruptly, even flippantly: 'You are coming a little too late.'[216] That stung, of course. But the important thing was to get her away from Paris. Once they were travelling together, the way would become clear.

The next time Polina visited Fyodor, they stayed up late talking. She was completely infatuated with Salvador, and could barely be induced to talk about anything else. When he was not seeing Polina, Fyodor wandered the streets. *I don't like Paris, although it's all terribly magnificent. There are a lot of things to see in it; but after you've looked around, an awful boredom sets in. Actually, the best things here are the fruit and the wine: one doesn't tire of them.*[217] Knowing no one else in the city, he dined alone, wrote a letter to his sister-in-law, and went to bed.

He was awoken at 7 a. m. by a banging at his door. Getting up blearily from bed, he opened the door to find Polina standing there distraught. She hadn't slept all night.* They went inside and he got back in bed, wrapping himself up in the blanket.

She told him everything and asked for his advice. Salvador's friend had written to Polina to say that Salvador couldn't see her because he had typhus. She had written to Salvador immediately, and then again the next day. She invited the friend to visit her, but he didn't reply either. Sick of waiting around in case he should

* According to Polina's story, 'She removed her veil, and he shuddered at the sight of her face. It was deathly pale and severe, the lips pressed together, the eyes looking straight ahead, but with an expression of horror and madness.'

write or call on her, she decided to go for a walk along the rue de la Sorbonne at about 6 p.m. It was there that she bumped into Salvador, who looked perfectly healthy if a little embarrassed. Back in her room, she screamed that she was going to kill him and then set about burning any of her letters and notebooks that might compromise her reputation. Even now she appeared capable of violence, and Fyodor warned her not to do anything stupid.

'I would not like to kill him,' she conceded, 'but I would like to torture him for a very long time.'[218]

'Enough,' he said. 'He isn't worth it. Really he ought to be exterminated with insect powder, but you would be foolish to ruin your life over him.'

Polina enjoyed saying such things for effect, but at the same time she sometimes expressed herself with such darkness and violence that he began to wonder what she was capable of. One day, as they were looking up together at the chapel of Saint-Étienne du Mont, behind the Panthéon, she told him that she had been to confession there – that she had confessed to a truly evil desire. The revelation was particularly disturbing to Fyodor, for whom Catholicism represented a kind of Antichrist, a worldly simulacrum of the true Church, leading its sheep astray.

'What is it? To kill Salvador?'[219] he asked.

'No, not him.'

'Who then? Me?'

'Oh no, not you,' she said indifferently. 'I tell you it is a grand and extraordinary plan.'

He pushed her to tell him more and her eyes burned with hatred.

'What difference does it make which man pays for the outrage that has been perpetrated against me? You are all guilty. All of you have betrayal and carnality on your consciences.* So if vengeance is to be wreaked, let the whole world hear of it. Let the revenge be without precedent!'

---

* Fyodor had once quoted Balzac at Polina to the effect that even a philosopher must go on a wild orgy once a month; perhaps not the right tone to strike with a young idealist.

'Do you really think you could kill a man?' he asked her.

'Without a qualm.'

'Whom?'

She looked at him almost with contempt.

'Haven't you guessed? The Tsar.'

This was Fyodor's worst nightmare. Could Polina, who represented a living link between the peasantry and the intelligentsia, really have succumbed to the Nihilists? How could a true Russian such as her want to destroy the Russian state? Did she not understand anything he had told her?

'Promise me you will never again even harbour such a thought,' he said to her.

She seemed suddenly very tired.

'No, I have already given up the idea.'

They talked more and he kept probing, asking questions, teasing out her thoughts and the way she thought. When he was sure that she really had given up the idea, he asked how she had conceived of such a thing.

'It is a fascinating thought,' she said dreamily. 'Such an enormous step, but so simple. Imagine, one gesture, one movement, and you are among the celebrities, the geniuses, the great, the saviours of mankind.'

'Fame is won by hard work,' he assured her glumly.

'Or by unprecedented daring,' she shot back.

It seemed that neither of them much wanted to stay in Paris anymore. Polina insisted on writing to Salvador again to send payment for a medical consultation he had given her when they had first met, but inevitably she didn't receive a reply, and so she resolved to go abroad with Fyodor.*

Fyodor suggested they stop off quickly in Baden-Baden for a few spins of roulette, before travelling on to Italy via Geneva. The two of them went along to the Holy Father's embassy to get their visas for

* 'Her eyelashes were closed, her arms firmly crossed upon her breast, her black hair sprayed across her pillow in long tangled strands. Her face bore a strange expression: that of calm acquired at the price of long suffering; an expression of the infinite.'

the trip, where they were met by a sour-faced little abbot who told them to wait. As they sat reading magazines, someone else swept straight through into the monsignor's office and the abbot didn't stop him – in fact, he bowed.

'We need to obtain our visa,' repeated Fyodor.[220]

'Wait please,' said the abbot in an icy tone.

They waited. A little while later, an Austrian chap came in and was led straight upstairs. Polina looked ironically at Fyodor. Fyodor got up and went over to the abbot.

'Look, since the monsignor is taking callers, he might as well take care of my visa.'

The abbot was taken aback. Measuring Fyodor from head to toe, he bellowed: 'Do you really expect the monsignor to abandon his coffee for you?'

Fyodor bellowed even louder: 'I spit in your monsignor's coffee! If you don't get our visa this minute I'm going in there myself.'

'What! With the cardinal in the room?' cried the little abbot, rushing to the door and spreading his arms like a martyr to bar the way.

'I am a heretic! A barbarian!' Fyodor declared. 'I don't care if he is the cardinal.'

The abbot glared at Fyodor with infinite malice, strode over and snatched up the passports, disappearing upstairs. A minute later and, voila – they had their visas.

He had, of course, made a scene for the benefit of Polina, to amuse her. *Perhaps there wouldn't have been any schoolboy pranks if it hadn't been for her. I don't understand – I simply don't understand – what I find in her. All right: she is beautiful, or she seems beautiful. She drives men out of their minds. She is tall and slender. In fact, very slim; she looks as though you could tie her in a knot or fold her in half. Her foot is long and narrow. Tormenting. Exactly so: tormenting.*[221] Sitting together on the train, he came clean and told her that he still harboured some hope for their relationship. She smiled but said nothing.

At Baden-Baden they had a little trouble finding a hotel with two adjoining rooms, but Fyodor was in a buoyant mood. He had been talking in verse the whole way there, and when they asked him to sign the guest register he put himself down as Officer. The town itself was an absurd place, really. There was a pavilion where an orchestra played a jumble of European and Russian songs. First it would be a medley from *La Traviata*, then a waltz by Strauss, then an instrumental version of the Russian song 'Tell her'. There was a particular tree where all the Russians had a habit of gathering – it was known locally as 'the Russian tree'. Opposite was Weber's coffee house, and then, of course, the casino, where Fyodor played a little roulette, trying to hold to his system, waiting for his luck to return.

They sat together in her room, that evening, talking on the bed. They had tea brought in around ten, and she asked him to sit close to her, and held his hand. Fyodor told her that he felt good, sitting with her like this. She apologised for her behaviour in Paris, and explained that it wasn't because she hadn't been thinking of him. He was almost overcome.

On impulse, he shot to his feet but immediately tripped over her shoe, which was lying on the floor, and sat down again, embarrassed.

'Going somewhere?' she asked.[222]

'I was just going to shut the window.'

'You can shut it if you want to.'

'No . . . You don't know what just happened to me.'

'What do you mean?'

How could he explain?

'Well, I was going to kiss your foot.'

'Ah – why that?' she replied, tucking her feet up beneath her.

'I had a sudden urge, and thought I would kiss it.'

They kept talking after that, but the atmosphere had curdled. She asked whether the maid might be coming in soon to clear up the tea; he said that the maid would leave them alone now until the morning. He looked at her; she hid her face in her pillow.

'All right then,' she said. 'Go back to your room – I want to sleep.'

'Right away,' he said. He stood there for some moments, watching her, then went over and kissed her. He suggested that she should undress before her candle ran down; she said she had a spare.

Eventually he got tired of playing cat and mouse and went to his room, leaving the door open in case she should change her mind. He lay listening to her getting comfortable among the bedsheets. He went in one last time – to close the window.

'You should get undressed,' he said.

'I will,' she said.

He left again, and came back again, and she sent him out again. This time, he closed the door on his way out.

The next day, Fyodor apologised for his behaviour and explained that he had been drunk.* He said she must find it unpleasant, the way he was badgering her. Polina smiled knowingly and said she didn't mind. *She doesn't bother to hide her aversion from me, but she also doesn't conceal from me either the fact that she is saving me for some future use. She knows that I am madly in love with her and actually allows me to speak of my passion; surely there is no better way to show her contempt for me than to allow me to speak freely of my love?* [223]

———

At first, the luck appeared to have followed Fyodor from Wiesbaden. On his arrival, he had walked straight up to the roulette table and won 600 francs in a quarter of an hour. *That fired me up.*[224] He started to believe that his system might solve all of his money troubles, even Mikhail's too. But then it went the other way: *Suddenly I started losing and could no longer restrain myself and lost my shirt.* Chasing the losses, he stacked up and staked and lost 3,000 francs.[†] All he had left in his pocket now was about 250 francs. As if this was not humiliating enough, it meant that he now had to write to his sister-in-law and ask her to return some of the money that he had sent on for Maria. He wrote to Mikhail, too, begging for 100 roubles to tide him over.

---

*This is the only time Dostoevsky ever claimed to have been drunk.
† A twenty-franc gold 'Napoleon' in 1863 contained 5.806 grams of gold, equivalent to about £183 today. So 3,000 francs would have represented about £27,500, not accounting for differences in purchasing power.

Mikhail had been keen that Fyodor visit Turgenev while he was in town to rustle up the manuscript of 'Phantoms', which would draw new subscribers, so Fyodor dutifully went over to visit. He didn't, of course, introduce Turgenev to Polina – though even if the two had met, Turgenev could hardly have judged, since he was in a ménage à trois with the French opera singer Pauline Viardot and her husband, an arrangement that had produced four children of uncertain provenance. Turgenev was still grieving over the reception of *Fathers and Sons*, though he handed over 'Phantoms'. Fyodor spent the rest of his time in Baden gambling and chasing Polina, which left very little time for reading. When he saw Turgenev again, Fyodor returned the manuscript to him unread. Offended, Turgenev said that he had written it for the Dostoevskys' journal, and offered to send it on to him in Rome. Fyodor demurred.

Before leaving Baden-Baden, he was determined to redeem himself at the roulette table. He made steady, serious gains, and within half an hour of play he had turned 80 francs into 700. It was such luck, such extraordinary luck, and it carried him away: he went all in. He lost everything he had brought with him, and everything he had won. After paying their bills, he and Polina had just 120 francs left for the road. *Blessed are they who do not gamble and who abhor the roulette table as a monumental folly.*[225]

In Geneva, Fyodor pawned his watch with an unusually honest pawnbroker who even refused to charge interest, though he gave them a pittance. Polina pawned her ring, too. In Turin, they checked into a hotel without knowing how they would pay the bill. With almost no money physically in hand, they opted to eat at the hotel restaurant and charge it to their room, but Polina attracted unwanted attention everywhere. Fyodor began to dread that the manager would bring the hotel bill while the two of them didn't have a copeck to their name. There would be a scandal, the police would be called – that was how things were done here.

Polina had been in a foul mood since the incident in Baden-Baden, but she seemed to soften towards him now. *A woman is capable of torturing a man with her cruelty and mockery without the faintest twinge of conscience, because she'll think every time she looks at you: 'I'm tormenting him to death now, but I'll make up for it with my love, later.'*[226] They sat together talking intimately, and his joy only seemed to make her more tender. She gazed up into his eyes.

'There is that familiar look,' Fyodor said. 'It's a long time since I saw it last.'[227]

She laid her head on his chest, and began to cry.

They waited three days in Turin for some word from Mikhail or his sister-in-law or indeed anyone else who might feel like bailing them out. When the reply came from Mikhail, he had sent enough money, but he was furious that Fyodor had been so rude to the one writer who was offering to help save their journal. 'Do you know what Turgenev means for us *now*?'[228] Mikhail wrote.

They arrived in Rome late on the night of 28 September. Polina was still stringing him along, but Fyodor was beginning to lose his patience. *If she found my love offensive, why didn't she simply forbid me to mention it? I was not forbidden; in fact, there were times when she prompted me to talk. She liked to listen to me and work me up until I was so excited it actually hurt – then send me reeling with a display of utter contempt.*[229]

'You know,' he said, 'if you torture a man this long, he will eventually stop trying.'[230]

She only smiled. Fyodor had had enough. He told her that he knew exactly what was happening, that she still held out hope for Salvador. At this, her whole demeanour changed. He probed at her weak spot.

'You are not objecting.'

After a sullen silence, she replied, 'I have no reason for hope.'

'That doesn't matter. You may know it rationally, but it won't stop you trying.'

She had nothing to say to that, so Fyodor left her there and went to his own bed for a while. *There were moments (especially at the end of our conversations) when I would have given my life to strangle her! If I'd had the chance to bury a sharp knife slowly in her breast, I probably would have reached for it with relish. And yet, if she had told me to throw myself off a cliff, I would have done it at once, and with pleasure.** When he went back to her room, he found her lying in bed, undressed. He tried his best to put on a brave face, but this only seemed to annoy her.

'I don't like you like this,' she said to him.²³¹

'What have I done?' he asked.

'I liked you much better in Paris and Turin. Why are you so cheerful?'

'It's a cheerfulness born of disappointment,' he said. The time for playing games was over. 'I am unhappy,' he told her seriously. 'I look at everything as though it were my duty, as though I were learning a lesson. I had thought at least that I would manage to distract you.'

She embraced him, then, and told him he had done a lot for her. But she still didn't invite him to stay with her, even though they were alone together on her bed at one in the morning. *Like that empress of antiquity who would undress before her slave because she did not consider him a man.*²³² It was time for him to go.

'It's humiliating for me to leave you like this,' he said, 'for the Russians never retreat.'

The next day, they went to see the Vatican, the great enemy of Orthodoxy, as Fyodor saw it, and it sent a shiver down his spine. The day after that, they looked around the Colosseum and the great fallen stones of the Forum. Fyodor still didn't write to Turgenev for the manuscript. In the giddy rush of unsatisfied lust and gambling, it had been impossible either to read or to write, though he did have a story idea brewing about a young Russian at large in Europe. *The main point is that all his lifeblood, energies, violence, boldness have been squandered on roulette.*²³³ There was probably enough for thirty pages, maybe more.

They took the boat for the last leg of their journey together, where they bumped into Alexander Herzen and his family. It was all perfectly amicable. Fyodor introduced Polina as a distant relative.

---

* *The Gambler*, Terras, p. 14, Garnett, p. 319. The qualities of limerence that Dostoevsky expresses in *The Gambler* are textbook: obsession and intrusive thoughts; loneliness and fear of rejection; hypervigilance; dramatic surges between joy and despair.

Any lingering intimacy had already begun to fade. *You look at the sunrise, the Gulf of Naples, the sea, and you can't help feeling sad. No, you're better off in the motherland.*[234]

They bickered a bit, but parted ways on good terms. And that was it. Fyodor was going home to Russia, travelling back into a long October. He said goodbye to Polina in Berlin and set off towards Vladimir to see Maria. Somewhere in between, he tried to cheer himself up by playing roulette. He lost everything, so Polina pawned her watch and sent him enough money to get back to his dying wife.

SEVEN

Epoch's End

1864–1866

S TUCK IN MOSCOW, FYODOR worked furiously on a new novella to help resurrect the journal. *Notes from the Underground* was a howl of spite in response to a novel that Chernyshevsky had published from prison, *What Is to Be Done?*, which, despite being utterly turgid, had made a great impression on the young radicals. It was almost incredible that the censors had allowed the book to be published – raising the interesting question of whether any of them had actually managed to wade through it. The novel was premised entirely on the idea that, if people truly understood what was in their self-interest, everyone would behave themselves and this would quickly fix the whole world. Fyodor heaped scorn upon the idea. *Have man's advantages been reckoned up with complete certainty?*[235] *And how do these sages know that man wants a rationally advantageous choice?*[236] *Shower upon him every earthly blessing, give him economic prosperity such that he should have nothing else to do but sleep, eat cake and busy himself with the continuation of the species, and even then, out of sheer ingratitude, sheer spite, man would play some nasty trick on you.*[237]

Chernyshevsky understood nothing about the perversity of the human soul. But Fyodor knew what lengths a person would go to in order to prove they were free to make their own choices. Chernyshevsky believed that rational egoism would save people, when the precise opposite was true: the pursuit of rational self-interest was the very thing holding society back from salvation.

The goal of life was to escape the ego and to love others as oneself, even if Christ was the only one who had ever achieved that on earth. In *Notes from the Underground*, Fyodor conceived a pure ego, a basement dweller, an underground man, to show the rational egoists what they were really working towards.

'I am a sick man . . . I am a spiteful man. I am an ugly man,' he spat onto the page.* Further down: 'To live longer than forty years is bad manners.' The manuscript was littered with these aphorisms. 'I am told the Petersburg climate is bad for me, and that with my small means it is very expensive to live in Petersburg . . . But I am not going away!' 'To be too conscious is an illness.' 'I have always considered myself cleverer than everyone around me, and sometimes I have been positively ashamed of it.' 'Another time, twice, in fact, I tried hard to be in love.' 'All my life I have not been able to begin or to finish anything. What is to be done if the sole vocation of every intelligent man is to babble, to pour water through a sieve?'[238] What is to be done, indeed?

With *Time* suppressed, Mikhail and Fyodor applied for a licence to publish under a new title, *Epoch*.† Katkov, who was an influential conservative as editor-in-chief of *The Russian Herald*, put in a good word for them with a sympathetic editorial about Strakhov's banned article. They had a good piece lined up about the slums of St Petersburg, and Turgenev's story 'Phantoms', which he had ended up sending straight to St Petersburg, was guaranteed to draw an audience (*though in my opinion it's full of rubbish; there's something morbid and senile about it*).[239] Polina had sent in a good story, too. But when the first issues of *Epoch* were

---

*The Underground Man speaks to us with *nadriv* (надрыв), a sort of herniated fervour, a raw, piercing, tearing voice, though the word is often said to be untranslatable because it is partly dependent on context. It amounts to an almost hysterical inner torsion. Constance Garnett translates the word, as the title of Part II, Book IV of *The Brothers Karamazov*, as 'Lacerations', which is quite a figurative, religious interpretation; Pevear and Volokhonsky translate it as 'Strains', which makes it sound as if Alyosha hasn't had enough fibre in his diet. Cf. *Reading Dostoevsky*, p. 155.

†Dostoevsky originally wanted to call it *Pravda* (*The Truth*), but this was rejected by the censors. The title was later used by the Bolsheviks for their own daily newspaper, though the notion of truth was a little stretchier by that time.

published containing *Notes from the Underground*, the critical silence was deafening.

Maria was growing weaker by the day. *Her face was skeletal, and the sweat stood out on her brow and temples.*[240] They were alone together now; Maria had sent Pasha back to St Petersburg and didn't want to see him until she was ready to bless him on her deathbed. It was just as well – the boy was useless – but every time Fyodor brought up the possibility of sending for Pasha, she took it as a statement that she was about to die and wept uncontrollably. *Why should I torment her in what may well be her final hours?*[241]

It is horrible to watch a person die of tuberculosis – *the blood gushes up and chokes you, about a pint of it*[242] – but it must have been particularly nightmarish for Fyodor, as if he were being forced to watch his mother die all over again, this time from the body of the husband. The only saving grace was that he wasn't a drunk like his father, like Isaev, though he was hardly a picture of health; he had a terrible bladder infection* and his fits weren't going away. *We sat side by side, sad and broken, as if we'd been washed up after a storm, alone on a lonely shore. How strange: I suddenly found it hard and painful to be loved so much.*[243]

It became clear that Maria was in her final hours. *Her breathing was hoarse and laboured; a kind of gurgle seemed to come from her throat.*[244] In the end, she managed to say goodbye and even asked to make peace with Mikhail, whom she had been convinced for some time was plotting against her. Fyodor sent a letter to Mikhail to ask him to get Pasha dark mourning clothes. At seven o'clock on the evening of 15 April 1864 she died.

In spite of the fact that we were so unhappy together (because of her strange, suspicious character and morbid imagination) we could not stop loving one another; the more unhappy we were, the more we clung to one another. Strange as it may seem, that's how it was. She was the most honest, noble and generous woman I have ever known. When she died, although I had suffered a whole year watching her die, I never realised the pain and emptiness I would feel when they covered her over with earth.[245]

*Usually sexually transmitted, in men.

As soon as Maria was buried, Fyodor rushed to St Petersburg to see Mikhail, who was suffering with some sort of liver infection. He'd had it for about two years, but it had grown worse since *Time* was censored and, with all the added stress of the new journal, he was struggling. Soon after Fyodor arrived, they heard that another article had been blocked by the censors. Mikhail collapsed. His body began to reject anything new; he was vomiting and also had diarrhoea. He tried to keep working, but the doctor told him in no uncertain terms that he was not to exert himself or leave the house. He started to feel better, but only for a day: the doctor explained that he had blood poisoning. He fell into a gentle sleep on the evening of Thursday 9 July, and never woke up.

I won't try to tell you how much I have lost with him. That man loved me more than anyone in the world, more even than his wife and children. My life has been shattered in a single year. These two were everything to me.[246] Fyodor found himself alone in the world, again.

My entire life broken in two. In the half I have left behind is everything I lived for, and in the other, still-unknown half, everything is strange and new, and there is not a single heart that could replace those two . . . Literally, I have nothing left to live for.[247]

When I have money, I shall become a highly original man. What's most debased and hateful about money is that even talent can be bought with it, and will be, till the end of the world.[248] Mikhail had died with only 300 roubles to his name, which barely covered the funeral, and in fact the situation was far worse than that, because he had accrued a staggering 25,000 roubles in debt.˙ Mikhail's wife and

˙A single rouble contained 4 zolotnik 21 dolya (i.e. 18 grams) of silver; at today's silver prices, he would have owed over £150,000, not accounting for differences in purchasing power.

children were destitute and in danger of ending up on the street. *I was the widow's only hope; she clung to me with her children and begged me to save her. I had loved my brother passionately. How could I abandon them?*[249]

Fyodor came up with a plan: he would take on the entirety of Mikhail's debt himself. He wrote to his wealthy aunt asking to borrow 10,000 roubles to keep the hungriest wolves at bay. *Epoch* was his only hope of making back the rest of the money, but working alone, it took him until August to produce the June issue. The subscribers began to complain. He worked twenty hours a day to keep *Epoch* afloat. All he did was edit, read the proofs, negotiate with the contributors, deal with the finances and logistics, sometimes until six o'clock in the morning. He had a new novel idea tapping away in his head, like a chick in its egg, but no one could produce their best work against the clock, purely to service debts. *Something demanded to be resolved at once, but it could neither be grasped nor put into words. As if everything were being wound into a ball.*[250]

He walked the streets alone, past people eating fine meals at Dussots, shopping at Gostiny Dvor, or taking hot-air balloon rides in the Yusupov Gardens. He ventured further into the stinking intestine of the city where he lived: the Ekaterininsky Canal, clogged with coal dust and building works; the stale waft of basement drinking dens; Finnish pedlars and decrepit cabs; Haymarket Square, with its flea market ringed by tables of young radicals, plotting to set up utopian communes over their sixth or seventh vodka. *It was as if I somehow felt better there, more isolated.*[251] On the corner of Konnyi Lane, there was Malinnik, an establishment set up over three floors and dedicated to worldly pleasures, starting tame and working towards depravity as you went further up, like a mockery of Dante's *Paradiso*. The first two floors were a bar and restaurant, but the third was a warren of thirteen rooms, separated by wooden partitions, each occupied by five or six young women who charged no more than 50 copecks for their services. *I suddenly and vividly realised the idea – revolting as a spider – of vice, which, without love, grossly and shamelessly begins where true love is consummated.*[252] It was impossible not to feel sorry for them, sitting around in such squalor, with only a dirty towel around their hips.

I want to get married. It doesn't do me much credit, though – rushing off to get married with a wife barely in the grave. What's more, I'm bound to make the wrong choice – we'll both be miserable and only make good people laugh.[253] It was true that he would be married again soon, but he was wrong about one thing: his new wife, a twenty-year-old named Anna, would make him happier than he'd ever been before.

As the anniversary of Maria's death came around in the spring of 1865, Fyodor found himself intervening in a rather sordid relationship between one of the contributors to *Epoch*, Peter Gorsky, and a fallen woman called Martha Brown, whom Fyodor had offered some translating work when it turned out she was destitute. Gorsky had been abusive towards her and, following a particularly bad row, Martha ended up staying in Peter and Paul Hospital rather than going back to him. Fyodor provided a shoulder to cry on and listened to her, assuring her that he didn't judge her, and they even found a private arrangement between the two of them for a month or two.[254] But it was clear it couldn't last. What Fyodor needed was to meet an eligible young woman without complications.

The magazine struggled on, Fyodor sifting the chaff of the submissions pile. He was sent one particularly good story by a young woman named Anna Korvin-Krukovskaya, and wrote to her to say that he would be delighted to publish it. She followed up immediately with a second story, better than the first, about a young man named Mikhail, brought up in a monastery by his uncle, who was a monk. Fyodor was quite taken with the setting – it was exactly the sort of character he might have written himself. Anna was the unmarried daughter of an elderly general, and had smuggled the stories out without her family's knowledge. She lived in the middle of nowhere, near the border with Poland, but Fyodor soon got a note inviting him to visit the family next time they were in St Petersburg.

On his first visit, Anna barely said a word, flanked as she was by her mother, her sister and two elderly Russo-German aunts for the excruciating half an hour that Fyodor spent there before making his excuses. *Have you noticed that, whenever two intelligent people who don't yet know each other all that well but, as it were, respect one another, come together, they are quite incapable, for at least half an hour, of finding a single topic of conversation?*[255] His mistake had been to give the matriarch advance notice to encamp the troops. Five days later, he sprang an ambush, turning up at the house without warning. To his great delight, only the two daughters were home. He and Anna quickly fell to chatting with the intimacy of old friends, which, in a certain sense, they were – for what else is a story but an invitation into the private rooms of a person's mind? By the time Madame Korvin-Krukovskaya came home, the two were getting on so well that it seemed only fair to ask him to stay for dinner.

Fyodor began an informal courtship, stopping to visit two or three times a week and chatting with the women of the household over tea. He was so immersed in these conversations that he fell into his old trap of forgetting his audience. *It is not enough to grow fond of people*, came the painful rebuke from his youth, *one must possess the art of making people fond of you.* On one visit, he revealed to them an idea he had once had for the perfect plot twist. Picture a man who, at the age of forty, has everything. A family man, a landlord, a collector of fine art. He wakes up in his beautiful house, the sunlight beaming in to wake him from peaceful rest. As he casts a contented eye over his furnishings, he has a vivid, jarring flashback: one evening after a party twenty years ago, egged on by his friends, he had raped a ten-year-old girl. Needless to say, Madame Korvin-Krukovskaya was deeply shocked and began to reconsider the influence that this forty-three-year-old man might be having on her daughters.

The courtship was becoming more serious even as it was going awry. Invited to a party which turned out to be full of stuck-up Russo-Germans, Fyodor conceived a furious jealousy for one of the young officers, convincing himself that Anna would be married off against her will and causing a scene. Anna stopped treating him as an inviolable authority and began to voice her dissent, particularly when he railed against the Nihilism of young people.

'The whole generation is stupid and backward,'[256] he said to her seriously during one argument. 'They would rather have shiny boots than Pushkin!'

Anna's response was perfectly calculated to wind him up.

'As a matter of fact, Pushkin is outdated.'

Anna was not nearly as pliant as Fyodor had assumed, but this only made his courting more fervent. He was attracted to people instinctually, almost magnetically, long before he knew whether they might be good for him, or even whether they would be able to remain civil with one another, and he reacted to any sign that the object of his affections was slipping away by making increasingly wild and grand gestures to recapture the tantalising prospect of intimacy.*

Matters came to a head one evening as Anna's sister Sofia was nearly finished butchering Dostoevsky's favourite sonata, Beethoven's *Pathétique*. The two slipped off alone to a small dining room curtained off from the lobby. They sat together on a love seat, with only the light of a small shaded lamp to bring their faces aglow. Even in the lamplight, Fyodor looked pale, but he was double her age, after all. He held her hands in his and whispered to her passionately.

'My darling Anna Vasilievna, please understand me. I fell in love with you from the moment I saw you. I even had this feeling before we met, from your letters. I do not treat you as a friend, but I love you with all my heart, with passion.'[257] He was building up to a proposal.

Just then, there was the clatter of a chair in the next room, and they looked up to see the curtain swinging. Sofia had been listening to everything.

April 1865 was a cruel month. Anna turned down his proposal and left St Petersburg. Then he received a letter from Polina's sister accusing him of 'treating himself to other people's sufferings

---

*Modern psychology might call his attachment style 'anxious-preoccupied'.

and tears', which was a bit rich coming from her. *She is a sick egoist. I love her even now, very much, but I already wish I didn't. I feel sorry for her because I can see that she will always be unhappy. A person who demands everything but won't take any responsibility will never find happiness.*[258] She had been offended that he had dared to express his unhappiness and now she wanted to punish him further. *Fine, don't love me, but don't torture me either.* Worse still, despite his best efforts, the number of subscribers to *Epoch* had been falling steadily and the only option was to close the magazine. It was madness to think he might pay off all his debt, but if perhaps he could get a book advance, he might pay off his most aggressive creditors and stay just shy of bankruptcy. *I must obtain at least three thousand roubles – though I don't know how. All I know is that if I do not get them I shall be ruined. Yet still I cannot help thinking that great things in life await me. Isn't that curious? I must have the resilience of a cat!*[259]

He decided to make a start on his new novel idea, *a psychological account of a crime.*[260] The protagonist would be a student who couldn't afford his university fees, but who believed himself truly great. This figure, Raskolnikov, believed like Napoleon that laws and morals were for other people. Turgenev's Bazarov had been praised as an authentic new Russian archetype, but Bazarov was only a wannabe Nihilist, an intellectual who was really all talk. Fyodor's main character, Raskolnikov, would make the perilous leap from words to deeds. The crime would come early, and the punishment late;* the real subject was the battle for Raskolnikov's soul, and by extension the soul of the young generation. Kicked out of university, living in a garret, behind on his rent and half-starved, Raskolnikov would see an opportunity: an old hag who hoarded money. To kill her and redistribute the wealth would be morally permissible, if you followed the cold moral calculus of the rational egoists and the revolutionaries, with their calls to 'take up axes'. *A fantastical, dark deed, a modern deed, a deed of our time, when the heart of man has*

---

* A full 80 per cent of the novel recounts events after the crime, but before the punishment.

clouded over; when there's talk of renewal through bloodshed.[261] Did any of them really understand what they were arguing for? Did they know what it was like to take an axe and to swing it down into a person's skull?

On the night of 29 June 1865 the Neva rose so high that it threatened to drown the inhabitants of basements across the city. The rats would swim up to street level as people's worthless possessions floated around in the wind and the rain. The government fired shots from its cannon at the Admiralty and Peter and Paul Fortress as a warning to the residents: something was about to burst, to overflow. Perhaps Fyodor heard them, or perhaps they merely disturbed his dreams.

My dreams are always so strange, no two the same – I can't begin to describe them.[262] *But how is it that you can always reason away the obvious absurdities and impossibilities overflowing in every dream? And why, too, when you wake up and return to reality, do you feel almost every time, and sometimes with extraordinary intensity, that you have left something unexplained behind? You laugh at the absurdities of your dream, and at the same time you feel that interwoven with those absurdities some thought lies hidden, a real thought, something belonging to your actual life, something that exists and has always existed in your heart.*[263]

Opening the notebook where he had been jotting down ideas for the new novel, he wrote, 'My first personal insult: the horse, the courier.'[264]

Stranded without an income while he began *Crime and Punishment*, Fyodor wanted to borrow more money from the Literary Fund, but there had been some slight unpleasantness about the fact that he was also on the executive committee and therefore pretty much granting himself loans. Someone had recently made an official complaint at a meeting, and faced with this attack on his character, Fyodor had done the dignified thing and handed in his resignation on 9 May 1865.

Less than a month later, he applied to the Literary Fund for a loan to pay off one of his other loans. He had sunk the 10,000 roubles from his aunt, which was effectively his inheritance, into the journal before it folded, and he was now being sued for the debts owing to two creditors – Demis the paper supplier and Gavrilov the printer – who were threatening to have him put in a debtors' prison. They even sent round a police officer to bully him (though they had a friendly exchange, and Fyodor ended up quizzing him about police procedures for the new novel). Whatever money he could get would have to go straight to the creditors, leaving him nothing to live on. With few alternatives available, Fyodor committed himself to the worst publishing deal of all time.

About a year before, he had been approached by a publisher, Fyodor Timofeevich Stellovsky, *a rather nasty man and a thoroughly incompetent publisher.*[265] Stellovsky would stalk impecunious writers like an endurance hunter running down a wounded beast. In 1861, for instance, he had bought the right to publish the complete works of the composer Glinka for just 25 roubles, an eye-wateringly bad deal.

Stellovsky had initially offered a flat fee of 2,000 roubles for a collected edition of Dostoevsky's existing works, which Fyodor had declined. But Fyodor had since become desperate. Now, when he came crawling back, Stellovsky made him a new offer: in return for 3,000 roubles, Stellovsky would have the right to publish the collected edition of Dostoevsky's existing work, and Fyodor also had to deliver him a full-length work of fiction by 1 November 1866, giving him just over a year to write it. If he missed the deadline, Stellovsky would gain the right to publish all his future work for the next nine years without payment. It was a clause so ridiculous that it didn't occur to Fyodor it would ever be enforced.

He divided the 3,000 roubles up among his creditors, keeping 175 roubles back to pay for a ticket out of town so that he might write in peace. He opted to go to Wiesbaden, where he had won money at roulette using his system, the idea being that he could win perhaps 1,000 roubles to get him through the next three months. *I've got into debt like a fool, and I want to win simply to pay it off.*[266]

Five days after his arrival, he had lost everything. *I can win – until now I've been playing at random, for the fun of the thing, like a fool, but now I'll tremble over every rouble.*[267] He pawned his watch, took the money to the table, and lost it. (Perhaps the protagonist for his new character should kill a pawnbroker. In the cold calculus of the Nihilists, that should count as a net gain – all they did was prey on others.)

He wrote to Turgenev to beg 100 thalers, promising to repay him as soon as possible, and after a few days Turgenev sent him 50 thalers.* A week later, Fyodor had run out of money to pay his hotel bills and, when he went into the restaurant, was told that orders had been given not to serve him dinner until he paid up. He called the manager, who explained that he did not 'deserve' dinner. Fyodor managed to persuade them to serve him tea, but tensions increased over the next couple of days. The staff stopped cleaning his clothes, or even answering his calls. In desperation, Fyodor wrote to his acquaintance Alexander Herzen asking for money, and didn't receive a reply. Now lacking even the money for postage, he wrote an unfranked begging letter to Polina, but she didn't have any to lend. She was in Paris, and he had originally thought of going to visit her, but now he was effectively imprisoned by his lack of funds. *I am still going without dinner and have been living on morning and evening tea for three days now – and it's strange: I'm not at all hungry. What's vile is that they deny me a candle in the evening if I have even a tiny little stump left from the day before. I leave the hotel at three o'clock every day, however, and come back at six so as not to let on that I haven't eaten.*[268]

He tried to write through the hunger, working on *Crime and Punishment*. He grew terribly thin and fell into a fever, shivering as he wrote and burning up at night. He finally got a reply from Herzen saying that he couldn't send the requested 400 gulden

---

* At this time, Germany was a mess of competing currencies, with individual cities minting their own coins. In the simplest terms: the thaler was worth almost a rouble; one thaler would get you 1¾ gulden; after unification in 1871, a thaler was worth three of the new silver Marks. Incidentally, Turgenev didn't get his money back until 1876, by which time thalers had become obsolete.

but that he could scrape together 150, though he pointedly didn't include the money itself, and even in his desperation Fyodor couldn't get over the embarrassment of writing back another time. He wrote to his old friend Wrangel, whom he hadn't seen in years, and also to Katkov asking for an advance on the new novel idea. Katkov was *a vain, conceited, and vengeful person,*[269] and not at all well liked in liberal circles, but *The Russian Herald* was second only to *The Contemporary* in subscribers and, as a consequence, they paid good money.

Fyodor was eventually released from weeks of hunger and misery when, after a second letter, Wrangel came through for him, sending a little money and inviting him to visit his family in Copenhagen on the way home. Sick of Wiesbaden, Fyodor went off to Pskov to pick up Pasha from his sister-in-law on the way to see Wrangel. His friend from Semipalatinsk was a different man now, no longer a youth, with a wife and children. That was what life was supposed to look like in your forties, though it was further out of reach than ever for Fyodor, taking the steamer back to St Petersburg with no money and a lazy, uneducated stepson who seemed bound for a life of dissolution. He arrived home to find the Neva freezing over, and that week he had three attacks of epilepsy. The doctor ordered him not to work so hard, but he was in the teeth of the idea and it wouldn't let him go.

Fyodor worked all winter on the novel. He didn't go out to see anyone, except for Polina, who was now in St Petersburg, but they only argued. He had actually proposed to her after the death of Maria, but she had only refused, and he had remarked bitterly that if she ever did get married, her husband would hate her within three days. By the end of November, he had already written most of a novel, but then he thought of a new plan that was even better, burned it all and started again. Katkov agreed to pay him a decent advance, so the novel would be serialised for a year starting in January 1866. Subscribers to *The Russian Herald* that year were either the luckiest or the most discerning in the history of literary journals, as they were now reading what would become two of the great works of world literature serially, one by Tolstoy, and the other by Dostoevsky. Both books pitted Napoleonic hubris and violence against Christlike redemption. Tolstoy's canvas for *War and Peace* was society;* Dostoevsky's *Crime and Punishment* depicted the war for a single soul. Arguably, Fyodor's book was the one that better captured the spirit of the times: on 12 January, the same month that serialisation began, there was a news report of a student named Danilov who had killed a moneylender in order to loot his apartment.

Fyodor wanted to try and write a hundred pages a month if possible, though he lost weeks at a time to illness. For fifteen days in February his haemorrhoids were so bad that he could neither sit nor stand, but had to lie motionless on his divan. Worse, if he was put in prison for his debts, he wouldn't be able to finish the serialisation, and he would lose his readers. Worse still, on 4 April 1866 someone made an attempt on the life of the Tsar himself, shooting at him while he was out walking his dog, Milord, in the Summer Gardens. The would-be assassin was an impoverished student, Dmitri Karakozov, who had been expelled from the university for failing to pay his fees. It was as if Fyodor's fictional protagonist had leapt the bounds of the book and was stalking the streets. As soon as he heard, he ran to his friend Maikov's house, trembling and pale, and burst in shrieking to deliver the news. This was the exact situation that his novel had been intended to pre-empt. He was well aware that he was still under surveillance, and now it was very likely that there would be a tightening of censorship. *But how can you fight nihilism without freedom of speech? If even the Nihilists were given freedom of speech, they would amuse everyone explaining their teachings. But at the moment people think of them as sphinxes, enigmas, wisdom, mystery, which entices the inexperienced.*[270]

Following the assassination attempt, a commission of inquiry was set up, and literary figures started to disappear in the night. *The Contemporary*, which had done so much to encourage radical ideas and had published half the revolutionaries in St Petersburg, was

---

* At the time Tolstoy's novel was being published as *1805* – perhaps he liked the dialectical force of a title like *Crime and Punishment*.

shut down for good. Through his new novel, Fyodor now appeared to be aligned with the reactionary Katkov, keeping him relatively safe, though he had so far only published the crime and not yet the punishment. The authorities refused to grant him permission to go abroad that summer to write as he had intended. It was probably for the best, since there weren't any casinos in Russia. *True – sad, vile, and stinking Petersburg, in the summer, suits my mood and might even give me a certain false inspiration for my novel; but really that's too depressing.*[271]

In the end, begging another 1,000 roubles from Katkov to pay off two different lawsuits by creditors and variously robbing Peter to pay Paul, he ended up going to write in peace in Liublino, just outside Moscow, where his relatives the Ivanovs were staying. The main house was noisy with a dozen young people coming home late from parties or getting up early to go fishing, so he rented his own little dacha nearby. The Ivanovs sent a servant to watch him in case of fits, though Fyodor inadvertently scared the life out of him by pacing back and forth throughout the night talking loudly of murder. He also drank vodka, as a traditional remedy for the cholera that had been sweeping St Petersburg. *I haven't yet got down to work on the novel for Stellovsky, but I will. I have worked out a plan – a quite satisfactory little novel.*[272] He was going to repurpose his idea for the short story about the gambling addict, though it would mean spreading the plot horribly thin.

Overall, he had a wonderful holiday. Fyodor so enjoyed having children around him – it brought out his mischievous side. Once, as they sat to lunch at a long table that easily fit the whole party, Fyodor, who was sitting at one end, accused a young girl at the other end of kicking him under the table. He kept an utterly straight face as she replied indignantly that her leg was not several metres long. He would join in all their games, though he would sometimes abandon them halfway through to go and write down an idea. He teased them mercilessly and they, in turn, teased him about his wispy beard, about which he was actually quite sensitive, though he tried his best not to show it.[273] One of the party was a rather beautiful twenty-year-old, whom he proposed to quite spontaneously one Sunday while everyone was out at church, but who put him down with a couplet from Pushkin and then burst out laughing. He also proposed to his sister Vera's sister-in-law, Elena Pavlovna Ivanova, whose husband was on his deathbed, but she put him off, too, given the circumstances.

Fyodor returned to St Petersburg to find that the serialisation of *Crime and Punishment* had the whole city in suspense. *And people had the nerve to think you'd gone crazy. The pathetic worms – who are they to understand what real intelligence is?*[274] But he had to put it on hold soon, because Stellovsky's deadline was looming and, amid all the excitement, he hadn't actually started yet. Deciding to settle the matter like a gentleman, Fyodor went to see the publisher and asked if he might buy his way out of the contract by paying a forfeit. Stellovsky refused. He asked for a three-month extension, but Stellovsky refused again. He even had the gall to tell Fyodor to his face that he was banking on Fyodor missing the deadline. To rub salt into the wound, Fyodor now discovered that it was Stellovsky who had bought the debts from Demis and Gavrilov and sued him for the money, which had forced Fyodor to agree to Stellovsky's contract in the first place. Stellovsky had effectively paid himself the 3,000 roubles; he now moved to his endgame and declared checkmate. Any sane human being would have admitted defeat.

So I have decided to perform an unprecedented and eccentric feat: to write 480 pages of two different novels within four months. * *I am not like other mortals. None of our writers, living or dead, has ever written under such conditions. The very thought of it would kill Turgenev.*[275]

* A printer's sheet or 'signature' is 16 pages according to *The Dostoevsky Encyclopedia*, making up about 5,000 words (cf. Figes, *The Europeans*, p. 147). Fyodor was aiming to write 30 signatures, and reckoned afterwards that he had written 47, which would be about 235,000 words or 752 pages – see his letter to Polina, 23 April 1867.

EIGHT

The Gambler

1866–1867

I'M EXCEEDINGLY ANXIOUS ABOUT *Stellovsky, and I even see him in my dreams.*[276] It was now the end of September and Fyodor still had not begun work on the new novel, which meant that he had just one month to write the whole thing, or his past and future works would be forfeit.

On 1 October, Fyodor wrote to his friend Miliukov asking him to visit after 9 p.m., when he might sneak home without fear of being hounded by creditors. He found Fyodor pacing the room, distraught.

'Why so dejected?' asked Miliukov.[277]

'You'd be dejected if you were on the brink of ruin,' Fyodor replied. He took the contract with Stellovsky out of his desk drawer and handed it to Miliukov, who read it while Fyodor paced up and down.

'Have you written much of the new novel?' Miliukov asked.

Fyodor stopped pacing and spread his arms wide.

'Not a line.'

Miliukov was shocked.

'But what is to be done? Something must be done!'

'What can I do when I have only a month until the deadline? It is already too late. It is impossible to write two hundred pages in four weeks!'

Miliukov sat down at the desk while Fyodor resumed his pacing, and the two fell into silent rumination.

'Listen,' Miliukov said eventually, 'You can't enslave yourself for all time. We must find a way out.'

'What way out? I don't see any way out.'

'You know what? You wrote to me, from Moscow I think, that you already had a finished plan for the novel, didn't you?'

'I have, but I'm telling you I haven't written a single line.'

'Let's get a few friends together. You tell us the plot of the novel. We'll outline the sections, divide it into chapters and write it up. Then you go over it and smooth out the rough spots and inconsistencies. Working together we can get it done on time.'

'No,' Fyodor said emphatically. 'I will never sign my name to someone else's work.'

Then Miliukov suggested an entirely different idea: a stenography school had started recently in St Petersburg, and they were training secretaries that could transcribe at the pace of normal speech. Perhaps instead of writing the novel, he could dictate it?

So it was that on 4 October 1866, at 11.28 a. m. (Fyodor had specified 'neither earlier nor later' than 11.30), the twenty-year-old stenographer Anna Grigorievna Snitkina rang the bell of Flat 13 of Alonkin's House on Stoliarny Lane. When the maid answered the door, Fyodor was wandering through the apartment in an unbuttoned shirt and slippers. As he locked eyes with the graduate standing there in her headscarf, holding sharpened pencils and a smart little portfolio, he cried out in embarrassment and flung himself behind a door.

He buttoned his shirt and threw on an old blue jacket, combed his hair, and asked for strong black tea to be brought into his study. (*The world can go to hell as long as I get my tea.*)[278] It was deeply unusual to have a young woman in his study alone with him. She sat on the old brown sofa, looking at a couple of large Chinese vases he'd brought from Siberia. He offered her a cigarette and she refused. He reassured her she needn't stand on ceremony, and she replied that she didn't smoke. He looked into her clear, grey, expectant eyes; she looked into his brown left eye and his black right eye. He had injured the latter in one of his epileptic fits, and the doctor had prescribed atropine, an extract of deadly nightshade, which dilated the pupil so much that the iris had disappeared entirely. Fyodor explained about his epilepsy. He wasn't sure this idea of stenography would really work. He had always worked alone, late at night, his hand scratching out lines upon lines of Cyrillic spiders.

'Well, let's try,' she said, 'and if it isn't working, I won't be upset – just tell me honestly.'[279]

'What's your name?' he asked.

'Anna.'

He forgot it the moment she had said it. Unsure quite where to begin, he picked up a copy of *The Russian Herald* and dictated a passage aloud to test her mettle. As she laboriously copied out her shorthand into longhand, he saw that she had missed an accent and a full stop. He prowled up and down the room for a long time, deciding what to do, while she sat there frozen like a rabbit. Finally, he announced that he couldn't possibly work now, and asked her to come back at 8 p.m.

When she came back that evening, he sat her down at his own desk, which seemed to please her, and asked her name again. She told him about her family: her father was a civil servant who had died in the spring; she lived with her mother; her sister was married to a censor; her brother was studying at agricultural college. Anna herself had started off studying science, but her flasks and retorts had a habit of bursting while she had her nose in a novel, so she'd decided to seek her independence through stenography instead.

'You must be very talented, considering that they recommended you out of your whole class,' he said.[280]

'It's not a question of ability,' she replied.

She had promised her father that she would persevere with it before he had died in April. As the original 150 students began to realise how difficult stenography was, and her peers flaked away, Anna did extra homework, determined to keep her promise. She was a serious, formal young woman. He liked that. She was so different from Polina, with her capriciousness and vanity – and what do we seek in a partner but the antithesis of the last? *I don't care half so much for good looks as for innocence.*[281]

Still, there was work to be done. He offered her a cigarette, forgetting that she didn't smoke; she respectfully declined. He picked up a paper bag with two pears in it, and offered her one; she took it. He chatted with her about the Petrashevsky days, told her about the mock execution. She started to get restless, and he assured her that he was about to begin dictation. He paced to the door, to the fireplace, and knocked on the fireplace twice with his knuckles, then again, to the door, to the fireplace, a lit cigarette in his hand.* He dictated a bit of the story that had been gestating, accidentally calling the city where it took place 'Roulettenberg', but deciding to leave it in. By the time they had finished it was late and Stoliarny Lane was full of drunken rabble, but Anna politely insisted that she didn't need to be accompanied by the maid, as she was staying with relatives nearby.†

The next morning, at the appointed time, Anna didn't appear, and Fyodor began to worry that he had scared her off, taking the first part of the novel with her. But she arrived half an hour later, having just finished writing up yesterday's work in longhand. They went to the study, tea was brought in, and he dictated for an hour, before declaring that he was tired of it and veering off into idle conversation. He asked her to remind him of her name, which she did. He offered her a cigarette again absent-mindedly. They talked a bit about the great writers of the day. Turgenev was talented but he had lived abroad so long that he'd forgotten his homeland. Nekrasov was no longer a close friend, but had been in his youth. Maikov he considered one of the wisest men in Russia. They did a bit more work but he couldn't settle down to it, and they gave up in the late afternoon.

As he was seeing her out, Fyodor couldn't help commenting, 'What large chignon you're wearing. Aren't you ashamed to have fake hair?'[282]

---

*The Russian cigarette of the time was a papirosa, an unfiltered tube of cardboard and paper with tobacco stuffed in the paper end. Dostoevsky's box of papirosi is on display in the drawing room of the Dostoevsky Museum in St Petersburg.
†That wasn't true – she ended up taking a cab home.

'I don't have false hair – this is my own,' she replied.

It wasn't a particularly auspicious start, either for their relationship or for the novel. It was already the fifth of the month and he had barely a few pages. But they began to fall into a rhythm: she would arrive at midday and stay until four in the afternoon; each evening, he would begin making notes in preparation for the next day, so that his dictations became more fluent as they went. As the stack of pages grew, Fyodor would ask her excitedly each day, 'How many pages did we do yesterday?'[283] They were barely interrupted, except occasionally by Pasha, who claimed to be interested in taking up shorthand, presumably in much the way he had taken up and abandoned everything else he had ever done, and Maikov, who wandered in through the open front door one day and seemed quite gratified to find Fyodor and Anna working together in the study.

Each day, when they took a break from dictation, they would talk about their lives. He talked to her about his courtship of Anna Korvin-Krukovskaya, and even told her about Polina, showing her a portrait.

'She is a remarkable beauty,' Anna said.[284]

'She has changed a lot in the last six years,' he replied.

Anna asked him questions and he told her about everything, about prison, the death of his wife, his debts (an unavoidable topic since the Chinese vases were now with the pawnbroker and they were eating with wooden spoons). Although he tried to conceal the stress he was under, he sometimes lost his temper with the maid. But Anna listened to him attentively, sympathetically. He began to call her 'my little dove'.

'Why do you only speak about your misfortunes?' she asked him. 'Why never mention the times you have been happy?'[285]

'But I have never experienced happiness,' he replied, 'I have always been waiting for it.'

The way he saw it, he stood at a crossroads: one path led to the holy land, Constantinople or Jerusalem, and devotion to a religious life; a second led to Europe and gambling; the third, to marriage. He asked Anna what she thought. Anna considered that it would be best to marry. She thought he should marry someone intelligent; Fyodor thought he should marry someone kind. He asked Anna why she had not yet married, and she responded that two men were courting her but, though she respected them, she didn't love either of them. Fyodor strongly agreed that she should marry for love.

The book was taking shape. Fyodor's protagonist was sometimes winning but mainly gambling away all the money he could get his hands on, all the while chasing a coquette called Polina who was stringing him along. It wasn't the most original story he'd ever written, but Stellovsky didn't deserve his best. Fyodor and Anna would argue good-naturedly about the characters, chatting happily between dictation. It began to seem as if they would actually make the deadline. But just as Fyodor had begun to understand how much he was enjoying Anna's company, the month was over.

Anna arrived to hand over the final pages for revision on 30 October, Fyodor's birthday. She normally wore black, but today she wore a lilac silk dress, and Fyodor found himself blushing as he fumbled around for 50 roubles to give her. He told her that lilac suited her very well, that she looked tall and graceful, and he shook her hand several times as he thanked her for all her work. But then Mikhail's widow Emilia turned up, and Maikov came to congratulate him, and the moment had passed. Fyodor asked when he might see Anna next (and suggested lightly that they might run off to Europe together). Anna suggested he visit her family in four days' time.

'Thursday?' he said. 'What a long time to wait. I shall miss you.'[286]

He finished his last revisions with just hours to go until the deadline and took the pages round to Stellovsky's house nearby, only to find that he wasn't in. He went to the publishing house, but the manager there refused to take delivery of the manuscript on the grounds that he had not been authorised to do so. By now, it was already evening and none of the notaries' offices were open. Not to be denied, Fyodor dashed to the nearest police station and, waiting for the district chief to return at 10 p.m., finally got a valid receipt for his new novel, *The Gambler*, with two hours to spare.

With Anna's help, he had achieved an almost impossible feat. Now all he had to do was finish *Crime and Punishment*.

When a girl's heart is moved to pity, we all know what comes next: she'll want to 'save' him and restore him to new life and activity – the usual fantasies. I twigged that the bird was flying into the net all by herself and prepared myself accordingly.[287]

It was bright and frosty on 8 November, but Fyodor could not enjoy it. Anna was half an hour late to his house, and by the time she arrived he was already worked up.

'I have been planning a new love story,'[288] he confided to her as soon as she was in the door.

'A new one? Is it interesting?' she asked.

'To me it is very interesting, but I don't know the ending. It is the psychology of the young girl that I'm finding difficult. I need your help.'

She seemed pleased that he thought it worth consulting her.

'Who is the hero of your novel?' she asked.

'An artist, not a young one; well, briefly, a man about my own age.'

The hero of this love story had a gloomy childhood, and lost his beloved father at a young age. He had a grave illness which had torn him away from his art for ten whole years. On his recovery, he had fallen in love with a woman, but the relationship had tormented him, and then both his wife and his beloved sister had died, leaving him burdened with terrible debts. The hero had grown old before his time, suffering with a paralysed arm. He was gloomy and distrustful; deep down he had a tender heart, but he was incapable of showing it. It was true that he had talent, but he had never succeeded in articulating his ideas.

'But why,' Anna asked, 'did you wrong the hero of your love story so much?'

'You don't find him sympathetic?'

'On the contrary, he's very sympathetic. He has a good heart. Surely any other man who had gone through so much would be embittered, but your hero still loves people. As a matter of fact, you are not being fair to him!'

'Yes, he has a kind, loving heart,' Fyodor agreed. 'And how glad I am that you understood him. It is at this decisive point in his life that the artist meets a young girl of your age – perhaps a year or two older. Let's call her Anna . . .'

'Is your heroine good looking?' she asked.

'She is not a beauty, of course, but she is not at all bad looking.' Anna could be forgiven if she looked a little put out at this. 'I love her face,' Fyodor added. Perhaps sensing that her patience was running out, Fyodor quickly outlined the conflict: the more the hero saw of Anna, the stronger was his conviction that he might finally find happiness with her. And yet, what could an old, sick man, burdened with debts, give her, a young, healthy, joyous girl? Wouldn't it be a terrible sacrifice for her, and wouldn't she regret it afterwards? Wouldn't it ring false for her to love him?

Anna spoke with conviction. 'If your Anna is not a shallow flirt, but has a kind, responsive heart, why shouldn't she fall in love with your artist? What does it matter that he is ill and poor? Does anyone love a person for looks or riches? And where is the sacrifice on her part? If she loves him, she will be happy and will never regret it.'

'And do you seriously believe that she could love him sincerely, for life?' he asked.

She hesitated.

Nothing in the world is harder than candour.[289]

'Put yourself in her place for a minute,' he said, his voice trembling. 'Imagine that the artist is myself, that I have declared my love to you and asked you to be my wife. Tell me, what would you say?'

Anna looked up at him.

'I should answer that I love you and shall love you all my life.'

Fyodor tried to keep the engagement quiet, as it would come as grim news to his growing number of dependants: not just the twenty-one-year-old Pasha, who showed no signs of getting a job; but Mikhail's widow Emilia and their four children; Mikhail's mistress and their son, who had come out of the woodwork; and Fyodor's alcoholic, infirm brother Nikolai. But despite knowing that his relatives would disapprove, this was the best thing that had ever happened to him, and he had to tell someone. Thus he found a time-honoured confidant in his cab driver, who told the maid, who told everyone she knew. The demands for money increased in pitch.

Anna had agreed to help him finish *Crime and Punishment*, and now that they were engaged Fyodor visited the Snitkin family home by the Smolny Monastery on the outskirts of the city. Fyodor got on well enough with Anna's mother and the engagement was not likely to last longer than the winter, when he hoped to receive an advance for a new book from Katkov. Unfortunately, in the meantime he no longer had a winter coat, having been forced by Pasha and Emilia to pawn it for money. So as it reached the end of November, he gritted his teeth and put on his thin autumn coat for the four-verst walk to Anna's house.

By the time he arrived, he was shaking with cold. Not normally given to drinking bouts, he downed three or four glasses of sherry in quick succession and asked for hot tea.

'Why didn't you wear your winter coat?' asked Anna anxiously.[290]

'Someone told me it was thawing today.'

'I'll send a servant at once to fetch it. He can take this one home for you.'

'No, please don't do that, please!' Fyodor cried desperately.

'Why not?' she asked. 'It will get even colder by nightfall.'

'I don't have a winter coat,' he admitted.

'What do you mean? Has it been stolen?'

'No, it hasn't been stolen. I had to pawn it.'

When she heard what had happened, Anna flew into a violent rage, sobbing hysterically. She screamed that his relatives were heartless, that Fyodor had obligations towards her, that she wouldn't survive his death. Fyodor held her, kissed her hands, and begged her to calm down.

'I am so used to pawning things that I didn't attach any importance to it. If I had known how you would take it I would never have let Pasha do it.'

Fyodor had tried to be honest that he was beset by debts and dependants. Showing an unwarranted degree of trust in Fyodor, Anna's mother suggested that he take over Anna's property as her guardian. She owned the house and its contents, after all. Fyodor was too honourable to accept, but the contrast with his engagement to Maria was striking.

The wedding date was set for Sunday 12 February at Izmailovsky Cathedral. In the meantime, Fyodor went to Moscow to see his relatives there and to get an advance from Katkov. He returned with 1,000 roubles, of which he gave Anna 500 for the wedding before relatives or creditors could make their own claims. He sent invitations out to his closest friends, not least Miliukov, who had set the whole train in motion. He also invited Strakhov, whom he hadn't seen in well over a year. Their friendship had never quite been the same after *Time* had been banned, but Fyodor asked Strakhov to be his witness in the hope that they might reconcile.

Fyodor had developed a toothache in Moscow, which had developed into a swollen cheek, and they had to put the wedding off for a few days. It did nothing to dampen his mood. *You can find enjoyment even in toothache. The enjoyment of the sufferer finds expression in moaning; if he didn't enjoy it, he wouldn't moan. Those moans express all the aimlessness of your pain, which is so humiliating to your consciousness; the consciousness that you have no enemy to punish, but that you feel pain; the consciousness that in spite of modern dentistry you are a slave to your teeth.*[291]

When the wedding day finally came, it went perfectly. It was 7 p.m. on Wednesday 15 February 1867 when Anna processed up the aisle in a white watered silk dress, bathed in candlelight and the voices of the choir. Fyodor Mikhailovich and Anna Grigorievna were married with Strakhov as their witness and Maikov, Miliukov and the others in attendance. That night, they toasted their family and friends with champagne. Fyodor couldn't stop looking at her. *The difference in our ages is horrible, but I am becoming more and more convinced that she will be happy. She has a heart, and she knows how to love.*[292]

Reality soon began to catch up with the newlyweds. He didn't have a fit on the night of his wedding but, as with Maria, he had not been entirely open with Anna about the severity of his illness. Two weeks later, while they spent the last evening of Shrovetide eating and drinking champagne at Anna's sister's house, Fyodor was telling a story when he paused mid-sentence. He turned pale and tried to stand, but began to subside towards Anna, and then howled in pain as he fell forwards. Anna caught him by the shoulders and got him back on the sofa, but he slipped off again and she didn't have the strength to lift him, so instead she pushed away the table and let him land gently on the floor and lay his head in her lap, cradling Fyodor as her sister sobbed, paralysed with fear. The convulsions gradually ebbed away and Fyodor began to come around. He didn't know where he was and his speech was mangled. They laid him on the sofa where, after an hour, the seizure returned. It was so forceful that, on waking, Fyodor screamed in pain for the next two hours.

He had now paid off 12,000 roubles of his brother's debt, but that only served to provoke those who hadn't yet been repaid – particularly two creditors whose rhyming names, Latkin and Pechatkin, call to mind a menacing pair of goons. On top of which, Fyodor was now financially supporting seemingly anyone with the surname Dostoevsky. His relatives had almost literally taken the shirt off his back, and Anna appeared determined that their life together wouldn't be sunk by Fyodor's generosity. She pawned all her furniture, including her piano, in order to buy them a trip to Europe. The trip would give them three months' respite from creditors and relatives, in which Fyodor could write, and pay off the remainder of his debts, and then their new life could begin.

It all made sense in a practical way, but Fyodor worried about leaving Russia, which was now the greatest source of inspiration to him. In Europe, he would be a fish on land, and he was sure his naive wife would be bored and tormented by his company. On top of which he had not wholly exorcised his passion for roulette. Still, it was Europe or debtors' prison. *I set off with death in my heart.**

Before a Russian travels, they 'sit on their suitcases', observing two minutes of calm and contemplation. Perhaps Fyodor and Anna didn't bother this time – after all, they were not intending to go away for long. Emilia would take the apartment on Stoliarny Lane, which Fyodor would continue to pay for. Before leaving, Fyodor called on Bazunov, the bookseller who handled Fyodor's publishing concerns. There, Bazunov handed him a letter from Polina. They hadn't spoken in over a year. She wrote of the great sadness of her life. She wasn't asking much about Fyodor; it was more that she was demanding to be understood. There wasn't time to answer the letter before leaving the city on 14 April 1867, when he and Anna bought their train tickets and climbed into their carriage.

Their first stop after Berlin was Dresden, where Fyodor wrote a long reply to Polina, *my precious friend*.[293] First he told her the whole story of the past year and a half, his debts, Stellovsky, publishing *Crime and Punishment*, his young and attractive stenographer and their subsequent marriage. By way of advice, he told Polina that it would be hard for her to be happy since she was so demanding and divided everyone into angels and scoundrels. He followed it up by noting that he would be in Dresden until 8 May if she wanted to reply. Little remained unsaid between them, but sometimes the urge to communicate outlives the exhaustion of the subject.

---

* Letter to Maikov, 16 (28) August 1867. The word used in Russian is *toska* (тоска). Vladimir Nabokov writes that 'no single word in English renders all the shades of *toska*. At its deepest and most painful, it is a sensation of great spiritual anguish, often without any specific cause. At less morbid levels it is a dull ache of the soul, a longing with nothing to long for, a sick pining, a vague restlessness, mental throes, yearning.' (*Eugene Onegin, a Novel in Verse*, Volume 2, Princeton University Press, 1991, p. 141).

Now that they were here, Fyodor soon began to feel restless. *Why was I in Dresden, specifically in Dresden, and not somewhere else?*[294] Other cities in Germany had soft green baize tables, on which notes and coins bred in piles or were decimated. He had seen people lose everything at those tables. He had himself lost everything more than once. In terms of poetic justice, therefore, the casino really owed him money. A thought experiment: *try not to think of a polar bear, and you will see that the damned thing is constantly in your thoughts.*[295]

Fyodor decided to go to cold, damp Homburg for a long weekend to gamble without his new bride, who was now, though they did not know it, in the early stages of pregnancy.* As the warning bell sounded on the train platform, Fyodor leapt up onto the train. Through the window he put one hand on his heart, and with the other he held up four fingers. Four days and he would be back. Tears came to Anna's eyes and he shook his finger – *don't cry.* The train began to leave, and Anna ran alongside it, crying, until she could no longer keep up.

Fyodor had promised to write to her each day, and was as good as his word. On Friday, he wrote that he couldn't stop thinking of her. On Saturday, he wrote that he dreamed of Anna all night, and admitted that he was also excited about his roulette system. On Sunday, he wrote that his nerves were worn out and he was taking too many risks. On Monday, he had pawned his watch, won his money back, and redeemed the watch. On Tuesday, he had lost the watch and couldn't pay his hotel bill. He asked Anna to send him money so he could buy a train ticket home.

The week dragged interminably on, each letter more painful than the last. On Wednesday, he staked the last of his money and built it up to 300 gulden, which made him so happy he bet big and lost it all. On Thursday, he sat at home with earache and toothache. Anna

---

*Anna wrote in her diary, 'If I am reconciled to his going there, it is not at all for the chance of his winning money at roulette, which, to tell the truth, I believe in very little; but I see that he is beginning to fret here, to become irritable.' (Anna Dostoevsky, p. 51)

sent him the money he had asked for that afternoon, enough to buy his way out of this self-inflicted nightmare. All he had to do was pay his hotel bill and catch the train to Dresden, back to his young, loyal, pregnant wife.*

On Friday, he wrote her a miserable, whimpering letter. 'Anya, dear, my friend, my wife, forgive me, don't call me a scoundrel! I have committed a crime: I have lost everything that you sent . . . I received it yesterday, and yesterday I lost it. Anya, how am I going to look at you now, what will you say about me now . . . Your judgement alone is terrifying to me! Can you, will you now respect me? And what is love without respect? . . . O my friend, don't blame me for ever! Gambling is hateful to me; not just now, but yesterday too, and the day before yesterday.'[296] He begged her to send more money for the journey home.

In Saturday's letter he spoke of a new work, one that would be magnificent, better even than *Crime and Punishment*, that would captivate the reading public and the booksellers. Katkov would give him more money and he would finally dig his way out of the pit of debt. He wondered idly whether Anna's mother might send some money over. In any case, soon they would go to Switzerland, where Fyodor would settle down to write.† Perhaps he had remembered the old proverb that what is good for the German is death for the Russian.

When the new money arrived, Fyodor quit Homburg without incurring further debts. Anna was waiting at the station, as she had been off and on for six hours, when he arrived. She looked at him with a fixed expression, almost unwilling to trust the evidence of her own eyes. Then she rushed up to him, brimming with happiness. Could it be that she hadn't judged him for going away, or for losing all that money?

---

* Anna confided to her diary: 'If only he could get out of his head that unlucky idea that he is going to win. I was very sad.' (Anna Dostoevsky, p. 52)

† As he wrote this, Anna was on the way to the train station. 'Today I really thought he would come.' (Anna Dostoevsky, p. 53)

At home, Fyodor enquired as casually as possible whether any letters had arrived from him. Anna passed him a letter from Polina, which he opened in front of her. He read the first page, silently, and then re-read it, blushing furiously. Anna appeared to think that the letter was from his niece, Sonya, and asked what she was writing about.˙ Fyodor smiled bitterly.

'It's not from Sonya,' he replied.

He and Anna kept talking but Fyodor couldn't concentrate. It really was the end for him and Polina. It is strange to think about love in this way. The person who will make you happy is sitting across from you with a cup of tea. She will forgive you everything; you can see that already. As well as offering an understanding and respect that you know you haven't earned, she has youth, grace, beauty. Her belly is beginning to swell with a pledge: I want half of me to be you. At the same time, you are holding a letter full of abuse from someone who gave you nothing and demanded everything, before whom you were abject. You are not angry, of course. You know she was bad for you. But we don't only want what we know is good for us; people are too complicated for that.

˙Anna had already read all his letters including this one, which she had wept over and resealed.

NINE

The Idiot

1867

THE REST OF THEIR time in Dresden was spent listlessly. Fyodor and Anna would wake up late, not simply because they were newlyweds but because they no longer had any way of telling the time; Fyodor's watch was in the pawnshop in Homburg. Anna wrote pages of obscure squiggles in a notebook, and wouldn't tell him what it said no matter how many times he asked. Some days, Fyodor would go out to the Café Français alone to read the newspaper. The only serious news came on 26 May, when they learned that another attempt had been made on the life of Tsar Alexander II, this time in Paris. Thankfully, the Tsar was only slightly wounded and the assassin's name was not Polina.

When it wasn't raining, they would go out and enjoy their honeymoon. Once or twice they went to a shooting range, where Fyodor turned out to be a crack shot, taking down nine of the ten targets. They went to the zoo, where the lioness paced in her cage, stopping only to headbutt the wall, and Fyodor stopped to stroke the camels' heads. Best of all was the museum, where they pondered the artworks, most of them depicting religious scenes in all the fleshly realism of the European tradition. They were overawed by Raphael's *Sistine Madonna*, which Fyodor stood on a chair to see better on account of his myopia. *You know, the Sistine Madonna has quite a fantastical face, the face of a mournful holy fool – don't you think?* Staring at it sparked off inchoate ideas for a new work of fiction, *ideas of the regeneration of all humanity, of eternal beauty, light interspersed with darkness – but there are spots even on the sun!*[297]

They heard that formal proceedings for debts had been issued against Fyodor in St Petersburg, meaning that they were now stuck on an indefinite holiday. They sampled the variable fare that Dresden had to offer, from chopped tongue to ice cream, rarely leaving each other's side. Fyodor told her she was the most generous creature on earth, but only because she was still young; soon, she would see that she had married a toothless old sinner. Anna replied that there wasn't a word of truth in it, that she loved him for ever and ever and was the happiest person in the world. After dinner they would take a turn around the gardens, arm in arm under the limes and the chestnuts, with their rose-coloured flowers, or race each other to the jetty on the Elbe, or listen to a concert.[298] Fyodor had bought a new brown hat and was delighted when Anna noticed how well it suited him. Each night he would spend an eternity getting ready for bed, as if steeling himself for a journey, and then he would go to kiss her goodnight and they would stay up talking, sometimes for hours. These were the happiest moments of the day for both of them. Fyodor asked Anna to tell him the story of their love and, when she was finished, he told her that he loved her ten times more now than when they had first met.

Anna was certainly pregnant now. *People say it's a trial to have children. Who says that? It is heavenly happiness!*[299] If it was a girl, they would call her Sonya, the name he had reserved for the heroine of *Crime and Punishment*,† and if it was a boy, Misha, in honour of

---

* *Crime and Punishment*, p. 577. Anna confides to her diary that 'never has any picture before made such an impression on me . . . Fyodor thinks there is pain in her very smile'. (Anna Dostoevsky, 1928, p. 36) She also approvingly notes the golden frame and the gallery's velvet seats, before reflecting, 'I do not care about the Child, as it sits on its Mother's arm. Fyodor was right in saying it was not a true child's face . . . I did not at all like St Barbara.'

† True, she was a prostitute, but the important thing was that she had a pure heart. Sonya is also the diminutive of Sofia, wisdom. It was the name of his favourite niece, to whom he dedicated *The Idiot*.

his brother. Mikhail had been dead for three years now, but Fyodor could have sworn he had seen him appear in a doorway after his latest fit.

They squabbled often and made up quickly. Anna was as proud and insecure as Fyodor, and this made each of them alert to any perceived slight. Sometimes one of them would storm off in the park, or the other would refuse to speak until they had received an apology, but neither could bear the uncertainty and they would soon find an excuse to break the tension with a joke or a kind gesture. The only enduring source of conflict was the daily trip to the post office. Katkov still hadn't sent any money; Pasha had had the nerve to ask Anna's mother for money; and the spectre of Polina hovered over any letter from an unknown sender.

It was clear by now that Anna must know about Polina's last letter, which had been quite rude about her. Once, during an argument, Anna told him she was drafting a strongly worded letter to 'a certain person' who had hurt her very much and Fyodor demanded to know who while she sat silently writing in the sitting room. Another day, as Anna was leaving to buy envelopes, Fyodor asked which post office she was going to. She told him she wasn't going to intercept his letters, if that was what he was thinking. As she stood at the front door, he rushed up, chin trembling, and told her she had no right to interfere, even if he were conducting a love affair. She replied coolly that his affairs were no concern of hers, but if he were more open with her she wouldn't have to conduct her own tedious correspondence. He asked who it was that had dared to annoy her, but she wouldn't tell him. So they both went to the post office together. There was one letter there marked for Dostoevsky – from Katkov. The money was on its way, which meant that they now had the funds to leave Dresden.

The plan had always been to go to Geneva, where Fyodor would write his next novel, but he wanted to stop at Baden-Baden on the way. *I was tormented by a tempting idea of maybe winning 2,000 extra francs. That's the worst part: I am wicked and too passionate by nature. Everywhere and in everything I go to the very limit; I've been overstepping the line my whole life.*[300] The real problem at Homburg had been that he had left Anna behind, which had distracted him – perhaps if he and Anna were together, the system would work again.

Baden-Baden was quiet for this time of year, since most tourists were off seeing the Paris Exposition.* The newlyweds checked into the grand Hotel Zum Goldenen Ritter in the centre of town and Fyodor wandered off to have a little look at the casino tables. *I am still convinced that, by keeping a completely cool head, and preserving your intelligence and calculation in gambling, it must be possible to overcome the crudity of blind chance and win.*[301] A day later, he had lost substantially and they moved into a more modest apartment on the outskirts of the city with an enthusiastic and useless maid. It was much cheaper on account of the ceaseless hammering of the blacksmith at his anvil, which began at 4 a.m. in the room below them. *All that night I dreamed of roulette, of play, of gold. I seemed in my dreams to be calculating something at the gambling table, some take, some chance, and it oppressed me all night like a nightmare.*[302]

Anna's morning sickness continued all the next day and she lay motionless on the sofa. Fyodor went out to buy her peppermints and currant juice, then took five of their remaining 45 ducats off to the tables. When he had spent those, he came back and took another ten, leaving them with 30 ducats. When he lost those too, he came back and sat sadly on the edge of the sofa where Anna was sleeping. He threw away his purse, which had brought him nothing but bad luck. *A hellish thought occurred to me: why not, when all's said and done, borrow more after my confession? So I prepared my confession as a sort of fricassee with a sauce of tears, to soften her up. The two thoughts came together; it is awfully difficult to struggle against these double thoughts.*[303] Waking Anna up, Fyodor began to tell her everything. Anna reassured Fyodor that she understood, and that he could have

---

* Among the exhibits, the American George Steinway presented his piano, the German manufacturer Krupp presented a fifty-ton cannon, and a newly opened Japan presented artwork that would have a tremendous influence on the French art of the period.

more money. She gave him another five ducats. He returned late. He had been up by as much as 400 francs, but stayed far longer than he had intended, and he begged her forgiveness, saying he was not worthy of her.

It went on like this the next day. Fyodor took another five ducats to offer up at the tables and lost them. Anna was crying, though she refused to criticise Fyodor himself. He asked for more money and she said no; he begged her and she gave him two ducats. He went and lost them. They agreed it would be best if they went to Geneva sooner rather than later. She gave him a last three ducats, leaving them with only 15, and Fyodor suggested it might have been better if she told him off instead of indulging him, and that it was painful to him, the way she was so sweet.

That day, they bumped into Ivan Goncharov, author of the novel *Oblomov*, who told Fyodor that Turgenev had spotted him at the tables the day before but hadn't said hello because he knew that gamblers don't like being interrupted.˙ Their relationship had cooled considerably since Fyodor had slighted him over 'Phantoms'. Fyodor had just read Turgenev's new novel *Smoke* in the March 1867 issue of Katkov's *Russian Herald* and hated it. *It's so artificial and confected. There's a terrible decline in artistry and he doesn't know Russia.*[304] As so often, Turgenev's most notable achievement in publishing the book was to unite both the radicals and the reactionaries in universal condemnation. In these turbulent times the deplorability of Turgenev was perhaps the only common ground among Russian intellectuals, though they all read every word he wrote. But this time, Fyodor wasn't going to come to his defence; on the contrary, he felt that Turgenev had spent too long in Europe and was losing touch with the motherland. *He is a spiteful old woman whose day is over.*[305] But propriety demanded that Fyodor pay a visit, lest he

˙Dostoevsky had first met Goncharov in 1846, as part of the Belinsky circle. He thought Goncharov had 'the soul of a bureaucrat', that he was 'devoid of ideas' and had 'the eyes of a boiled fish', but recognised that 'God, as if for a joke, has bestowed a brilliant talent' on him. (Letter to Wrangel, 9 November 1856)

seem to be avoiding repaying the 50 thalers he still owed Turgenev from two years ago.

Turgenev now lived in the house next door to the love of his life, Pauline Viardot, and her husband Louis, with whom he was on good terms. Although he earned more than Fyodor from his writing, there was also the 5,000 francs a year he now received from his estate at Spasskoe, near the Tolstoys. He had always been better known, better paid and better connected. In his more generous moments, Fyodor even had to concede that Turgenev wrote better prose. But when he called on Turgenev at noon on 10 July, their often productive antagonism now threatened to brim over into open hostility.

He was wearing a sort of indoor wadded jacket with pearl buttons, but it was too short, which was far from becoming to his rather comfortable stomach and the solid curves of his hips. But tastes differ. Over his knees he had a checkered woollen plaid reaching to the floor, though it was warm in the room.[306] *I knew from experience that, although he made a show of kissing me, he really only proffered his cheek, and so this time I did the same and our cheeks met. He did not show that he noticed it, sat down on the sofa, and affably offered me an easy chair.*[307]

Turgenev immediately began to complain, in his high-pitched voice, about the reception of *Smoke*. The main idea had ruffled feathers: if Russia were to suddenly vanish from the face of the earth, it wouldn't be any great loss; indeed, the world would go on exactly as it had before. Apparently the rest of Russia had taken it badly and the English Club in Moscow was even collecting signatures to have him expelled. But Fyodor was the wrong person to complain to. A staunch patriot, he couldn't stand the liberal game of insulting Russia in the name of love. *One can't listen to such criticism of Russia from a Russian turncoat who might have been useful.*[308]

Fyodor picked up a copy of the book.

'*Smoke* should go in the fire,' he said.[309]

Turgenev had the nerve to ask why he should do such a thing, and Fyodor told him that he hated Russia and did not believe in its future. Turgenev saw only one way towards civilisation, and couldn't see any special purpose for Russia – indeed, he had mentioned that he was planning to write an article condemning all Slavophiles and Russophiles.

'For the sake of convenience, you should order a telescope from Paris,' Fyodor told him.[310]

'What for?' asked Turgenev.

'It's a long way. You can train your telescope on Russia and examine us – otherwise we'll be hard to make out.' Turgenev had begun to flush with anger. Fyodor continued with assumed naivety, 'But I really didn't expect all this criticism and the failure of *Smoke* to irritate you so much. Honest to God, it isn't worth it, forget about it.'

'But I'm not at all irritated. What do you mean?'

Fyodor changed the subject and they talked a little about their personal lives, but when the subject of Germany came up Fyodor let loose, berating German people as dishonest and questioning the idea that they were any more civilised than the Russians.

If he was red before, Turgenev was now very pale.

'In talking like that, you are offending me personally. You should know that I have settled here permanently, that I consider myself a German, not a Russian, and I am proud of that!'

'Although I've read *Smoke*, and have been speaking with you now for a whole hour, I could not at all have expected you to say that,' replied Fyodor somewhat disingenuously. 'Please forgive me for having offended you.'

Their parting was stiff. *I vowed to myself never again to set foot at Turgenev's.* According to custom, Turgenev offered to call on Fyodor in return and Fyodor mentioned that he would not be ready to receive anyone before noon. Turgenev left his card the next day at 10 a.m.

―――――――

It is impossible to speak of Anna's goodness and her patience without understanding the pit of addiction and desperation

---

*Letter to Maikov, 16 (28) August 1867. They might have fallen out, but at least not so badly that one challenged the other to a duel, as Tolstoy did when Turgenev swore at him once in an argument.

that Fyodor dug for them that year.* Soon, their 12 ducats had dwindled to five. Fyodor pawned his wedding ring. They were down to two gold pieces; he gambled his way back to 21 gold pieces and redeemed the ring. Fyodor would go out all day while Anna lay on the sofa at home, staring at the wall, or attempting to satisfy cravings for particular foods. He was so well known to the casino that the attendants would bring him an armchair when he arrived, and the other gamblers had marked him out as the man who picked fights when he was jostled. *I did, of course, derive acute enjoyment from it, but this enjoyment was at the cost of torture: the whole thing, the people, the gambling, and, most of all, myself in the middle of them, seemed horribly nasty.*[311] One day he won big and came home with a fruit basket and a bouquet of red and yellow roses for Anna. She often felt queasy, and Fyodor brought lemons and sugar to make her lemonade. For her cravings he tracked down caviar, French mustard, bilberries, ryzhiki mushrooms.† Even amid the gambling, he was besotted with Anna. *Some women fascinate by their beauty or charm in a minute, while you may ruminate over another for six months before you understand what is in her.*[312]

At times, the gambling seemed like a brute fact in much the way that fish swim; at others, it seemed to be a desperate leap at a life that was hopelessly out of reach. At one point, they had as many as 166 gold pieces, but of course the only reliable rule in gambling is that your pot trends towards zero. By 18 July they had only one gold piece left. Fyodor returned to Anna for the fifth time in as many hours and asked her to hand over anything he could pawn. Anna took off the earrings and brooch that he had given her and looked at them, sadly, for a long time, and then kissed them, before handing them to Fyodor. He pulled her onto his lap, told her she was the sweetest person in the whole world, and kissed her breasts

---

*The 5th Diagnostic and Statistical Manual lists nine possible signs of gambling disorder, of which Dostoevsky matched eight (the only thing he didn't do was lie about how bad it was).
† Known to us as saffron milk caps.

and her hands. Then he took off to gamble.* *Whenever I have found myself in some exceptionally shameful position, some more than usually humiliating, despicable and, above all, ridiculous situation, it has always aroused in me not only boundless anger, but at one and the same time an incredible sense of pleasure, an intoxication that came from the agonising awareness of my own depravity. I confess that I often sought it out, because for me it was the most powerful of all such sensations.*[313] Three hours later, he had lost everything again. He slumped down in a chair at home, covered his face with his hands, and wept.

'Now I have stolen your last things from you and played them away!' he cried.[314]

Anna kneeled by him and tried to comfort him, but they were both miserable beyond words. Fyodor told her that he had gambled for the last time. They lay on the sofa together, went to get cigarettes and then lay down on the bed, Fyodor running through acquaintances who might lend him money. At 11 p. m. he decided that the only thing for it was to try his luck again the next day, one last time. Fyodor told Anna that he loved her unspeakably, loved her and worshipped their growing child.

The next day Fyodor pawned his wedding ring and lost the money. He spent most of that day trudging around in the rain trying to find someone who would take Anna's scarf. After dinner, he took her wedding ring to pawn instead. He won some money and redeemed the rings. The pawnbroker told him not to play any more, but Fyodor didn't listen. By the end of the week the rings were back in pawn. Fyodor pawned Anna's fur. He borrowed money from Goncharov, while Anna wrote to her mother, whose finances were hardly better. Meanwhile, they restricted themselves to free activities to pass the time. They wandered around the grounds of an

---

* Anna relates: 'No sooner had the door closed behind him than I was prey to such insufferable thoughts that I could no longer control myself, but began to cry bitterly. It was no ordinary weeping, but a dreadful convulsive sort of sobbing, that brought on a terrible pain in my breast, and relieved me not in the slightest ... There are moments when I cannot help thinking it would be better if Fyodor didn't come back for three whole days on end, and I could lie asleep all the time in a darkened room.' (Anna Dostoevsky, 1928, pp. 265–6)

old castle, taking breaks for Anna to rest, and up some little stone steps to a high fort from which they had a magnificent view of the town and the forested mountains. Fyodor stood at the edge of the precipice.

'Goodbye now, Anna,' he said. 'I'm going to throw myself down.'[315]

Anna didn't smile.

Their poverty began to grate. Anna would cry often and it got on Fyodor's nerves. Her shoes were torn and they couldn't afford to replace them. She was clearly enervated by the heat, the sound of the smithy, the landlady's children, who woke them up every morning at six o'clock, Fyodor's coughing fits and his attacks. One late afternoon in early August, he had a severe fit, during which he could speak only in German. Anna tried to wedge him, half-standing, half-sitting, between the bed and the wall, but his convulsions were too violent. He bashed his right foot painfully against the wall as Anna eased him back onto two pillows on the floor and undid his buttons. His lips went blue as he fell unconscious. When he woke some time later, he apologised in French, still disoriented, and put on his hat to go out. Anna insisted on accompanying him. Deserted by language, Fyodor kissed her hand over and over, and they drank hot chocolate together.

Anna's mother came through for them, sending 172 francs. Fyodor lost a little of it, then won a little more. Once they had paid a couple of the bills that had heaped up, and Fyodor had lost some more, they had 30 francs left. He won quite a sum one day. Most days he lost. Anna began to beg him not to return to the casino on the same day, not to go at all, and Fyodor punched the wall in frustration. They soon had no money for breakfast, let alone rent. Fyodor pawned some of their clothes and gambled away most of that.

Anna had picked up a deck of fortune-telling cards, and no matter how many times she shuffled them she kept getting the coffin, which signified either death or loss of property. One day Fyodor told Anna he hated her; another, Anna told him the very idea of him winning money at roulette was utterly ridiculous. Once, Fyodor caught Anna at the tables and scolded her, telling her that she would only lose whatever she won. Later, he told her he only wanted to make sure that she didn't get overexcited, given her condition.

When Anna's mother sent another letter containing 150 roubles, they began planning to leave for Geneva. Fyodor hit a streak of luck and before long they had 1,300 francs! They were both over the moon and went to buy sausages and doughnuts. Fyodor thought that if he could get as many as 3,000 gulden they might even send for Anna's mother. He started staking big money. He lost. He asked for some of the money that Anna's mother had sent to redeem the brooch, the earrings and the ring. Anna was distraught, but she gave him the money. He returned that night inconsolable, having lost it all.

They decided to leave the next day. Anna escorted Fyodor to the pawnshop to redeem their things, but he then continued gambling and pawning. An hour and a half before their train left, Fyodor went back to the tables, returning twenty minutes later having lost everything he had with him. Anna told him curtly not to be hysterical but to help her fasten the trunks. At the train platform, Turgenev was there, but the two men didn't so much as bow to one another.

Everything would change once the baby was born, little Sonya or Misha. Everything would be better then.* The birth was due in January or February 1868. They stopped off in Basel to see Holbein's *The Body of the Dead Christ in the Tomb*. This was Christ as Fyodor had never seen him before: so frail, so unutterably human, with his lumpy navel, the protrusion of his hip bone, the scuffs of blood on his hand and rib. His face vacated of sense and already turning blue. Christ in the world, brought down to our level. A perfectly beautiful man thrust into a world of compromise and vanity.

And then they reached Geneva, where Fyodor would get to work on the most ambitious story he had yet conceived: a second coming, the arrival of a Christ-like figure in modern-day St Petersburg. Whether Fyodor could realise such an audacious theme was

---

* Anna writes in her diary, 'Any child would make me as happy as happy could be, and if anything went wrong I should be in despair.' (Anna Dostoevsky, 1928, p. 413)

doubtful, but despite his illness, his poverty, his moral inadequacy, he would try. *I have ideas, very great ideas, of which I ought not to speak, as I would be sure to make everyone laugh. I am certain that I am more loved than I deserve. But I know for certain that twenty years' illness must leave traces, so that it's impossible not to laugh at me sometimes.*[316]

I have six months of ceaseless work ahead. But by then it will be time for my wife to give birth.[317] When they arrived in Geneva in mid-August 1867, they took a quiet, furnished room that might allow him the peace to write. Their two elderly landladies were always boasting about Geneva, but other than the lake, Fyodor couldn't see what was so great about the place. For one thing, it was expensive, and for another, everyone was always drunk. The drunkenness was worse even than in London, if such a thing were possible. *One doesn't live here; one serves a sentence here.*[318] The couple rarely socialised with the other Russians in the city, except to see Herzen's cousin Nikolai Platonovich Ogarov, who was no less a revolutionary than Herzen himself.

Having scrounged a little money from Maikov, Katkov and Fyodor's old doctor, Stepan Yanovsky, they decided to stay in Geneva at least until the baby was born, since Fyodor could communicate better with the doctors in French. On money matters, Anna was also plotting against Pasha whom she now acknowledged as a nemesis, concocting a story about him going directly to Katkov in Moscow to beg for money. Fyodor was angry while the ruse lasted, but he insisted on supporting Pasha financially come what may. He had more than once called in a favour to get Pasha a job, but his stepson had found office work to be beneath him and tended to quit the moment he was asked to do anything.

Having escaped the terrible orbit of the roulette wheel, Fyodor re-established a proper work routine. Get up late, light a fire, have coffee. Sit at desk, contemplating this good soul, this Prince Christ, and what might await him in St Petersburg, the city to which

Fyodor would dearly have longed to return. *I need Russia, need it for my writing and my work.*[319] At 4 p.m., Fyodor would go out for dinner, while Anna stayed at home. He'd sit in a café to read the *Moscow News* or *The Voice*, all the while gathering material to write about Russia and its unfounded faith in European civilisation. Then, before going home to bank the fire, drink more tea, set down a few ideas, Fyodor would permit himself a little wander around for half an hour to clear his head.

While he was plotting his new novel, Giuseppe Garibaldi and Mikhail Bakunin came to Geneva to attend a meeting of thousands of European revolutionaries somewhat optimistically called the League of Peace and Freedom.* At the conference, they were all talking about getting rid of large states and their large armies, to be replaced by small republics. Religion was to be abolished, world peace achieved (by fire and sword, of course). It was precisely this sort of utopianism that Fyodor wanted to demolish. And the book had to be good, because by now Katkov had advanced him 4,000 roubles.

Fyodor sat at his desk, probing at ideas, but the plot wouldn't come together, and he wouldn't receive any more money until he had at least sent off a completed section. *Worst of all I fear mediocrity; I think it's better a thing be either very good or quite bad.*[320] He tried taking a short trip to Saxon-les-Bains for a little flutter at roulette – and then another – but he lost his money without gaining any inspiration. He wrote quite a lot, threw it away and started again, scouring the newspapers every day for the flash of lightning that would briefly illuminate the whole silhouette of the novel to him. He read the headlines as if they were one long prophecy filled with lacunae. The murders, the obsession with money, the way that Western ideas like Nihilism were corrupting the young generation. *The visible connection between all matters, general and private, is becoming stronger and stronger and more obvious. I definitely want to publish something like a newspaper when I get back.*[321]

---

* One of Bakunin's house guests was a young terrorist by the name of Sergei Nechaev who, for now, was lying low.

The air was frigid, particularly when the icy northeasterly *bise* would blow in all of a sudden, rushing down from the mountains across Lake Geneva. It would grow more common in the spring – another reason to leave as soon as the baby was born. As winter approached, it was impossible to heat the houses sufficiently for Fyodor's comfort, let alone for poor Anna. Even with the fire blazing, it was 6°C.* On top of which, he was having fits every ten days here. It took him days to recover, and although he trusted his imagination, his memory sometimes failed him in the aftermath. He had given his word of honour that he would send Katkov a chunk of the novel for the January issue, and it had to be done.

There were so many ideas he wanted to express in *The Idiot*. He had been writing six different plans a day for how it would go. Now he had to start writing it even though he hadn't really worked out the plot. *I've been tormented by one idea for a long time, but I was afraid to make a novel out of it, because the idea is too difficult and I'm not prepared for it, although the idea is quite enticing and I love it.*[322] It all centred around his beautiful man, Prince Myshkin, a naive and kind and generous soul. He had something of Don Quixote in him, a good person who was nevertheless sympathetic because his behaviour was out of place and he couldn't see it. Prince Myshkin would be a sort of holy fool, regarded by some as a common idiot, but piercing through his simplicity to the heart of matters. The idealist in Fyodor wanted a redeemer, but the realist in him demanded an unhappy man. *For me the whole comes out in the form of a hero. That's how it's worked out for me. But will he develop under my pen? And it has turned out that in addition to the hero there is a heroine, too, and that means TWO HEROES!! And besides those there are two other characters as well – absolutely major ones, that is, almost protagonists.*[323] The heroine around which the plot revolved was Nastasia Filippovna, a fierce, beautiful woman whose pure character was ignored by a high society that regarded her as 'fallen'. Her suitor, Rogozhin, was a wealthy but coarse merchant driven to distraction by his passions; and there was also Myshkin's own love interest,

*Fyodor measured it five degrees according to the Réaumur scale.

144

Aglaya, whom Fyodor had not sketched out properly yet, but who was modelled somewhat on Anna Korvin-Krukovskaya. As ever, the plot would descend into a love triangle, or perhaps a square. Myshkin would be torn in two, his Christian love for Nastasya in an intractable conflict with his all too human love for Aglaya. *And how can one love two at once? With two different kinds of love? That's interesting . . . Poor idiot.*[324]

A Messianic tenor ran through the whole. *The whole world shall be renewed through Russian thought, and this will come to pass in some future generation – that's my passionate belief.*[325] First Rome had fallen, then Byzantium; Russia was to take up its destiny as the third Rome come the Millennium, with a Russian Christ to lead the world. *We are living in the age of the Third Horse, the black one, and the rider who has the balance in his hand, seeing that everything in the present age is weighed in the scales and by agreement, and people are seeking for nothing but their rights. But by rights alone they won't keep their hearts pure, and afterwards will follow the pale horse.*[326]

By this time, there were perhaps more atheists in Russia than anywhere else, because, as Fyodor saw it, Russia had gone further than Europe in spiritual matters. Russian Liberals like Turgenev or Herzen were useless now – *the shitheads!*[327] They were not even Russian, but citizens of the world, and they only took intellectual positions on socialism as a way of passing the time. In any case, they had been surpassed entirely by the new generation.

The problem was not that material progress had not been made. Famines used to be frequent. Looking up at the feudal castles perched precariously in the Swiss mountains, some of them half a mile up, one could not help but think of the poor people who had been forced to haul up the stone. And yet, for all the prosperity of the modern era, the infrequency of famine and the rapidity of communication, there was no idea binding humanity together with anything like the power it had in centuries past. *There is more wealth, but there is less strength. There is no uniting idea; everything has grown limp, and everyone is limp!*[328] The whole edifice of materialism was founded on a house of cards, *without recognising any moral basis except for the satisfaction of individual egoism.*[329]

The fallacy of rational egoism was to believe that the human heart naturally desired what was good, when really it was a battleground between good and evil. *The law of destruction and the law of self-preservation are equally strong in humanity!*[330] The answer was faith – deep, instinctual, unbidden faith – and for that, you had to look to the Russian people, the peasantry. The simple love of one's fellow creatures, rather than the love of lofty abstractions. *In abstract love for humanity one almost always loves no one but oneself.*[331] All this he wanted to express through his characters, but Fyodor knew he must make the approach obliquely or risk being called a madman. His most outlandish ideas he could put in the mouths of characters he had already disowned, so that he might speak without seeming to endorse their views. But first he had to set up the conflict between the lovers.

Fyodor sent the first part of *The Idiot* off to Katkov at the end of 1867, hoping it might still make the crucial first issue of the year. He was afraid it would be boring. The first part hadn't said much – it had only introduced the mysterious figure of Myshkin – but it hadn't compromised the rest either. The important thing was to arouse the reader's curiosity.

TEN

Death for the Russian

1868–1871

W *E LIVE ON A pittance. We've pawned everything. Anna is now in the final hours. I wonder whether she won't give birth in the middle of the night. I'm terribly anxious myself, but meanwhile I need to write without pause.*[332]

The weather was stormy on the night of 3 March 1868. Bad weather often affected Fyodor's nerves and, true to form, he had a severe epileptic fit. The next morning he could barely stand, and the day passed in a fog of half-thoughts. He went to bed at 7 p.m., but was woken four hours later by Anna gently tapping him on the shoulder.

'I think it's started – I'm really suffering!' she said.*

'How sorry I am for you, my darling!' Fyodor replied in the tenderest voice, before falling back asleep.

He was woken again at 7 a.m. by Anna, who had been suffering through his sleep, praying that he would be well enough to get to the midwife in the morning.

When he realised what was happening, Fyodor threw on his clothes and dashed off to get the midwife. He rang the doorbell a number of times before a servant came to the door to explain that the midwife was sleeping after returning from a visit. Fyodor threatened to go on ringing the bell or break the glass, at which

---

*Anna Dostoevsky, *Reminiscences* (1975), pp. 140–1. She had been having labour pains since 8 p.m. but was determined not to wake him until she absolutely had to.

point the sleepy midwife was roused and brought to Anna's bedside. She looked Anna over and pronounced that she would be back in seven or eight hours.

When she did not return, Fyodor went out to hunt her down. He discovered her at dinner with friends and dragged her back to Anna, where she further pronounced that labour was progressing badly and delivery was not likely before late evening. She nipped out again for a quick parlour game with her family until, following both threats and enticements of hors d'oeuvres and wine, she was persuaded to remain at Anna's side.

For his part, Fyodor's frantic attentions were not helping to set a calm and reassuring mood. At one point, his sobbing began to distress Anna more than the contractions, and he was escorted from the room by the midwife, who then latched the door from the inside to stop him coming in. In the other room, he prayed and prayed. Every now and then, Anna would send the midwife out to see how Fyodor was coping.

From the room came no longer groans but awful animal cries, unendurable, incredible. Then suddenly I heard a cry, the cry of a baby, a weak, discordant cry.[333] *My child's. That's a strange sensation for a father, but of all human sensations it is one of the best; I now know that for myself.*[334] He crossed himself, broke the lock and burst in. *The midwife held in her hands a little red wrinkled creature, screaming, and moving its little arms and legs, fearfully helpless, and looking as though it could be blown away by a puff of wind, but screaming and seeming to assert its full right to live. Anna was lying as though insensible, but a minute later she opened her eyes, and bent a strange, strange look on me: it was something quite new, that look. What it meant exactly I was not yet able to understand, but I had never known such a look on her face before.*[335]

Fyodor threw himself on his knees and kissed Anna's hand. It was a little girl, Sonya. *The mysterious coming of a new creature, a great and inexplicable mystery. There were two and now there's a third human being, a new spirit, finished and complete, nothing like the handiwork of man. It's positively frightening, and there's nothing grander in the world.*[336] He would ask Maikov, who had been such a good friend, and was now the only one he corresponded with regularly, to be the godfather. Anna's mother would be godmother.

In her exhaustion (and because the baby was enormous), Anna had trouble feeding her. She wouldn't countenance a wet nurse, so she supplemented Sonya's diet with cow's milk and nutritional powders. Fyodor didn't give much of a damn about his work; he'd put down his pen the moment he heard Sonya's voice and rush to her. *She is very cute – in spite of the fact that she looks impossibly, even ridiculously, like me. She lies there and looks as though she's composing a novel!*[337] She was his first thought when he woke up in the morning. The best time of the day was now bath time, when he and Anna would wash little Sonya, and Fyodor would wrap her in a cotton piqué blanket, fastening it carefully with safety pins, and rock her in his arms. Sonya's first smile was positively beatific, and the thought occurred to Fyodor: When a sinner prays to God, it is exactly like a mother seeing the first smile on her baby's face. *It is a thought in which all the essence of Christianity finds expression; God is our Father and as glad of us as a father in his own child. It's the fundamental idea of Christ.*[338]

Being a father, and beginning to know this new creature who was certain only of the need for love, affected Fyodor profoundly. He had always had a sentimental streak in him, but through fatherhood it became a part of his world view.* All these socialists with their grand conferences, debating over the ideology that would extinguish countries or abolish property, knew less than this little baby. The idea of the beautiful man, the simple goodness of the Russian people, the Nihilists and the materialists and the socialists, it was all connected, but the world would not be healed by ideology alone. *Individual kindness will always remain, the living impulse of one personality to exert a direct influence upon another.*[339] How might anyone tell what seed they had planted in the soul of another by one smile, one small

---

* Anna noted that he returned from his European exile 'so much milder, kinder, and more tolerant to others' (Anna Dostoevsky, *Reminiscences*, p. 169). In his biography, Strakhov credited fatherhood, as well as the couple's relative solitude, for what he considered a marked spiritual maturation.

act of kindness, a seed that might only begin to bear fruit many years in the future? The most skilful chess players could look only a few moves ahead, but a person's actions throughout their lifetime contained an incalculable number of moves. *In scattering the seed, in your kind deeds, you are giving away a part of your personality, and taking into yourself part of the other; you are in mutual communion with one another.* In this way, your life itself might become your greatest work. You could look on it almost as a science, this scattering of the seeds of kindness, some to be passed into other hands, others to fall and take root long after you have forgotten them, or been forgotten. *How can you tell what part you may have in the future determination of the destiny of humanity?*

Worrying came naturally to Fyodor, and he was constantly asking Anna whether Sonya was all right, whether she had slept well and eaten well. Having just lost all their money again on another gambling trip to Saxon-les-Bains, he wanted to write to Katkov to ask for a further advance so they could move to Vevey at the other end of Lake Geneva. There, both he and the baby would be safe from the *bises*. Perhaps they could even ask Anna's mother to join them. *I'm now so cheered, so certain that we'll move to Vevey. Honest to God, that's better than winning money!* [340] While they waited for the funds to come through, Fyodor would sit by Sonya's crib for hours at a time, talking to her or singing her songs (*in my funny voice*),[341] and by her third month he could swear that she already recognised him. She always smiled and stopped crying when he came over to her. The weather began to improve over the course of that spring and, on the advice of the doctor, they put her in the pram every day and took her for a turn in the Jardin des Anglais.

It was on one of these days that they were caught out by the *bise*, the icy wind that Fyodor most wanted to escape, which froze poor Sonya stiff before they could get her inside. That night she ran a temperature and started coughing. They had the doctor visit every day, and he was still reassuring them that Sonya would recover the day she stopped breathing, on 24 May. *The baby's little tongue and lips and whole mouth were covered with a minute white rash, and towards evening she died, gazing at me with her big black eyes as though she understood already.*[342] It was so sudden as to be nonsensical. Sonya had just begun to live; Sonya was dead.

Fyodor was desolate. He stood in front of his beautiful daughter sobbing, covering her little hands and face in tears and kisses, as she grew cold, as the body grew cold. *I howled as I have never let myself do before.*[343] It did not seem possible that they would survive this.

They went together to the government office to register the death. They dressed her in a white satin dress. They put her in the smallest coffin with its white satin lining. *I bought flowers and strewed them on the baby.*[344] They cried uncontrollably. They sat in the Russian church while the rites were spoken and stood, hollow-cheeked, while the coffin was lowered into the grave. *And now people tell me by way of consolation that I'll have more children. But where is Sonya? Where is that little person for whom I would accept crucifixion if only she could live?*[345]

Every day they went back to lay flowers on the white marble cross. Sunk in their bottomless grief, after a few days they received a visit from the neighbour's servant, who had come to ask them to stop crying so loudly.

Geneva had become unimaginably bitter to the Dostoevskys, who were now joined by Anna's mother, and they moved as far away as they could afford, which was to the other side of the lake. On the steamer, Fyodor retold Anna the whole story of his life, this time as a succession of curses: a dismal, lonely youth after his beloved mother died; the cruel mockery of the literary circle, who he had thought were his friends; hard labour in Siberia; an unhappy, childless marriage with Maria; and now, he said, fate had taken away 'this great, this *only* human happiness – having a child of your own'.[346]

Vevey was one of the most picturesque places in the world, and it was cheap. It was a small town and there was nothing to do there but grieve for the duration of that miserable, haunted summer.

Every conversation led back to Sonya. Fyodor did not raise a single smile for the duration of their stay. Despite his grief, the only way that he and Anna would get the funds to leave Switzerland would be to deliver more of the book. Maikov had written to him that he had found the world of Part One fantastical and didn't believe in the characters, but Fyodor was so far in debt now that he had to plough on. In any case, he'd had several other letters of admiration, and perhaps it would work out.

He and Anna would go on walks to get out of the house. On one sunny day, Fyodor went up into the mountainside alone. Below him was the lake, and all around him the horizon, bright and boundless. *My mind was possessed with an agonising but unformulated idea.*[347] He stretched his hands out into the cold, infinite blue. He stood taking in the sun, the rainbow in the waterfall, the snow glowing on the tip of the mountain, and felt outside all of it, utterly separate. Everything had its place, down to the last blade of grass. Everything except for him. *A terrible longing came upon me to leave everything here and go away at once without even saying goodbye to anyone. I had a foreboding that if I remained here even a few days longer I would be drawn into this world irrevocably and that my life would be bound up with it for ever. But I did not consider it for ten minutes; I decided at once that it would be impossible to run away, that it would be cowardice. Absorbed in such thoughts, I returned home after a walk of less than a quarter of an hour. I was utterly unhappy at that moment.*[348]

Part of the difficulty with Fyodor's finances was the ongoing effort of supporting his extended family. Everywhere he went, it was as if he were dragging Emilia, Pasha and the others behind him on a sled. On the advice of Anna, Anna's mother, and by this point even the normally discreet Maikov, he decided that he could not keep giving away his last copeck to others. Pasha was twenty-one now and would have to give up on his notion of being completely idle as if it was a point of honour.[349] First he'd worked at the Address Bureau, then at the Archive of the Kingdom of Poland, but he never lasted in any of these jobs. And neither he nor Emilia had even written to congratulate Fyodor on Sonya's birth while she was alive.

I think that not only will none of them feel bad about my child, but perhaps even the contrary, and just the thought of that enrages me. What harm had that poor creature done them? Let them hate me, let them laugh at me and at my love – I don't care.[350] With death never far from his thoughts, he drew up a will granting the copyright in all his works unequivocally to Anna. But he wouldn't completely abandon his dead wife's son, nor his brother's widow. *I sometimes dream of Misha; he takes part in my affairs, and yet all through my dream I quite know and remember that my brother is dead and buried.*[351]

In the day, Fyodor and Anna distracted themselves with work as best they could, she taking down his dictation. In the evenings, Anna would cry to herself, and the sadness was stripping the flesh off her bones. For Fyodor, too, the grief seemed to be intensifying. *There are moments that are unbearable. On the day of her death, I left the house to read the papers, having no idea she would die in two hours. She knew me already. She followed me with her eyes, looked at me in such a way that I can still remember it, more and more vividly in fact. I'll never forget her and never stop grieving! Even if there's another child, I don't understand how I'll love it, where I'll find the love; I need Sonya.*[352]

The novel stuttered along, and the odd letter came in, though Fyodor believed that the secret police were intercepting his correspondence, as some of it was going missing. It seemed a cruel irony, when he had betrayed his former convictions in order to come out firmly as a tsarist, and when he was simultaneously accused of being too conservative by the liberals. He had half a mind to make an official complaint, but instead he allowed himself to call these nameless officials scoundrels in his next letter to Maikov, which inevitably they read.

Come autumn, escaping Switzerland became a matter of survival. They travelled to Milan, taking a mountain pass by foot, gathering Alpine wildflowers as they went and admiring their hardy beauty. *The world will be saved by beauty.*[353] They stopped in Milan for only a couple of months, staying down an alleyway so narrow that the neighbours would chat through the open windows. *I am growing dull and limited; I'm not keeping up with Russia. There's no Russian air and Russian people here. I really don't understand Russian émigrés at all. They're all mad!*[354] It was too cold and rainy to go walking for any length of time, and despite the change of scenery, and the hodgepodge beauty of the Duomo, Fyodor decided to push on to Florence, which he remembered fondly from his trip with Strakhov in 1862. They moved around between apartments, one of which they rented from Napoleon's nephew, Antonio Bonaparte.[355] The weather was better there, and they would go for walks in the Giardino di Boboli, where the roses bloomed in winter, or stroll through the galleries of the Uffizi, the walls covered with endless interpretations of the *Madonna e Bambino*. Everywhere they looked, they saw mother and baby, mother and baby.

It was there, in Florence, that beauty saved them. Anna began to swell with new life. The two of them talked about having a new daughter – they were certain it would be a daughter – and they would name her Lyubov, meaning Beloved. Little Lyuba, darling Lyubochka. If Fyodor had been nervous about his firstborn, he was positively paranoid about this second pregnancy. Then more good news: after a long silence, Strakhov resumed his correspondence with Fyodor, who prevailed upon him to send over the new complete edition of *War and Peace*. Fyodor devoured it, passing each volume on to Anna as he finished it. When he reached the book where Prince Andrei Bolkonsky's wife dies in childbirth, he decided to hide it. Anna looked everywhere for it and told him off for losing it. Fyodor apologised for his absent-mindedness. She could have it back once the baby was born. *I wait with excitement, and with fear, and with hope, and meekness.*[356]

Fyodor had finished writing *The Idiot* now, and its final scene was published, ending in the image of Rogozhin and Myshkin, standing together over the body of the murdered Nastasya. So much of the novel was written with that scene in mind: Rogozhin the passionate, jealous lover, about to enter the penal colony; Myshkin, whose compassionate love did nothing to save Nastasya, bound for the madhouse; and the heroine herself, perhaps his greatest heroine, a noble soul who refused to acknowledge the role imposed upon her by society. He wasn't entirely happy with the novel as a whole. *A lot was written in haste, much is meandering and unsuccessful, but there are some successful things too. I'm not defending my novel, but my idea.*[357] He had poured a part of himself into the book, narrating the experience of epilepsy, as well as the horrifying last moments before his mock execution. He had created some of the defining set pieces of his fiction, too; and yet the numerous minor characters and tangential plots made it hard, at times, to follow. *I sense that, compared to Crime and Punishment, the effect of The Idiot on the public is weaker. And therefore all my vanity is now roused: I want to make an impression again.* Immediately upon finishing he began sketching out ideas for another, better book, which would properly develop this idea of a hero on a metaphysical journey. He'd call it *Atheism*, or *The Life of a Great Sinner*. He wanted to model it after George Sand's *Spiridion*, which follows the life of a young monk, Alexis, torn between faith and spiritual doubt. It would be an epic, composed of five books, and it would take him the rest of his life, six or seven years, he thought. *I cannot, must not tackle it, because I'm not yet ready for it: I haven't thought it out and I need material.*[358]

They travelled on, first to Bologna and Venice, then Prague, and back to Dresden so that they might be somewhere familiar in time for the birth. This time, Anna's mother was with them, and labour went easier. On 26 September 1869 their second child was born, a daughter, Lyuba, just as they had hoped. *The baby is big, healthy, a beauty.** That winter, after many long months of grief and anticipation, their happiness returned to them. Fyodor dashed off a novella, *The Eternal Husband*, which almost served as a mature, realistic development of the idea he had been pursuing in *The Double* – the two men whose destinies are intertwined, two men with a shared fascination for the same woman, the peaceful man and the predator.[359] He published that one in *Dawn*, a new journal which Strakhov was working on. Despite Fyodor hating the novella

---

* Letter to Maikov, 17 (29) September 1869. Anna was more circumspect about the latter assessment: 'Only an infatuated and ecstatic father's eyes, of course, could see "a beauty" in that tiny pink morsel of flesh.'

and having written it purely to keep the three of them alive – by the time he finished writing it he couldn't afford the postage to send it – *The Eternal Husband* actually got very good reviews, and even went some way to repairing the damage that *The Idiot* had done to his reputation. But it was a distraction from the real prize, the big novel that was gestating.

As Fyodor waited for his epic to take shape, an entirely different story materialised in whole before him, ready to be written: while investigating a murder, Russian authorities had uncovered a conspiracy of Nihilists, and with it a secret terrorist cell of an organisation known as the People's Vengeance. *It's one of those ideas that have an undeniable resonance among the public. Like Crime and Punishment, but even closer to reality, more vital. I hope to make at least as much money as for Crime and Punishment, put all my affairs in order and return to Russia by the end of the year.*[360]

Desperate for news of what was going on in Russia, Fyodor had been reading three newspapers a day – *St Petersburg News*, *The Voice*, *The Moscow News* – as well as reading the two thick monthly journals, Strakhov's *Dawn* and Katkov's *Russian Herald*. It was during this daily ritual that Fyodor came across the story of a young student, Ivan Ivanov, whose body had been recovered from a pond in the Petrovsky Park in Moscow. It was easy to see how Ivanov had died, since the body was frozen in a block of transparent ice: his feet were tied down with bricks, and he had been shot at point-blank range in the back of the head, making an exit wound of his eye. *This is a sort of sequel to Nihilism, not in a direct line, but obliquely, and they don't express themselves in newspaper articles, but directly in action.*[361]

The victim had been a student at the same agricultural college that Anna's brother attended. It transpired that his only transgression had been to get on the wrong side of the secret terrorist cell he was a part of – some said that he was planning to denounce them, others that he only objected to the dictatorial approach of their leader, Sergei Nechaev.* A rumour went around that Nechaev had been the first prisoner ever to escape Peter and Paul Fortress some years earlier, and it was now known that he had been plotting revolution from Bakunin's spare room in Geneva.† How strange, to think that Fyodor had been bored stiff in Geneva with all this going on under his nose. But the idea of the conspiracy of five young men burgeoning into a popular movement was, finally, laughable. *Why don't people of consequence join their ranks? Why are they all students and half-baked boys of twenty-two? And not many of those.*[362]

Still, the logic of liberalism led to Nihilism, and Nihilism could only end in violence. That was what all of the so-called realists didn't understand: one only had to open a newspaper to see that these were extraordinary times. *What the majority calls fantastical and exceptional sometimes constitutes the very essence of the real. Taking a banal view of ordinary phenomena is not realism, in my opinion, but rather the opposite.*[363] So many novelists wrote the same old thing, over and over. *Only in realism is there no truth.*[364]

In this new novel, Fyodor would trace the evolution of beliefs from his generation of 1840s socialists to the generation of Nechaev – he would show how such utopianism ended in bloodshed. Nechaev would be the basis for Peter Verkhovensky, the ringleader of his young revolutionaries. He would write of the ageing forties generation without mercy, leaning on *literary recollections, Belinsky, Herzen, Turgenev and the others.*[365] The young generation of revolutionaries, for their part, were not tortured and poetic souls, they were devils that had possessed the Russian people. It was like the Gospel of Luke: when the demons had been exorcised, cast into the swine and run off a cliff into the sea, the possessed man would

---

* Dostoevsky must have started when he saw who was responsible: Nechaeva was his mother's maiden name.
† The theme of this new novel must have pleased Katkov, who had fallen out with Bakunin back in 1840, when Bakunin had (correctly) accused Katkov of having an affair with Ogarov's wife and, at Belinsky's salon, Katkov had (more or less correctly) called Bakunin 'a eunuch'. After much spitting, slapping and whacking of canes, they agreed to fight a duel, though it never took place.

wake up and sit at Jesus' feet in wonder. *And if you want to know, that's exactly what the theme of my novel is:*[366] Devils.

His routine was the same every day: sleep until one in the afternoon; work from three until five; go to the post office in case some letter brought news from Russia; take the same route home through the Royal Gardens; dinner at home; walk at seven; tea, then work from 10.30 p.m. to 5 a.m. His epileptic fits came infrequently in the winter and the spring. Still, he would feel the blood rushing in his head and heart. The work on *Devils* stuttered and he could sense there was a flaw in it, but he couldn't pinpoint exactly what it was. The murder plot was ultimately a risible intrigue, and Verkhovensky was turning into a half-comic figure. The book needed ballast. *The whole problem is that I keep taking up topics that are beyond me. The poet in me always usurps the artist.*[367]

In the middle of July 1870, he suffered a series of epileptic fits, one after another. In the aftermath, he was nervous, his memory weak and his thoughts abstracted, and a peculiar sadness came over him. It used to take him three days to recover from a severe attack; now it took six. When he began to piece his head together and return to work in August, he read through the 240 pages he had written and saw that he would have to throw a lot of it out. He had come up with a completely new plan for the novel, a better one. There would be a second hero named Stavrogin, drawing a little from the Great Sinner of his unwritten novel, this one more mysterious and withholding, a fallen Lucifer – or a Mephistopheles. Fyodor remembered Speshnev, how he had led the others in the Petrashevsky circle astray without even seeming to participate. *I've wanted to portray him for a very long time.*[368] Stavrogin would be a tragic figure, a true Russian but also representative of a trend that was spreading across Europe. And he would meet his match in Bishop Tikhon, a radiant Orthodox elder who would light the path to deliverance. This added great depth to the plot, but it also meant not delivering the first section for another few months, which meant no windfall, which meant they could not afford to return to Russia until the following spring. He wasn't prepared to publish weak material again, even if it meant putting the rest of their life on hold. *If you only knew how onerous it is to be a writer. If I had two or three years of support for the novel, the way Turgenev, Goncharov or Tolstoy do, I would write the sort of thing that people would still be talking about in a hundred years!*[369]

Fyodor made good progress on *Devils*, the first part of which he reworked twenty times before it was published in *The Russian Herald* in January. The timing could not have been better, at least when it came to proving the book's relevance: the Franco-Prussian War was just that month concluding after the capture of Napoleon III, and was swiftly followed by the Paris Commune, a socialist government run on revolutionary principles, which was put down after three months by the national army.* *Can you really say that it failed again for a lack of the right people, the right circumstances, and so on? For the whole nineteenth century the movement has either been dreaming of paradise on earth or, when it comes close to action, it demonstrates a humiliating impotence. Wanting something is not the same thing as achieving it.*[370]

In the spring of 1871, Anna was so homesick and drained from nursing Lyuba that she barely got out of bed, and she was now pregnant for a third time, so they would need to travel before she gave birth. Meanwhile, Stellovsky was up to his old tricks and had been selling a new edition of *Crime and Punishment* while refusing to pay anything to the author. With that money, they could have afforded to return to Russia straight away, but Maikov's polite visits to enquire about payment were no match for an artful weasel such as Stellovsky.

I resolved to try my luck for the last time. Apart from my need to win, I had an intense longing to play.[371] Fyodor would take one last trip to Wiesbaden, all or nothing. They told Anna's mother, who disapproved of gambling, that he was travelling to Frankfurt on business. If Fyodor lost everything, as seemed inevitable, their code for his asking for the train fare home would be: *write to me.* Needless

---

*The Commune counted among its prominent feminist members Anna Korvin-Krukovskaya, who was now calling herself Anne Jacquard. After helping to run the Montmartre Committee of Vigilance and writing for *La Sociale*, she escaped the so-called 'Bloody Week' of suppression and crossed over to England, where she hid out in the home of Karl Marx.

to say that he immediately lost 100 thalers he'd brought, and the next day lost the 30 thalers she sent him for the train fare. Falling asleep, he had a nightmare involving his father, which seemed to augur a terrible disaster. Would Anna die of grief when she heard what he had done to her and Lyuba? Fyodor ran off in the middle of the night to find a priest, but got lost in town and instead went home and wrote a long letter to Anna:

> I know that you have every right to despise me and to think: 'He's going to gamble again.'... I won't, I won't, I won't, and I'll come straight home! Believe me. Believe me one last time and you won't regret it. Now I'll work for you and for Lyubochka, without sparing my health, you'll see, you'll see, you'll see, my whole life, AND I'LL ACHIEVE MY GOAL!... It's as though I've been reborn morally (I'm saying this to you before God)... You mustn't think I'm insane, Anya, my guardian angel! A great thing has happened to me, I've rid myself of the vile fantasy that has tormented me for almost ten years. For ten years (or, rather, since my brother's death, when I was suddenly crushed by debts) I kept dreaming about winning money. I dreamed seriously, passionately. Now that's all finished with! This was QUITE the last time![372]

It was a promise he had made before, but it was different this time: it was not that he wanted to quit, but that he had lost his compulsion.*

On his return, he settled down to work on the next part of *Devils*, and in June 1871 a chunk of money came through from Katkov. They now had the funds to return to Russia. Their three-month honeymoon, which had been prolonged in a sickening limbo of debt and itinerancy, was finally coming to an end after four years.

---

* In a second letter the next morning, Fyodor suggested that, if Anna's mother asked why she was pawning off her possessions for money, she should say he'd had an epileptic fit and soiled his hotel mattress.

They went to retrieve their things from pawn. It was a near-certainty that Fyodor would be searched at the border and that they would confiscate his papers, so Fyodor gave Anna all of his draft material from the past four years to burn in the fireplace – for *The Idiot*, *The Eternal Husband*, the first part of *Devils*. But Anna couldn't bear to burn the notebooks, so she gave them to her mother to carry across the border that autumn. They prepared to reclaim their missing days from the Julian calendar. At the start of July in Europe, Anna was burning manuscripts; at the start of July, she would already be back in Russia.

The journey from Dresden took 68 hours in total. Fyodor entertained Lyuba the whole way, playing games with her, taking her out to stretch her legs on the platform at each stop, and keeping her amply supplied with milk and snacks. As expected, they were the only people stopped at the border, where customs officers rifled through all their bags and suitcases, peering at their books and manuscripts. They were only saved from missing their St Petersburg connection by Lyuba's screaming, which eventually annoyed the officers enough that they were waved through – and stepped 12 days into the past, back to 7 July 1871.

They spent a full 24 hours rolling through the Russian countryside. After hundreds of versts of identical swamp and forest, dotted at long intervals with isolated peasant huts, they emerged suddenly and without warning into the heart of the imperial city, with its horse-drawn tramcars, uneven pavements, broad roads with lumbering carts, peasants in their red shirts and sheepskins, bearded coachmen, and the golden dome of St Isaac's looming over it all. The train slowed to a halt, and they set foot in St Petersburg for the first time that decade. *I've lived through a lot in these four years. I've lived intensely, though in isolation. Whatever God sends from here on in I'll accept without a murmur.*[373]

They found two rooms on the third floor of 3 Ekaterinhof Prospect, near the Yusupov Gardens. They were reunited with Mikhail's family, who seemed to have found their feet, and Pasha, who had just married a short, pretty young woman called Nadezhda that April. The bad news was that he had sold off all of Fyodor's rare and signed books, which was quite upsetting, though not entirely out of character. Still, overall it was a happy time. Eight days after they arrived, Anna gave birth to their first son, Fyodor, whom they called by his diminutive, Fedya. *In spite of everything I have lost, I love life ardently, I love life for life's sake. I will be fifty soon, yet I cannot make out whether I am ending my life or only beginning it.*[374]

ELEVEN

The Citizen

1872–1877

O NE THING I DO *know: the second half of the novel will be incomparably easier than that first.*[375] Fyodor had returned to a St Petersburg gripped by the trial of 84 of Nechaev's followers in open court from 1 July to 1 September 1871.* During the trial, a manual for revolution, *Catechism of a Revolutionary,* was presented as evidence. The scale of ambition on display was breathtaking: *Efforts to injure the prestige of local authority, to reduce the villages to confusion, to spread cynicism and scandals, together with complete disbelief in everything and an eagerness for something better, and finally, by means of fires, a pre-eminently Russian method, to reduce the country to desperation.*[376] Fyodor was midway through publishing *Devils,* and the high-profile trial of what now appeared to be a widespread conspiracy ensured a huge and committed readership for the rest of the book. Sending off the pivotal chapter, in which the nihilistic Stavrogin makes confession to Bishop Tikhon, he was dismayed to find that Katkov wouldn't print it. Stavrogin confesses to terrible crimes, including the rape of an eleven-year-old girl who subsequently committed suicide. Like the rumoured crimes of Svidrigailov in *Crime and Punishment,* but still more intense, Stavrogin has bowed to the power of the intellect and ideas,

---

* When he was eventually extradited from Switzerland, Nechaev was publicly sentenced to 20 years' hard labour in Siberia, but he was never sent. Instead, he was secretly held in solitary confinement under a life sentence in Peter and Paul Fortress where, in 1882, he died of scurvy.

untethered from God and morality, which has turned all of life into a sort of game in which everything is permissible. It is at this crucial moment that Fyodor explicitly wanted to offer Orthodoxy as a counterpoint and even a solution to Nihilism. This was the beating heart of the book – without it there was only immorality with no hope of redemption. Fyodor explained all this, but still Katkov refused to print it.

The public didn't miss what they hadn't seen, and its anti-revolutionary message burnished his reputation in conservative circles, where he was beginning to be regarded as one of the foremost writers living in Russia. Maikov introduced him to a new literary circle that had formed on Wednesday evenings around the flamboyant reactionary Prince Vladimir Meshchersky and his new journal, *The Citizen.** Strakhov was already in its orbit, as well as Konstantin Pobedonostsev, a balding, clean-shaven man with beady little spectacles and a fondness for bow ties, who served as tutor to the Tsarevich Alexander.† Through Meshchersky and Pobedonostsev, Fyodor managed to obtain a sum of money directly from the Tsarevich to pay off the worst of his remaining debts, relieving him of a huge burden. Around this time, Fyodor was also invited, along with Turgenev, the playwright Ostrovsky and a few others, to have his portrait painted by the celebrated Vasily Perov for a series on Russia's leading writers.‡ Before he even lifted his brush, Perov spent hours with Fyodor, chatting to him and observing him, and the portrait captured him faithfully. Fyodor looked serious, lost in thought, clasping his knee, his thinning hair raked across his head, his cheeks lined and sagging. *But what a job he did on my warts in the portrait – they're as good as life! That's what they call realism.*377 A mean-spirited article in *The Voice* called it 'a portrait of a man exhausted by a serious ailment'. *My face may well*

---

* Both unscrupulous and intelligent, Meshchersky was funding the journal with 80,000 roubles that he had inveigled from the Tsarevich Alexander. He would soon fall out of favour after embezzling funds that the Tsarevich had allocated for a school.
† Imagine Philip Larkin transposed to tsarist Russia, with bigger ears, and you will find yourself startlingly close to Pobedonostsev's portrait.
‡ They also included Maikov on Fyodor's suggestion.

be like that, but do they have to say it in print? He could at least have said it indirectly – that's the whole point of style.[378]

That spring, the family decided to go on holiday to Staraya Russa, a spa town in Novgorod province, 300 versts south of St Petersburg, near Lake Ilmen.* When they arrived to catch their steamer, there were so many mosquitoes by the river that the other travellers' children looked like they had smallpox. Lyuba had also hurt her wrist and it looked so disconcertingly lumpy that they had to go back to St Petersburg to have it set by a proper doctor. When, finally, they were all settled in Staraya Russa, Anna caught a chill and developed an abscess in her throat. Confined to bed, her temperature kept rising and the doctor refused to say definitively that she would survive. Soon she was unable to speak; when she needed something, Anna passed Fyodor little handwritten notes. They were visited by the local priest and his wife.

'What will I do without her?'[379] Fyodor sobbed. 'How can I live without her? She is *everything* to me.'

'Don't cry,' said the priest's wife, putting an arm around him. 'God is merciful. He won't leave you and the children orphans.'

Very weak now, Anna beckoned over Fyodor and the children to give her blessing, kissed them, and wrote down instructions for what Fyodor should do when she passed away. That night, the abscess burst, the pus draining into her throat. Slowly but surely, she began to recover, and a few weeks later, the family was well enough to return from their thwarted summer holiday, hardly relaxed but grateful to be alive.

In the autumn of 1872, Fyodor got up each day at 2 p.m., washed his face, combed his hair and sat at his writing desk in an old coat. He would roll a cigarette and then smoke it leisurely, accompanied by two hot cups of coffee or, if not, the strongest possible tea. *The samovar is the most essential thing in Russia.*[380] The majority of his

---

* The town was founded over a thousand years ago, originally to harvest salt. Recently archaeologists discovered a trove of birch-bark letters from as early as the twelfth century – an almost unique opportunity to gain insight into life in medieval Rus'. When translated, Letter 35 read, 'Yakove, brother, lie down when you fuck', the earliest known example of a Russian obscenity.

writing was done late at night, once the children and Anna were in bed – he would often stay up until seven in the morning. His task now was to write around the unpublished confession as he tied up *Devils*, a task made all the harder by his ongoing battle with his own memory. Every time he had a fit, Fyodor found himself re-reading the published sections of his own book for clues to how it would end and even to remind himself of the main characters' names. He had always struggled to create a sense of unity in his books – *many separate novels and stories get squashed into a single one, so that there's neither proportion nor harmony*[381] – but now he had begun to fight against the unravelling of his mind.

Yesterday a friend came to see me. 'Your style is changing,' he said; 'it is choppy: you chop and chop – and then a parenthesis, then a parenthesis in the parenthesis, then you stick in something else in brackets, then you begin chopping and chopping again.'

The friend is right. Something strange is happening to me. My character is changing and my head aches. I am beginning to see and hear strange things.[382]

Fyodor had been toying with the idea of starting a new journal, and it made perfect sense: you could speak directly to the people without getting caught up in literary cliques. In the short term, however, there was the practical matter of setting up an income. He didn't like the idea of Anna taking up stenography again – after all, look where the first job had got her – but he didn't have another novel idea ready to start so soon. Anna had originally hoped to take over the house of her mother, who had died not long after they returned to St Petersburg, but unfortunately Fyodor had absent-mindedly signed over management of the house to a friend, who had allowed tax arrears to build up on the property, waited until it went to public auction, and then paid off the taxes in order to take ownership of the house.

Thankfully, Anna was far more shrewd than her husband, and she now took over all management of their finances. Having already successfully threatened Fyodor's remaining creditors, she conducted a campaign of minor industrial espionage, casually enquiring about paper costs and commissions until she had everything she needed to cut out the publishers and produce the first complete edition of *Devils* herself. They decided to print 3,500, a significant outlay but with much better gains to be made than handing over the rights – Bazunov the publisher had only offered them 500 roubles.

Another opportunity for income came when the editor of *The Citizen* was fired by Prince Meshchersky in late 1872, apparently over creative differences. Fyodor took the opportunity to ask whether he might act as editor and Meshchersky was keen, so Fyodor suggested he take a modest salary of, say, 3,000 roubles, plus payment for any articles he wrote. The deal was done there and then, and *The Citizen* had a new editor for the 1873 subscription in the person of F. M. Dostoevsky.

Fyodor was always excited when it came to Christmas, and this year he insisted they get a tall, bushy tree, which he lovingly decorated, climbing up on a stool to attach the last candles and a star to the top. *There were ever so many lights, gold papers and apples and little dolls and horses.*[383] On the day, he gleefully handed out the presents. Lyuba got a doll and a little tea set; Fedya got a trumpet and a drum. And then the pièce de résistance: toy horses and a sleigh. The two delighted children sat inside while Fyodor shook it for realism. Little Fedya grabbed the reins and urged the horses on, and then began whipping the horses with the reins as he had seen peasants do. That evening, as Anna was dropping off and Fyodor was reading in bed, they heard Fedya screaming and Fyodor ran through to find the little boy wide awake. He was obsessed with the sleigh and distraught that he had been snatched so cruelly from his adventure. And so, while the rest of the family went back to sleep, Fyodor watched over his son in the nursery, cackling away even as the tears dried on his cheeks, driving like the wind down the frozen river of his imagination until, around 5 a.m., he started listing to the side and could finally be gathered up for bed. Fyodor was worn out, but he didn't mind; the great promise of children is that your suffering will be mirrored in their happiness.

On 22 January 1873, the Dostoevskys announced the first complete edition of *Devils* in the newspaper. Soon couriers began arriving from various bookshops to buy 10 copies, 20 or more from the stacks that were piled up in the apartment. Some of them tried to haggle, seeing that they were dealing with a diminutive housewife still in her twenties. But Anna stood firm and, if necessary, closed the door on them. Others tried to get hold of Fyodor, hoping to negotiate with a softer touch, only to be told that he was asleep and they would have to deal with Anna. Soon, someone turned up asking for 300 copies.

Reviews began to appear, too. The liberal consensus was that Dostoevsky had used his narrative powers to bolster the cause of the reactionaries, making a wholesale mockery of students who mostly wanted to change Russia for the better. The radicals responded with predictable horror to the idea that Fyodor was now working for the arch-conservative *Citizen*. At the same time as Fyodor was being vilified as a powerful enemy, he was being written off in the same journals as a sick man who had lost his mind. Among it all, one critic stood out: Nikolai Mikhailovsky, the new chief critic of *Notes of the Fatherland*. His criticisms of *Devils* were well aimed – how, for instance, could you talk about the problems bedevilling society without mentioning capitalism, industrialism, factories, banks? – but tempered by genuine admiration for its literary achievement. Mikhailovsky represented the views of the Populists, a new movement that was just beginning to coalesce around a belief in the Russian 'People', not dissimilar to some of Fyodor's own arguments, a decade earlier, that the elites should get 'back to the soil'.*

Arriving at the offices of *The Citizen*, Fyodor laid down his ground rules: he must be obeyed without question and there was not to be so much as a comma out of place. He would often spend an hour or more in silence, contemplating the proofs of an article, while

---

* Much ink has been spilled over the true meaning of the powerfully evocative Russian word народ (*narod*), but depending on context, in English we would say 'a people', 'the people', or perhaps 'the common people', 'the masses' if there weren't an implied pejorative. This is a different word from the bog-standard люди (*lyudi*), which is generally just a collection of persons, as in *Poor Folk*.

the young secretary, Varvara Timofeyeva, looked meekly on. Prince Meshchersky turned out to be impossible to work with. He wrote up one of the Tsar's private conversations without receiving official approval; he argued that all reform must now come to a full stop;* the last straw was when he tried to publish an article suggesting that student dormitories should be surveilled by the police. *I have my reputation as a writer and I also have children. I do not intend to destroy myself. Besides, the idea is deeply opposed to my convictions and fills my heart with indignation.*[384]

Despite being a Romanov-funded publication, the magazine was briefly censored for criticising the government response to famines in the provinces, and Meshchersky's indiscretion with the Tsar's utterances landed Fyodor in the guardhouse for two days (it was, after all, Fyodor's name on the masthead). Anna visited to keep him company, as did Maikov and a more recent acquaintance, Vsevolod Soloviev, a serious, religious young man who was convinced that Dostoevsky's genius was not yet fully understood by his peers. Fyodor passed the two nights quite peaceably, praying with his hands crossed on his breast, reflecting on his prison years. *Perhaps I never spent moments more consolatory to my soul than those moments of reflection in the middle of the night on that prison bed. This will perhaps strike the reader as strange, and he may be inclined to set it down to bragging and the desire to be original – and yet it was just as I have said. Yes, those moments were the light of my soul.*[385]

After just over a year as editor of *The Citizen*, Fyodor decided to hand in his resignation. He had underestimated the stress of editing a weekly magazine, especially one owned by Meshchersky, and the trouble with the authorities had taken its toll on his health. He was constantly catching colds and his lungs were beginning to feel tight. The doctor prescribed compressed air baths, where he and a few other patients would sit under a gigantic metal bell, pressurised by a steam engine, for two hours at a time, three times a week. The treatment helped with the shortness of breath but it meant waking

---

* After this, the radicals nicknamed him Prince Full Stop – at the time it was rather droll but perhaps you had to be there.

---

up early, which Fyodor hated. Worse than the toll on his health, he simply didn't have time to work on fiction. There were two good things to come out of his time as editor of *The Citizen*, however. First, Fyodor's column, *A Writer's Diary*, had been a huge success – many said it was the best thing in the journal. Second, through his conversations with Varvara the secretary, he had begun to be convinced that the new generation of Populists were not necessarily opposed to Christianity, and indeed from the right perspective the two ideologies might even be complementary.

Fyodor's relationship with Varvara had been terse, at first, but he had opened up a great deal once he established that she was a Christian. They talked about the Gospels, about realising Christ's teachings and about the afterlife. He would sometimes treat her to a recitation of Pushkin's poem 'The Prophet', which he knew by heart. He could see the influence of the Westernisers on her, and tried, at opportune moments, to school her about the dangers of turning too far towards the decadence of Europe. When an article about Bismarck and the papacy crossed his desk, he confided to her: 'They don't suspect that soon everything will come to an end – all their "progress" and chatter! They have no inkling that the Antichrist has been born, and is coming ...'[386]

When Varvara began to object, he slammed his fist down on the desk.

'The Antichrist is coming! It is coming! And the end of the world is closer than they think!'

Fyodor knew that Varvara had contacts at *Notes of the Fatherland* and charged her with approaching them discreetly to see whether he might write them a novel. He wanted to speak to the radicals from their own pulpit. This time, it was his conservative friends' turn to be dismayed, having believed with some justification that Fyodor was now a hardened Slavophile. How could someone go from editing *The Citizen*, probably the most reactionary journal in Russia, to writing for *Notes of the Fatherland*? The truth was that Fyodor refused to subscribe to any readymade ideology and would much rather invent his own. He had always supported some of the stated aims of the socialists, and he had for years been championing Russia's unique and sacred mission under the Tsar. At different times, all ends of the political spectrum had allowed themselves to believe that he spoke for them, and by this point almost everyone had criticised him as a spokesperson for the enemy. But although Fyodor's personal philosophy had evolved alongside certain individuals at different times, from Nekrasov to Maikov to Strakhov and now the young Vsevolod Soloviev, he valued his intellectual independence above all else. And what he most wanted to do now was to resign as editor of a right-wing journal to write a landmark novel for the mouthpiece of the radical left.

Fyodor had in mind a new kind of novel that would speak to young people like Varvara. The novel of aristocrats squabbling among themselves was finished. *It has said everything that it had to say (superbly in the case of Lev Tolstoy). But that was the last word.*[387] Instead, Fyodor wanted to write about modern life: broken families, unusual arrangements, the unexplored clashes between different social strata. *New characters will appear, unknown to us as yet, and a new ideal; but what sort of characters?*[388] *One may make serious mistakes, exaggerations, misjudgements. But what else can a writer do if he doesn't want to confine himself to the historical form, and is possessed by a longing for the present?*

In April 1874, Nekrasov called on Fyodor and formally invited him to contribute to *Notes of the Fatherland*. Not only that, he was offering 250 roubles for each signature – a hundred more than Fyodor had received for any of his previous novels. Fyodor said that he would have to run the offer by his wife.

'I would never have imagined you were under her thumb,' said Nekrasov.[389]

Before Fyodor could open his mouth to explain the situation, Anna, who had been eavesdropping in the next room, told him to say yes.

Out of loyalty to Katkov, Fyodor put off giving Nekrasov a firm answer and went to Moscow to give *The Russian Herald* first refusal. But Katkov didn't have the money to commit to a big new novel, since he was paying Tolstoy 500 roubles a signature for the serialisation of *Anna Karenina*.

Tolstoy was the talk of the town, and although Fyodor had never met him, he seemed to be well acquainted with everyone Fyodor knew. Turgenev had known him since the 1850s – their estates weren't far from one another's, and they had been shooting together, though they had once quarrelled to the point of almost fighting a duel.* Strakhov was in regular correspondence with Tolstoy, who considered him a valuable critic. But Count Tolstoy hadn't deigned to make himself known to Fyodor.

In the summer of 1874, Fyodor travelled alone to the German spa town of Bad Ems – *to drink the waters and to observe the English.*[390] His doctor felt that the climate and the mineral waters there would help his lungs; Fyodor had developed emphysema and was having trouble breathing. Once he was in Europe, he was possessed by the idea of visiting Sonya's grave, so he took the 600-kilometre train journey to Geneva expressly for the purpose. On arriving, he found that the headstone was already obscured by a cypress that had sprung up in the six years since he last stood on this spot. New life, but not his Sonya. He broke off a pine-scented sprig to give to Anna as a keepsake.

The family spent the winter in Staraya Russa. It was cheaper there; the children liked it; it was easy enough to get to St Petersburg when necessary; and crucially, it was a calm place to write his new novel, *The Adolescent*. He had tried narrating in the first person as a young man of illegitimate birth, Arkady Dolgoruky. The voice was painfully self-conscious. The aristocratic birth father, Versilov, was one of the 'superfluous men' of his generation, but he was also sympathetic and there was depth to explore there. The plot, however, was thrown together too hastily, and the later parts

---

* Later, after reconciling, Turgenev visited Tolstoy on his estate, Yasnaya Polyana, where he ingratiated himself with the family, entertaining the growing horde of Tolstoy children with charades and gamely undertaking forfeits. Tolstoy's diary entry that evening read: 'Turgenev. Can-can. Sad.'

revolved increasingly around the threat of a compromising letter being made public.

Nekrasov was complimentary about the first part as soon as it was published: 'I got so carried away that I sat up all night reading, and I'm not supposed to do that sort of thing at my age, and with my health what it is.' Vsevolod Soloviev, too, wrote a glowing review in the *Petersburg News* under a pseudonym. But when Fyodor next saw Maikov and Strakhov, they were distinctly cool with him. *Not a word about my novel, clearly because they didn't want to pain me. Instead they talked about Tolstoy's novel, only a little, but with ridiculous enthusiasm.*[391] He asked why they were so against him publishing in *Notes of the Fatherland* when their beloved Tolstoy had done exactly the same thing, but Maikov simply frowned and said nothing. At parting, they couldn't seem to find a good date to meet next.

When Soloviev paid a social call on Fyodor, he found him more than usually preoccupied.

'Tell me honestly: do I look like I'm jealous of the glory of Lev Tolstoy?'[392] Fyodor asked the moment he had stepped over the threshold.

'I don't exactly know whether you are jealous of Lev Tolstoy, but you don't have to be,' Soloviev replied judiciously. 'You both have your own ways. There is no competition between you, and therefore no cause for jealousy from your side. Please tell me, who accused you of this?'

'Yes, accuse is the word,' Fyodor said, pacing the room. 'They accuse me, my friends who have known me for a long time, probably about twenty years.'

'They asked you about it to your face?'

'Yes, almost. They are so obsessed by the thought that they can't hide it, and they speak about it all the time,' Fyodor told him irritably. 'Well, the thing is I really do feel jealous, but not in that way. It is more about my working conditions.' He outlined the difficulty of writing for money, always being in a rush to finish. He had recently re-read *The Idiot* as he and Anna wanted to publish their own edition, and although he found certain scenes that were just as he had planned them, there were others that could have been so much better if he'd had time on his side. Tolstoy, on the other hand, had all the time in the world. 'He is a wealthy man, he has everything, he doesn't have to worry about where his next payment is coming. He can take his time writing and improving his works, and that's very important . . . So yes, I am jealous of him in that way.'

Since he couldn't do any proper work while he was under the bell having his two-hour compressed-air treatments, he brought *Anna Karenina* in with him to pass the time. *The novel is rather boring and so-so. I can't understand what they're all so excited about.*[393] His life was now arranged around these health treatments, compressed air in the winter and the mineral springs at Bad Ems in the summer. Three of the four weak spots on his lung from the previous summer had healed, but the fourth had got bigger.

It was difficult, leaving Anna and the children, and he worried about them, particularly as Anna was expecting their fourth child. When he caught the steamer, Fedya and Lyuba waved for a long time from the shore, before their pinprick forms turned away to head back to the house. In his first letter, Fyodor asked Anna to write to him every three days, and told her to try to be cheerful. He wrote to remind her to have a bath, to tell her to look after the nanny, and to bathe the children, and she replied that she hadn't bathed herself or the children in over two weeks.ˑ The letters were always held up by a day or two, which was perhaps to be expected, since an official at the passport office had revealed the insulting fact that Fyodor was still under government surveillance after all these years.

Fyodor hardly knew anyone in Ems, but he did meet one person he got on with particularly well, through Katkov's sister-in-law: a poet named Pelageya Guseva. *I was at the spa, drinking the waters. She made an impression on me at the first meeting, cast a sort of spell on me. It was a case of fate. I did not choose it – I did not want to love her. My whole soul was in revolt at the fact that this could have*

ˑ He was still writing to ask her to bathe 'at least a little' four years later (Letter to Anna, 25 July [6 August] 1879).

happened to me.˙ She was a forty-year-old widow, a faded beauty whose tendency to sickly pallor appealed to the old Romantic in Fyodor. She was also an admirer of his writing. They had wonderful conversations together and argued amiably and Fyodor made sure to tell her stories in which his wife featured prominently. When Anna wrote to Fyodor with the bad news that her brother had caught his wife in flagrante, Fyodor composed himself and replied: 'Just like you, Anya, he's filled with a sense of duty. He knows that he's bound by the children.'[394]

It was just as well that he soon had to return for Anna's confinement. When the couple were reunited, Fyodor discovered that some miscreant had published a rumour in the *Petersburg Gazette* that Fyodor was on the brink of death, which had not exactly set Anna at ease – she had telegrammed him immediately and received a response that he was quite well, but the German and Russian had been garbled, causing further confusion. In any case, the birth went well, and on 10 August 1875 they had a son, Alexei. It was a beautiful Indian summer that year and, despite nearly losing a suitcase containing the manuscript of *The Adolescent* on the way to the steamer, it was a pleasantly uneventful autumn for the family of five in St Petersburg. Fyodor finished correcting the last chapters of the book, which he handed to *Notes of the Fatherland* to go into their last issue of the year. *I see that the novel is a loss, however: it will be buried with full honours amidst universal contempt.*[395] Readers, it seemed, would rather keep reading books about high passions among the gentry.

Soon after the conclusion of *The Adolescent* was published, Fyodor bumped into a friend on the street, who immediately began gushing about Part 7 of *Anna Karenina*, which had also just come out.

˙ *The Adolescent*, pp. 307–8. In 1880, Guseva wrote to him asking for a favour and explaining that in Ems she had 'heroically concealed' her feelings (history does not record how successful she was in the attempt). He shot back: 'I remember you *too well* ... But don't write to me about that in your letters. I shake your hand firmly, like a friend.' (Letter to Pelageya Guseva, 15 October 1880) *NB For a wife it is important only that her husband remain true to her in fact; his fantasies of other women must not disturb her at all.* (*The Unpublished Dostoevsky*, Volume 2, p. 150)

'It's completely unprecedented. Are there any of our writers who could rival it? Could anyone imagine anything like it in Europe? Is there any work in all our literature in recent years, or even earlier, that could stand next to it?'[396]

Well, undeniably there was nothing like Tolstoy in Europe – but he was no Pushkin, after all.

Ever since *Time* was banned and *Epoch* folded, Fyodor had thought about publishing a journal or diary of some kind again. He had always enjoyed writing feuilletons, whether they were unsigned articles on life in St Petersburg during the 1840s or notes on his travels around Europe with Strakhov; indeed, the most enjoyable part of editing *The Citizen* had been his *Writer's Diary* column, which had received an enthusiastic response from its readers. But what he was planning now was altogether more ambitious, a stand-alone publication that would chart the life of Russia, month by month. *You could leave out a great deal and confine yourself to a selection of events more or less characteristic of the moral life of the people, of the personal character of the Russian people at the present moment.*[397] The idea would be to intersperse recollections from his undeniably eventful life with opinion pieces on court trials and military conflicts, short stories and fables. *Everything would be put in with an idea that would illuminate the whole. The very selection of facts will suggest how they are to be understood. And it ought to be interesting even for light reading, apart from its value as a work of reference. It would be, so to say, a presentation of the spiritual, moral, inner life of Russia. I want everyone to buy it, I want it to be a book that will be found on every table. It's an immense undertaking.*[398] In 1876 he decided to take up this long-held ambition in earnest.

The owner of the house they rented at Staraya Russa died around this time, and Fyodor bought the two-storey wooden house for 1,150 roubles. At last, he owned a property he could leave to his family. Nestled on one bank of the Pererytitsa River, it had six rooms upstairs, hundred-year-old trees, a garden and an orchard, as well as a stable, an icehouse and a bathhouse. Here, Fyodor worked on *A Writer's Diary*, wading into any and every debate with his opinions on belligerents in Europe, 'the woman question' and the need for women's higher education, Jewish people.˙ He was the sole author of every word of the issue, and he and Anna published it themselves. Finally, it didn't matter what the critics said, nor whether he subscribed to a particular tendency, or published in a particular journal; with *A Writer's Diary* he was talking directly to the people. It was an immediate success, and Fyodor soon got an enquiry from a journalist as to whether he had ever considered writing his memoirs. *At the moment I'm incapable of doing that. As a result of my falling sickness (which, however, hardly troubles me any more), I have forgotten the plots of my novels. I do remember the general outline of my life.*³⁹⁹

He and Anna were perfect collaborators, and their home life was now quite contented. In Staraya Russa, they rented a cow so that the children could have fresh milk every morning, which Fyodor would sometimes have to track down when it wandered off to find its friends. The only source of marital tension was Fyodor's jealousy, which was particularly pronounced on 18 May 1876, when he received an anonymous letter from a 'well wisher', claiming that Anna had been bewitched by a dark stranger. The letter suggested that, if he didn't believe in the truth of it, he should look at the portrait in her locket. When Anna came in to his study after dinner and sat down beside his desk, he paced around the room heavily.

'Why are you so gloomy, Fedya?' she asked.⁴⁰⁰

He stopped directly in front of her.

'Do you wear a locket?' he asked, choking with rage.

'Yes, I do.'

˙The best a modern biographer might say about some of these interventions is that they were of their time. Like his beloved Dickens, he was a champion of many social ills, but too ready to found his edifices on stereotypes. His ideal of an explicitly Orthodox Russian nation left no room for what he perceived as non-Orthodox, internationalist (or indeed stateless) people, and he was deeply suspicious of what he called 'yids'. We must remember that, for many years, anti-Semitism was official policy in Russia.

'Show it to me!'

'What for? You've already seen it many times.'

'Let – me – see – that locket!' he roared, ripping the chain off her and cutting her neck. It was a locket he had bought her in Venice, after Sonya had died. His hands trembled and the locket almost slipped from his grasp as he opened the catch. The portraits inside were of Lyuba and, on the other side, himself.

The letter, it turned out, had been written by Anna. She had copied it word for word from a fictional letter in the latest *Notes of the Fatherland*, which Fyodor had read the previous day but hadn't recognised. It was a practical joke – that was all it was. She tried to make light of it, dabbing at the blood on her neck, but Fyodor was in no mood to join in.

'Just think what might have happened! I might have strangled you in a rage!'

After nine years of marriage, they still desired each other very much and were sometimes overcome with the need to possess one another. When he went to Bad Ems for his summer treatments, the two wrote passionate and, in Fyodor's case, detailed letters about the contents of their dreams. He apologised for grumbling and being impatient after their quarrel, and wondered at the fact that, over the course of their marriage, he had fallen in love with her four or five times over. He promised to kiss her all over, her lips and then her toes. Fyodor couldn't stand the thought of Anna talking to another man and was beside himself when she wrote teasingly that she had bumped into her former fiancé. He was also upset to learn that three nannies had quit in the space of one month, having been successively terrorised by the unruly Dostoevsky children. By August, Fyodor was desperate to get back – Anna wrote to him about a certain special purchase she had made in preparation for his return, and he wrote back, 'My treasure, my angel, I kiss your little feet, which I fantasise about passionately.'[401]

A Writer's Diary was gathering a following greater than anything Fyodor had written up to this point. Pobedonostsev asked Fyodor to add the Tsarevich Alexander to his subscription list, so it could hardly have been any more influential. And yet, all of this sifting of life's specificities, following trials, participating in the chaos of national life, putting out a new issue every month, meant that there wasn't time to develop fiction longer than a story. For the next year or so he worked hard, seeing little of his family, back in miserable St Petersburg, where he would pour whole bottles of cockroach powder around the apartment to try to rid himself of an infestation. Once, he woke from a seizure to find Anna gone and couldn't shake the feeling that something had happened to her, despite assurances from the maid that she hadn't been there in the first place. A telegram reassured him she was well, but the episode cast a pall over his work. The novel that he had developed and abandoned a long time ago began to come back to him now, and he felt by instinct that the only way to ground himself and bring out the novel was to go back to his family's old estate, where his father had died, to retrace his footsteps, so that he could tell his last big story. *The damned trip to Darovoe! How I would like not to go! But I can't: if I deny myself those impressions, how can I be a writer after that, and what is the writer to write about?*[402] And so he travelled to Moscow and took the rickety train out to the countryside, trundling along at 15 versts an hour.

Arriving at Darovoe, Fyodor was astonished to discover that Agrafena Lavrentieva, the village idiot, was still alive and approaching her seventies. He remembered her as a young woman. Incapable of speech, she would wander the fields all year round except on the very coldest nights, when the villagers would forcibly bundle her into a hut. Even in winter, she could often be found standing barefoot in the cemetery where her only child was buried, her grey hair covered in frost, talking indistinctly.[403] Many of the peasants remembered him, too, and invited him in for tea – helpful little Fedya, who had once run two versts back to the house just to get a glass of water for a peasant mother working in the fields, who had helped gather firewood when one of the others was injured. Although he only spent a few days there before returning to St Petersburg, he shored up so many memories, scribbling them down whilst seated a tree stump.

On 28 December 1877, Fyodor learned that Nekrasov had died. He had last seen him a month before. *At that time he already looked almost like a corpse, so that it even seemed odd to see him move his lips and speak.*[404] When he went to view the body, it was gnarled by suffering. Returning home, he could not settle down to work. Instead, he took all three volumes of Nekrasov's poetry off the shelf, and began reading at the first page. The first four poems had appeared alongside Fyodor's own first published piece. *As I went on reading – I read one poem after another – it seemed as if my whole life were passing before me.* He read through the night, volume after volume, remembering the way they talked through the White Nights as young men. A memory rose from the deep: Nekrasov had opened up to him about his father's violence, the way he would steal a hug from his mother when they had the chance. Nekrasov had been one of the few who understood as well as Fyodor the way violence was inherited, and had refused this inheritance; instead, his poetry had been a crucible which transmuted its fierceness into love.

There were several thousand people at the funeral, many of them students. The procession of the coffin began at 9 a.m. and there were still people there when it got dark at around 4 p.m. Walking beside Anna in the cemetery, Fyodor said, 'When I die, Anya, bury me here or wherever you want, but don't bury me in the writers' section of Volkov Cemetery. I don't want to lie among my enemies – I suffered enough from them while I was alive!'[405]

Anna promised him a huge funeral, a procession of tens of thousands, a burial at the Alexander Nevsky Monastery, rites by a bishop, but only if he promised to live for many more years to come. Fyodor smiled. 'All right, I'll try to live a while longer.'

At the open grave, Fyodor said a few words about Nekrasov. *I began by saying that his was a wounded heart, wounded once for his whole life, and that this unhealed wound was at the same time the source of all his poetry, all this man's love for everyone who suffers from violence, from the cruelty of the unbridled will, from all that oppresses Russian women and children.*[406] In a spirit of generosity, he spoke of Nekrasov's greatness as a poet – that he stood second only to Pushkin and Lermontov. A voice from the crowd shouted out that Nekrasov was greater than either of them. Well, it was his graveside; Fyodor let that go.

His contemporaries were dying and Fyodor was frail. He had been predicting that his health would fail him even in his early twenties; now he was beset by haemorrhoids and by epilepsy, his voice hoarse, his lungs eaten up with emphysema. Other men, healthier men than him, had been broken by the hardships of Siberia. But for all the work he'd produced since returning, he had yet to write his magnum opus, the book that had been gestating in the back of his mind since the late 1860s. The novel now filled his head and his heart; *it's begging to be written.*[407] It would mean putting *A Writer's Diary* on hold for the time being. Might he really live long enough to produce a truly great work at his own pace, a work that would place him unquestionably in the pantheon of Russian writers? Sometimes he felt that death was stalking him through the misty streets, and yet perversely he sometimes felt he was only just getting started. *In the prime of life, fifty-six, not more, and we know that is the very flower of manhood; the age at which real life begins.*[408]

TWELVE

The Prophet

1878–1881

FYODOR'S GREATEST PLEASURE WAS spending time with his young family. *The soul is healed by being with children.*[409] He would call them in as he had his first coffee of the day, and sit happily listening to them as they related their morning adventures. The family always ate dinner together. Sometimes the children would knock on their father's study door while he was working and he would offer them a sweet. Once, he dressed as a white polar bear and the children sat on stools as if stuck on ice floes. Fyodor crawled around the floor on all fours, hunting for tasty children, who squealed in glee as he rushed to them and hugged them. If he had a favourite, it was little Alyosha, their youngest. He was a happy child, always babbling away, and Fyodor felt somehow sure that Alyosha was special, perhaps even like his father.

The spring of 1878 had begun with the exciting news that Fyodor had been invited to attend the International Literary Congress in Paris by none other than Victor Hugo. But he never got the chance to attend. On 30 April, Alyosha had a fit. Although the boy convulsed, he didn't cry out; the fit lasted only four minutes. Fyodor was struck with foreboding. Had the boy inherited epilepsy from him? Two weeks later, on 16 May, Alyosha was laughing with his nurse when his face began to twitch. At first the nurse thought it was because his molars were coming through, but the boy soon began to convulse. After a lifetime of having fits, this was the first time Fyodor had been made to witness one as an observer. *A terrible scream that is unlike anything else breaks from the sufferer. In that scream everything human seems obliterated and it is impossible, or very difficult, for an observer to admit that it is the sufferer himself that is screaming. It seems as though it were someone else screaming from within the sufferer.*[410] Alyosha's face was horribly distorted, especially the eyes, jerking and contorting. It was uncanny, horrifying, almost unbearable. The fit lasted 12 hours and, at the end of it, Alyosha never woke up. Fyodor kissed him, made the sign of the cross over him three times, and broke down in tears. He spent the whole night kneeling beside the body.

Yesterday he was still having fun, running around and singing; today he's laid out on the table.[411] The weeks after Alyosha's death were desolate. *I look at his little clothes, his little shirt, his little boots, and I wail. I lay out all that is left of him, all his little things.*[412] *If only I could look upon him one last time, without going up to him, without speaking, if I could be hidden in a corner and only see him for one little minute. If only I could hear him pattering about the room with his little feet just once, only once. But he's gone, and I shall never hear him again.* If grief is unspent love, it is hard to imagine how much it hurts to lose the second of your children.

Fyodor had always intended to visit the holy monastery at Optina Pustyn as part of the research for his new novel, and the notion of unburdening his grief on the famous elder there, Father Ambrose, finally gave him a reason to go. After the funeral, he set off for Moscow, and then travelled on with Vsevolod Soloviev's brother, Vladimir, towards the monastery about 200 versts away.* It meant taking a train to Sergievo and then a series of bumpy country roads for two long days.

Cut off from the advances of the nineteenth century, the monastery appeared just as it might have done when it had been founded hundreds of years earlier, its white towers topped by blue cupolas with golden crosses, sparkling brightly against the thick

*Vladimir Soloviev was already becoming a noted philosopher.

forest.* It was this monastery, more than any other, that had come to represent the true heart of Russian Orthodoxy, and Fyodor was travelling in the footsteps of Gogol and Tolstoy, who had already made their own pilgrimages before him.

Many of those who had travelled to the monastery were there to see the famous elder. Born Alexander, he had first entered Optina in 1839, taking the name Ambrose, and having become the principal elder of the monastery in 1860 was now considered one of the holiest men in all Russia. Not only erudite, but emanating great spiritual calm, mildness and humour, he made a great impression on everyone he met.†

Fyodor met with Father Ambrose three times. Only once did they meet alone. Fyodor explained his grief over Alyosha, and Father Ambrose offered his condolences.

'Be not comforted. Consolation is not what you need. Weep and be not consoled, but weep. Only every time that you weep be sure to remember that your son is one of the angels of God, that he looks down from there at you and sees you, and rejoices at your tears, and points at them to the Lord God; and a long while yet will you keep that great parent's grief. But it will turn in the end into quiet joy, and your bitter tears will be only tears of tender sorrow that purifies the heart and delivers it from sin. And I shall pray for the peace of your child's soul. What was his name?'[413]

'Alexei, Father.'

'A sweet name. After Alexei, the man of God?'

'Yes, Father.'

'What a saint he was!'

But Fyodor couldn't maintain this deferential tone for long. He rarely met his intellectual equal even in literary circles, and probing Father Ambrose on matters of faith made him so excitable that he began to interrupt the elder, disputing with him on certain

---

*The recent history of Optina Pustyn has been more changeable: in Soviet times, the monastery was turned into a gulag; then, in 1993, after its restoration as a monastery, three monks were stabbed to death by a Satanist.

†In 1988, on the restoration of the monastery, he was canonised as Saint Ambrose of Optina.

points, then raising heated objections, even beginning to explain his own religious ideas to the elder. While there, he also browsed the monastery library, taking down a number of passages from *The Life of the Elder Leonid* by Father Zedergolm for use in his novel.

This trip, and the death of Alyosha, were the catalyst for one of Fyodor's most important ideas, which would be, as he saw it, the simplest, most persuasive argument for atheism that there could be: if God exists, why does he permit the suffering of innocent children? Why would he create a world in which blameless horses were lashed across the eyes, in which invading armies sometimes threw babies in the air and caught them on the tips of their bayonets? He had read a case of a young girl whose parents punished her by smearing excrement on her face and in her mouth, and another child torn apart by a pack of dogs for sport. *Imagine that you are creating the fabric of human destiny with the aim of making humankind happy in the end, giving them peace and rest at last, but that it is necessary to torture to death only one tiny creature, and to found your edifice on its unavenged tears. Would you consent to be the architect under those conditions?*[414]

The shape of the book was coming into focus now. It would be the greatest novel he had written yet, perhaps the greatest novel in the Russian language. It would contain every theme, every conflict, every archetype and new idea that Fyodor had gathered over the decades: Fyodor Karamazov, the alcoholic father cooped up in a crumbling estate in the countryside, who raped a local girl, and who was murdered in an intrigue involving 3,000 roubles. There would be four sons of Fyodor, each of them four compass points on the two thematic axes of Dostoevskian fiction: Dmitri would represent the life of the body, and Ivan the life of the brain; the bastard Smerdyakov would represent nihilism and the fourth brother, faith. That last brother would be a pure young monk, a beautiful soul, whom he would call Alyosha. A naif, almost too good for this world, and yet that was what protected him: his incorruptibility. In the monastery where he lived would be a wise elder who would reveal profound truths about God and Russia. Poor Dmitri would be carried away by his passion for women, money would pour through his hands like water, and he would desperately need 3,000 roubles from his father to pay a debt. He had an honest heart, but that might not be enough to save him from prison. Ivan would be led by the force of his own intellect to doubt his faith – he would imagine outlandish scenarios and thought experiments. What if Jesus returned to earth during the time of the Inquisition? Would the Catholics not suppress him as a radical? As he retreated further into his own mind, Ivan would even hallucinate the Devil himself, one dark night, and the two of them would exchange truly dangerous ideas. Lurking in the background, Smerdyakov, the perverse soul, the half-brother, the one who eluded rational explanation, the fifth member of a four-person family, the five in the two plus two.*

Fyodor returned to St Petersburg with the clarity he needed to begin work on *The Brothers Karamazov*, but he couldn't work in their old apartment. The doors failed to burst open with the arrival of Alyosha; the floors refused to patter with his feet. Now a family of four, they moved into a set of six rooms at 5/2 Kuznechny Lane, the same building where he had lived when he was writing *The Double* back in 1846. Fyodor's study was sparsely furnished as ever, containing a desk and a clock, an icon, a large cupboard, and a couch along the back wall opposite the windows, above which hung a reproduction of the *Sistine Madonna*.

Freed in some measure from the immediacy of his grief, Fyodor threw himself into his work. By the end of 1878 he already had a full plan for the book and had written the first 160 pages, which he sent off to Katkov for the all-important January issue. At the end of each long night of work, his thoughts were now firmly on his legacy. *I lie here and think constantly that I will die soon, in a year or two, perhaps, and what will become of my three precious little heads after I'm gone?*[415]

---

* *Let's conclude our reflections, which are beginning to be suggestive of newspaper criticism.* (*The Idiot*, p. 417)

Through the publication of *A Writer's Diary*, Fyodor had become one of the pre-eminent names in Russian literature, and as he began to publish *The Brothers Karamazov* in Katkov's *Russian Herald*, the name Dostoevsky took on an almost mystical significance. For the first time in his life, he was being taken seriously by everyone, from the students to the literati. The government even ended its decades-long surveillance of his letters and activities, which was just as well since he was now in the Tsar's inner circle.

In the spring of 1878, Fyodor had been invited to dine with the Tsar's children, Grand Dukes Sergei and Paul, on whom their tutor believed he would have a beneficial influence. After being picked up in a royal carriage, Fyodor got on quite well with the young nobles, who kept up a good conversation, and he was soon being invited to the Winter Palace on a regular basis. He participated in one of the amateur plays put on in court, playing the part of a monk in a production of *Boris Godunov*. He was introduced to another of the Grand Dukes, Konstantin, who Fyodor felt was perhaps better suited to the creative arts than to his navy career. Finally, he got the chance to meet the Tsar Alexander II. Despite being a passionate monarchist, Fyodor didn't remotely follow court etiquette: he would be the first to speak in front of the Tsar; he sat down without permission; he even turned his back to the royals when he left a room. He accidentally made one of the Tsarinas cry, and on another occasion he was so emphatic in making a point that he found he had been holding onto the button on her dress for the whole time they had been standing together.

In any given week, there was barely an evening that wasn't accounted for by a salon or a dinner: on Sundays he might have Strakhov or Maikov over; on Mondays there was Sofia Tolstoy's salon; on Tuesdays it was Elena Stackenschneider's; on Wednesdays everyone went to Prince Meshchersky's; on Saturdays he would often pay a visit to Pobedonostsev; and once a month there was a dinner for the Society of Writers, where ideological enemies put aside their differences in the name of a hearty meal.

It was at Sofia Tolstaya's salon, one Monday night, where he met the Devil mingling among the other guests. He had come in the person of a pleasant, fashionable young man, smartly dressed like a French ambassador. Something told him that this young man was the Anti-Christ and, just as he had the thought, he saw a beautiful, furry tail snaking out from under his suit jacket. *I didn't trust my eyes and decided to rely on my sense of touch.*[416] As the young man gracefully approached Fyodor's end of the room to kiss a woman's hand, Fyodor reached out and grabbed the tail. *And what do you know, it was definitely a real tail, almost like sable, living, warm and even containing some electricity.* The Devil turned around and looked at Fyodor welcomingly, like an old friend, as if to say, 'Did you recognise me?' And then he was gone.

That week, Fyodor bumped into Maikov at the offices of *The Word*, where he had been shaking down some overdue royalties, and told him the whole story.

'How do you explain it?' Maikov asked.[417] 'Was it a hallucination or real life?'

'A hallucination? It was a fact!' Fyodor replied. 'Draw your own conclusions, but I have no doubt that he is coming and the Kingdom is at hand.'*

As they were still standing in the middle of the editorial office, Maikov drew his friend aside and invited him for a cup of tea.

'Tea? Why would I want tea? This is slander! I'm trying to share the news with you: the Anti-Christ is coming to this world. Who will chop away his tail?'

Everyone had begun to look at me strangely. Everyone had begun to behave with me not as before – not as to a healthy man. This impression never left me even at the liveliest social functions. I was tormented by the idea that everyone suspected me of being mad.[418]

But Fyodor knew he was not mad. The Anti-Christ was at large in Russia, and his servants were hard at work. In 1878 someone had shot the governor of St Petersburg in his office, though he thankfully survived; in the same year, the head of the Third Section had been stabbed to death in the street, and months later

---

* *If you are so corrupted by modern realism and can't stand anything fantastic, let it be a case of mistaken identity. (The Brothers Karamazov, p. 274)*

his replacement narrowly avoided being shot in his carriage. In February 1879 the governor of Kharkov was killed, and then, just after 8 a.m. on 2 April, while the Tsar was strolling back to the Winter Palace through the square, a terrorist by the name of Alexander Soloviev shot at him. The Tsar ran off in a zigzag as Soloviev shot four more times at him, swallowed poison, and was arrested. Alexander II had now survived his third assassination attempt, and it wouldn't be the last.

On 26 August 1879 a new terrorist organisation calling itself People's Will published the Tsar's death sentence. They attempted to carry it out on 19 November, when they detonated a mine underneath what they thought was the Tsar's train outside Moscow; but he had taken a different train when the first had broken down. Meanwhile, a People's Will operative was working as a carpenter inside the Winter Palace itself. Each night, he smuggled a little more nitroglycerine into the cellar, until he had amassed a potent stockpile of 300 pounds directly under the Yellow Room, the Tsar's dining room. As the court settled down to dinner on 5 February 1880, a huge explosion lifted the floor and blew out the windows. Eleven were killed and over 50 wounded; the Tsar, however, had been running a little late for dinner, and was unhurt.

Despite the strains of his illness, the last year of Fyodor's life was undoubtedly his apotheosis, as *The Brothers Karamazov* unfolded in all its complexity and beauty before the reading public. The highlight of that year was a festival in Moscow to mark the unveiling of a new statue to Pushkin. The festival would gather together for the first time not only countless nobles and high officials, but all the literary luminaries in Russia, with the conspicuous exception of Tolstoy, who had been invited three times but replied only that he considered festivals to be a sin. Pyotr Tchaikovsky was there, as well as the mayor of Moscow and the president of the Moscow Commerce Bank. The Tsar himself might have been there if he weren't mourning the death of his wife.

On the eve of the festival, Fyodor checked into Room 33 of the Loskutnaya Hotel on Tverskaya Avenue. Turgenev was due to read on the first day, 7 June, though Fyodor didn't go to hear him – he preferred to spend the time preparing for his own speech the next day. Besides, he couldn't stand Turgenev's style of oration: *the gentleman read with a sort of melancholy condescension, as if it were a favour, so that it was almost insulting to the audience.*[419] From what others said, the speech went down well enough, though Turgenev stopped short of actually pronouncing Pushkin a national poet on the level of Shakespeare, Goethe or Homer.

Reportedly a group of about a hundred students clapped Turgenev's speech more enthusiastically than anyone else, and Fyodor suspected they were claqueurs, professional applauders hired to make him appear more popular than he really was.

On 8 June it was Fyodor's turn to give his speech. He got up, white tie askew, coat hanging off him, and limped up to the front. The auditorium was packed and, as he stepped onto the stage, the audience thundered with applause. He bowed and gestured to the crowd to stop clapping, but the applause continued for some time before he had a chance to speak.

Dostoevsky had mastered a certain way of speaking at readings: *tersely, calmly, precisely, clearly, firmly.*[420] His voice was rasping, but the audience was rapt. He talked about Pushkin as a national prophet at a time when Russian civil society was just beginning to stir. *If a lecturer keeps an audience for longer than twenty minutes, they won't go on listening. Not even a celebrity can hold his own for half an hour.*[421] Fyodor spoke for over 40 minutes, first about Pushkin's early poetry, then about the great genius of *Eugene Onegin*, the alienated hero and the selfless heroine, Tatiana. Although she loves Eugene, she will not abandon her marriage. 'What kind of happiness can there be if it is founded on the unhappiness of another?'[422] Fyodor asked the gathered audience. 'And now imagine as well that it is essential and unavoidable to torture to death just one human creature; let that creature be not entirely worthy, even ridiculous – not some Shakespeare, but simply an honourable old man.' Wouldn't it be better to suffer yourself than to inflict suffering?

It was this sort of insight that made Pushkin unique. Fyodor could see no one else who understood and embodied the spirit of the Russian people in a way that was truly universal. Here, Fyodor came around to the real thrust of his argument: that the Russian spirit was uniquely placed to fuse together the genius of all world cultures.[423] Since the reforms of Peter the Great, which began to hybridise Russian culture, there had been a great, unconscious purpose: 'It was then that we at once began to strive towards a truly vital reunification, towards the universal brotherhood of peoples!' All these arguments over Westernisers and Slavophiles – it was all a misunderstanding.* To be a Russian was to be a brother to all people, a pan-human. *There was violent applause at this passage from many parts of the room, but I waved my hands as though imploring them to let me finish without interruption and the room relapsed into silence at once.*[424]

This was Russia's destiny! To reconcile Europe's conflicts, 'to enfold its neighbours with brotherly love, and in the end, perhaps, to utter the great and final word of universal harmony, the brotherly, lasting accord of all tribes according to the Gospel!' He pronounced the last words of the speech in an excited whisper and then stepped down from the podium, the whole auditorium around him perfectly silent. Then someone screamed from the back, 'You have solved the mystery!' And with that, *the enthusiasm of the audience burst like an irresistible storm.*[425] There was an ovation, true, but it was not simply a matter of the audience standing and clapping. *It was out of the question to stop it: the women wept, many of the men wept too.* Fyodor's speech had triggered a great outpouring of pent-up emotion in the room, a catharsis amounting almost to religious ecstasy. *Strangers sobbed, embraced each other and swore to be better people, to love one another.*[426] He was mobbed by grand dames, students male and female, state officials, hugging and kissing him; one young man came up, shook

---

* *You cannot understand me so I won't explain any more precisely, but know that I am nevertheless more liberal than you. My convictions are not Slavophile so much as Orthodox, i.e. peasant, Christian convictions. I don't like their superstitions and ignorance, but I love their heart and all that they love.* (The Unpublished Dostoevsky, Volume 2, p. 98)

Fyodor's hand and promptly fainted. Two old men came up to him excitedly and told him, 'For twenty years we've been enemies and refused to speak to each other, but we have just embraced and made up. It's all down to you. You're a saint, a prophet!' Even Turgenev crossed the stage towards him, his arms wide, to congratulate him.

When Fyodor tried to get away, the crowd forced its way backstage and wouldn't let him alone for another hour while the chairman rang his bell in a futile attempt to call the meeting back to order. The next writer due to speak, Ivan Aksakov, declared that they hadn't witnessed a speech so much as a moment in history. He didn't want to read his own piece – Dostoevsky had pronounced the last word on Pushkin and there was nothing left to say. When the others eventually prevailed upon Aksakov to read, Fyodor attempted to slink off but was detained by fans. As soon as Aksakov had finished, the stage was stormed once again by a horde of women who had somehow procured a real laurel wreath one and a half metres wide, with which they now crowned Fyodor, while the mayor thanked him on behalf of the City of Moscow.

Back at the hotel, he wrote to Anna to tell her everything, his head swimming, his hands and legs trembling with excitement. Nothing like this had happened to him since that first White Night in his youth, when Nekrasov and Grigorovich had burst in with tears in their eyes and proclaimed him a genius. *It was a complete, total victory!*[427]

At breakfast the next day, Fyodor was seated next to a young woman. By way of small talk, he asked her whether she had ever read Dickens, and she admitted that she hadn't. Fyodor raised his voice, addressing the whole table: 'Ladies and gentlemen, we have the happiest person in the world among us!'[428] The young woman looked quite flustered and the greybeards around the table confused, so Fyodor explained: 'She hasn't read Dickens and has it all to look forward to! How I would like to be in her place.' *When I am tired, or unwell, nothing calms me down better or gives me more joy than Dickens. He's one of the best writers in the world.*[429]

Later that day, at the closing of the festival, Fyodor read out Pushkin's poem, 'The Prophet'. By this point the audience were perfectly clear that they considered Dostoevsky the true prophet, but much as the suggestion privately gave him pleasure, Fyodor publicly demurred.* That evening, before returning to Anna and the children, he took a cab to Strastnaya Square, the horses clopping through the warm, quiet streets, and stood looking up at the Pushkin statue. He laid the comically large wreath he had been given at Pushkin's feet, bowing deeply to his great teacher. It was a gesture of humility, but also of reassurance, perhaps the first of humanity's great superstitions: if we take the trouble to honour the dead, perhaps one day someone will remember us.

———

It is dark now, six in the morning, the city is awakening, and I have not yet gone to bed. My doctors tell me that I must not over-exert myself, that I ought to sleep at night and not sit for ten or twelve hours bent over my writing desk. Why am I writing at night? Because as soon as I get up at one o'clock the doorbell starts ringing: someone comes asking for a favour; another insists that I solve some insoluble problem for him or he'll shoot himself; a delegation of female students arrives, followed by schoolboys and charitable societies. What time is there left for me to think, to read, to work, to live?[430] Dostoevsky's emphysema was getting worse. *Damn these papirosi! They do nothing but harm, but I just can't stop. I'm always coughing and now I've got a tickle in my throat and I'm short of breath. But how am I to give up?*[431] He wanted to work but he needed to rest. For some years now, he had lived only in apartments that overlooked a church, and he would sometimes take breaks in the gardens at Vladimirskaya Church to watch the children play. *I always was attracted by children. I had a sort of intense happy sensation at every meeting with them. I stood still and laughed with happiness, looking at their little legs flying along, at the boys and girls running together, at their laughter and tears, and then I forgot all my mournful thoughts.*[432] But even the short walk

---

*Somerset Maugham once commented drily that the role of prophet is one 'which few authors have been disinclined to play'. (*Sunday Times*, 18 July 1954)

to the church was difficult these days, dragging his carcass along in exhaustion past the stalls selling fragrant firewood, leaning on an umbrella.

The important thing was to complete *The Brothers Karamazov*. He had ideas for a sequel called *The Children* and he was also planning to pick up *A Writer's Diary* in 1881, but first he had to finish *Karamazov*, even if it meant writing by night and sacrificing the last vestiges of his health. Fyodor had buried his heart in its pages, and those of *The Idiot*, *Crime and Punishment* and *Devils*, and even if he never got around to writing his memoirs, those who knew him could unearth him there.*

He still socialised that autumn, though even at other people's houses he was often to be found sitting silently on a chair in the corner. He reprised his reading of Pushkin's poem 'The Prophet' at a couple of soirées and, at the start of November, caught up with Strakhov, who passed on some praise that cheered him up greatly. Tolstoy had just re-read *The House of the Dead* and had written to Strakhov: 'I don't know a better book in all our new literature, including Pushkin . . . If you see Dostoevsky, tell him that I love him.'[433] Fyodor was over the moon when Strakhov showed him the page, and asked if he could keep it. Moments later, however, Fyodor was affronted: what did Tolstoy mean by 'including Pushkin'? Strakhov diplomatically responded that the Count was a hardened freethinker. In any case, Fyodor kept the letter.

A few days later, on 7 November, Fyodor sent off the last chapters of *The Brothers Karamazov*. Over the three years of his work on the novel, he had secured his legacy, and he knew it. *This is a significant moment for me. But allow me not to say farewell. After all, I intend to live and write for another twenty years.*[434] He was dreadfully sick and worn out, but there had hardly been a time in his life when

---

* Dostoevsky had tried to write his memoirs once, for a series the journalist Pyotr Bykov was compiling on Russian writers, but he made a false start and then abandoned it: *I sensed that the piece was taking too much out of me, raising up before me the life I had lived, and required great love to carry out. If I am free and well, I'll definitely write it, because I want to and feel a need to – but when I'll get it written, that I do not know.* (Letter to Bykov, 13 January 1877)

this wasn't true. Life, for Fyodor, had been a constant negotiation with myopia, haemorrhoids, bladder infections, seizures, the limp he had developed in Siberia, and the hoarseness exacerbated by his emphysema. The only thing holding him together for most of his adult life was determination. As the year reached its darkest days, Fyodor worked on a new issue of *A Writer's Diary* for publication at the start of 1881. He published the first complete edition of *The Brothers Karamazov* in December to mixed reviews, but was cheered by a letter from Pobedonostsev suggesting that he present a copy of the book to the Tsar and his family. The work of little Fedya Dostoevsky, born in a hospital for the poor and sent to Siberia for sedition, sitting on a shelf in the Tsar's study! In a literary milieu filled with the concerns of the gentry he stood alone as a voice of conscience for the weak, the poor, the sick, the abused. His whole life, he had leant into the prevailing wind. He was so very tired.

The day of Sunday 25 January 1881 was typical. Fyodor accepted an invitation to the Winter Palace, caught up with Strakhov and Maikov, and went to the printers to hand over the final pages of his new issue of *A Writer's Diary*. In the evening, he went for a brief stroll before setting to work. That night, Fyodor had a nosebleed, the first sign of a tear in his pulmonary artery. At the exact same time, the apartment next door was being raided by the police. They were looking for any evidence that might help them identify the inhabitant as Alexander Barannikov who, as one of the leaders of People's Will, was one of the most wanted terrorists in the country.* Fyodor was no longer the young revolutionary being arrested in the night, but the old man who lived next door.

---

* Barannikov had previously been involved in a number of unsuccessful attempts to assassinate Tsar Alexander II and his capture was overdue. On the morning of 25 January he and his accomplices had been tunnelling under a cheese shop for reasons that would soon become clear. Barannikov was arrested that afternoon when he tried to visit another member of the cell, and the police caught one of his accomplices, Nikolai Kolotkevich, at 4 a.m. on 26 January when he entered Dostoevsky's building.

The last twenty-four hours of my story have come and I am at the end.[435]

Awareness of death and its presence has always contained for me something oppressive, some mystical dread, ever since childhood.[436] He had always been afraid he might die in the night, or sleep so deeply that he would be buried alive, and would leave out notes asking not to be buried for three days just in case. He worried, too, about leaving his body in a presentable condition. The healthy man didn't think about death, nor what might be lurking on the other side of it. *But at the first sign of sickness, the possibility of another world instantly comes to the fore, and the sicker he becomes, the greater his contact with this other world.*[437] Most people imagined eternity as something vast, something entirely beyond our understanding, but what if it was just a little room, with spiders in the corners?

He knew he was leaving behind a humanity forever caught between two imperatives: what had to happen, and what ought to be. *All those not belonging to the ruling class suffer.*[438] *They are given equal rights to prevent their suffering. It's an excellent thing, but there follows a weakening of the sense of honour and duty. Egoism replaces the old consolidating principle and the whole system is shattered on the rock of personal freedom. The emancipated masses, left with no sustaining principle, end up losing all sense of cohesion, till they give up defending the liberties they have gained.* The future of Russia unfurled before him. *Communism will triumph (whether the communists are right or wrong).*[439] *But their triumph will be the farthest point of removal from the kingdom of heaven. One must expect this triumph, yet none of those who rule the destinies of this world is expecting it.*

If pressed to say whether he had achieved what he wanted with his life, Fyodor might easily have pointed to the raptures of the crowd following his Pushkin speech, when the audience had cried that he was a prophet, crowning him with laurel. But what was he next to Pushkin?* Not only had Pushkin created the very language of Russian literature, but he had turned his life into an art, cutting a swathe through society, seducing the wives of the gentry and fighting duels. It sometimes seemed as if Fyodor had spent his whole life at his desk, his hand cramped in a fury of writing, of logorrhoea, insisting upon a great idea and yet, like Cassandra, destined not to be truly understood.

If, before his discovery of America, Columbus had begun telling his idea to other people, I am convinced that for a very long time people would not have understood him.[440] There is something at the bottom of every new thought of genius that can never be communicated to others, even if one were to write volumes about it and were explaining one's idea for thirty-five years;† there's something left which cannot be induced to emerge from your brain, and remains with you for ever; and with it you will die, without communicating to anyone, perhaps, the most important of your ideas. But if I have failed to convey all that has been tormenting me, it will in any case be understood that I have paid very dearly for my convictions. And serving this idea did not release me from the moral obligation of making at least one creature in my life happy, in a practical way.[441]

On 28 January 1881, Fyodor Mikhailovich Dostoevsky lay on the sofa in his study underneath the *Sistine Madonna*, his head propped up by a cushion, his face pale, a dark spot of blood on his chin, surrounded by his family. His breath whistled. He asked for the parable of the prodigal son to be read to the children: transgression, repentance, forgiveness. It was the only story. His son and daughter knelt in prayer. He saw Pasha and Maikov. The sky was dark and Anna was beside him. She held his hands, a finger gently probing for his pulse, which was receding like footsteps in a mist.

---

* *Many strong natures seem to have a sort of natural craving to find someone or something to which they can do homage. Strong natures often find it difficult to bear the burden of their own strength.* (*The Adolescent*, p. 390)
† *The Idiot*, p. 357. Writing this in 1868, Dostoevsky could have had no idea that his publication history would last exactly thirty-five years.

'Remember, Anna, I always loved you passionately and was never unfaithful to you, even in my thoughts,' he told her.[442] He tried to sit up but this was the end.

Often I couldn't look at the setting sun without shedding a tear.[443] I have seen and I know that people can be beautiful and happy while they live on earth. I will not and cannot believe that evil is the normal condition of mankind. Let's say that paradise will never come to pass – I do understand that, and yet I'll go on preaching. It's so simple: in one day, in an hour it could all be arranged! The main thing is to love others like yourself, that is the main thing; there's nothing else we need. It's been said a billion times, but it hasn't yet become part of our lives.[444]

I love and can love only that earth which I am leaving behind. Never, never have I ceased to love that earth, and even on the night I part from it I love it more than ever. Is there suffering in the next world? On our earth we can only love with suffering and through suffering. We cannot love otherwise, and we know no other sort of love. I want suffering in order to love. I long, I thirst, right now, to kiss the earth that I am leaving behind.[445] I don't want, I won't accept life on any other!

Epilogue

A ND NOW, *I WILL pass on to the description of the subsequent incidents of my chronicle, writing, so to say, with full knowledge, and describing things as they became known afterwards, and are clearly seen today.*[446]

The day after Dostoevsky's death was a whirlwind. The apartment on Kuznechny Lane was packed with well-wishers jostling to see the body. Countesses and Grand Dukes who never normally had to wait for anything were stuck queuing for hours. There were even a few undercover revolutionaries there to pay their respects. The body was laid in an open coffin on a table, the face, so often creased in suffering, now tranquil. Around the coffin were flowers and candles. At one point, the candles flickered out, leaving only the dim light of the incense burner, and a surge from the crowd on the stairs knocked people against the coffin, which Anna had to grab to stop it falling off the table.

As word of Dostoevsky's death spread through St Petersburg, student groups organised collections to buy wreaths for the funeral; Anna was awarded a pension of 2,000 roubles a year, the first pension ever to be granted by the Tsar for 'services to Russian literature'; meanwhile, there was a frantic search behind the scenes for a cemetery that might agree to take Dostoevsky's body for free, since Anna didn't have the funds to buy a plot herself. Friends of the family suggested the cemetery of the Alexander Nevsky Monastery and, after some arm twisting by the powerful Pobedonostsev, the Metropolitan there agreed to take him for a fee (though privately he didn't see why they should bury a mere novelist on such holy ground).˙

Anyone arriving in St Petersburg on 31 January 1881 might have assumed the city was burying a Tsar rather than an ex-convict. A huge crowd, numbering in the tens of thousands, carried the coffin covered with a golden cloth for three versts from Kuznechny Lane to the Alexander Nevsky Monastery. There were dozens of wreaths bobbing along over the heads of the procession as it stretched out along Vladimirsky Prospect, each carrying a message from a different organisation: 'to a Russian man'; 'to the Great Teacher'; 'to the Friend of Truth'. Around the coffin, mourners carried chains of flowers and sang hymns. On Nevsky Prospect, horse-drawn trams were forced to a halt as bystanders climbed onto roofs for a better view. To many present, it felt as if they were burying a part of Russia.

Just a month later, on 1 March 1881, revolutionaries finally assassinated Tsar Alexander II. For months they had been digging a tunnel, starting from the back room of a cheese shop on Sadovaya Street, underneath the road that the Tsar crossed on his way to the military roll call each Sunday at the Mikhailovsky Manège. The plan was to undermine the Tsar, detonating a bomb under the road as he passed over, but the assassins weren't taking any chances – this was the sixth attempt on his life. Three other assassins stood nearby at street level ready to finish the job, armed with paraffin cans filled with nitroglycerine.

On the day in question, the Tsar took his bulletproof carriage on a different route that didn't pass by Sadovaya Street, instead taking the alternative route via the Ekaterininsky Canal. At the parade he was in good spirits, and chatted amiably with the English ambassador about the Duchess of Edinburgh. On the way

---

˙In 1797 it had become one of only three monastery complexes in the Russian Orthodox Church to be given the highest rank, becoming a *lavra* (Лáвра). The other two are in Kiev and in Sergiev Posad, 70 kilometres outside Moscow.

back to the palace, the three assassins were waiting for him, their bombs painted white to blend with the snow. At 2.15 p.m., as he approached Konyushennaya Bridge, the first assassin threw a bomb underneath the horses, killing a pedestrian and one of the Cossack guards and damaging the carriage, but leaving the Tsar unharmed. Instead of taking the driver's advice to make their escape, the Tsar opened the door to confront his assassin.

'Are you all right?' one of the guards asked.

'Yes, thank God,' replied the Tsar, crossing himself.

The second assassin was waiting in position.

'It's too early to thank God,' he said, hurling the second bomb.*

The Tsar lost his legs and bits of his torso. They dragged him to the Winter Palace in a sleigh but the severed legs were like a burst pipe and he died shortly after his arrival. The terrorists who had conducted the assassination, People's Will, wrote respectfully to the new Tsar Alexander III petitioning him for reform and warning that, if it did not come, 'a revolutionary earthquake throughout Russia will complete the destruction of the old order'.[447]

In fact, the destruction of the old order was already well underway, and the new had already been born. A three-year-old Iosif Vissarionovich Dzhugashvili was growing up in Georgia. Later, trying to sound like a strong man, a man of industry, he would adopt the name Stalin, Man of Steel, and would read *Devils* not as a warning, but as a manual for revolution. (Lenin preferred Turgenev.)

In the wake of the assassination, Pobedonostsev advised his erstwhile pupil, now Tsar Alexander III, to tighten restrictions on Russia's Jewish population. This resulted in the May Laws, with the explicit intention that a third of the population be converted to

---

*This is the cinematic version; other accounts say that the first bomb had cut the Tsar's face and he had asked to borrow a handkerchief from one of the Cossacks, who was still worrying about whether it was too dirty to give to a tsar when the second bomb exploded.

Christianity, a third emigrate, and a third die of hunger. The Jews were blamed for the assassination of Alexander II and in the three years after his death there were over 200 anti-Semitic incidents including horrific pogroms in Warsaw, Kiev and Odessa, in which thousands of homes were destroyed.

In 1884, Konstantin Sergeevich Alexeev adopted the stage name Stanislavsky so that his parents wouldn't find out he had an amateur theatre company. In the years before creating the Moscow Art Theatre, the Stanislavsky Method, and his world-famous production of Anton Chekhov's *The Seagull*, he adapted Dostoevsky's *The Village of Stepanchikovo*, which Dostoevsky had originally conceived as a play, but had been unable to stage in Semipalatinsk. Taking the part of the benign Uncle Rostanev, Stanislavsky felt that it was the first time he had really become the character: 'In all previous roles to a greater or lesser extent I merely aped, copied or mocked other people's images or my own.'[448] When *The Village of Stepanchikovo* was first published, the motiveless, controlling malignity of Foma Fomich hadn't seemed very realistic, but the stage production would come into its own with the arrival in court of the infamous Rasputin.

Meanwhile, in the decadent West, Sigmund Freud had just qualified as a doctor and was working as a clinical assistant at Vienna's General Hospital, where he took a keen interest in cocaine. Always intrigued by the hidden recesses of the mind, the life and works of Dostoevsky held an instinctive appeal for him. They would soon provide part of the inspiration for Freud's most influential theory, and another less influential idea: first, that all men, to some extent, wish for the death of their father figures and sexual union with their mother figures; and second, that addiction to gambling is a substitute for masturbation.* Freud considered *The Brothers Karamazov* 'the most magnificent novel ever written'.

---

*His theories were spectacularly wrong, of course, but they undoubtedly provoked new avenues of thought. As the anthropologist Tanya Luhrmann has memorably put it, 'Freud's theories were like a flashlight in a candle factory' ('Why Freud Survives', *New Yorker*, 28 August 2017).

A year after Dostoevsky died, and three years after he had written that 'without God, everything is permitted', Friedrich Nietzsche declared that 'God is dead'. He had just embarked on the decade in which he would write all his best-known works of philosophy. In 1887, just over a year before he went mad, he encountered Dostoevsky's *Devils*. He wrote in *Twilight of the Idols* that Dostoevsky was 'the only psychologist . . . from whom I had something to learn; he ranks among the most beautiful strokes of fortune in my life.' In January 1889, legend has it, Nietzsche saw a horse being flogged in the Piazza Carlo Alberto in Turin and ran over to it, weeping as he threw his arms around its neck. It was his first act of insanity, or perhaps his last act of sanity.

As a new century dawned and Modernism destroyed the conventions of art, the significance of Dostoevsky as a novelist became clear to a new generation. Thinking back on the Russian suppression of the Polish uprising and the imprisonment of his father, Joseph Conrad wrote *Under Western Eyes*, explicitly responding to *Crime and Punishment*. Virginia Woolf found that 'outside of Shakespeare there is no more exciting reading', and James Joyce saw Dostoevsky as 'the man more than any other who has created modern prose, and intensified it to its present-day pitch. It was his explosive power which shattered the Victorian novel.'

When the scholar Leonid Grossman met Anna Grigorievna over the course of the winter of 1916 in the newly renamed Petrograd,* she was still as sharp as a tack. 'I am not living in the twentieth century,'[449] she told him. 'I have remained in the 1870s. My people are the friends of Fyodor Mikhailovich, my coterie a band of people

---

* There is a melancholy joke about the many names the city went through in this era. In the joke, a KGB officer is interrogating an old refusenik. *Where were you born?* The old man answers, 'St Petersburg.' *Where did you grow up?* 'Petrograd.' *So where do you live now?* 'Leningrad.' *And where would you like to die?* The old man fixes his interlocutor with a stare. 'St Petersburg.'

who are gone. I live with them. And everyone who is studying the life or the works of Dostoevsky is a near relation.'

She lived alone, for the most part, helping to promote the works of Dostoevsky in Russia and abroad, delivering a comprehensive bibliography for a museum in Moscow, arranging the letters that she had meticulously kept and writing notes in the margins, transliterating parts of her diaries into longhand. 'There are moments in the life of everyone, when one needs to be alone, to tear oneself from the habitual rut, to endure one's sorrow away from the everyday bustle ... I am deeply convinced that this continuous realisation of one's designs is the only road to happiness. No, I can't complain – I have known happiness.'

In 1917, the revolution that Dostoevsky had predicted half a century before came to her hotel, but the soldiers knew who she was and left her alone out of respect. That summer, she travelled to the Caucasus, where she caught malaria along with most of the village. Her son, Fyodor, wrote to tell her to move away – the nearby railway works were throwing up clouds of mosquitoes – so she went to Yalta.*

Anna soon became too weak to return to Petrograd. At the start of 1918, Russia adopted the Gregorian calendar, and Anna stuttered out of existence along with the rest of the country between Wednesday 31 January and Thursday 14 February. In the spring, the German army cut the line of communication with her son. With no money, and no way of getting money, she found herself starving. One day, a well-wisher gave her two pounds of black bread and she ate it all immediately, inflaming her intestines.†

---

* By coincidence, Polina was also on the Crimean Peninsula that winter, in Sevastopol. The two women would die within months of one another.
† She and Fyodor had argued about wolfing bread before, in May 1867. Feeling sick, Anna had been eating bread with salt to try and calm her stomach. Fyodor told her that would only make her sicker; Anna said she didn't think so. Fyodor started shrieking that she was a wicked woman, which Anna found hilarious. (Fyodor did eventually concede that his reaction was comical.) Anna Dostoevsky, *Diary* (1928) pp. 135–6.

On 5 June a letter was sent to relatives explaining that she was in a critical condition, but in the confusion of the war, the post was all going missing. 'So,' a relative explains, 'sadly and in complete loneliness, without her children or relations, almost in poverty, died in the seventy-third year of her life Dostoevsky's most devoted friend, who had done so much for the writer's happiness during his life and for his name after his death.'[450]

It would be 50 years before, in accordance with her will, her body was laid to rest in the monastery, alongside her husband's.

———

The memory of a man is limited to a hundred years. For a hundred years after his death his children or his grandchildren, who have seen his face, can still remember him, but after that, though his memory may still remain, it is only by hearsay, in thought, for all who have seen his living face have gone. His grave is overgrown with grass, the stone crumbles away, and everyone forgets him; afterwards they forget even his name, for only a few are kept in the memory of men – and so be it! You may forget me, dear ones, but I love you from the tomb.[451]

NOTES

1   See *The Dostoevsky Encyclopedia*, p. xvii, Grossman, p. ix, Sekirin, p. 288.
2   Letter to Katkov, 8 July 1866.
3   Kjetsaa, pp. 309–10; Catteau, p. 118.
4   Orest Miller, from Sekirin, p. 48. More recently, the scholar Kenneth Lantz has noted that Dostoevsky 'exploited his biography for considerable literary power . . . Dostoevsky took considerable pains to let the aura of his life lend vibrancy to his art. The reader becomes aware of a region beyond the novel's story where the work seems to extend into a penumbra of textuality.' (*A Writer's Diary*, Volume 1, pp. 21–2)
5   'The Meek One', from *A Writer's Diary*, Volume 1, November 1876, p. 677.
6   'The Meek One', from *A Writer's Diary*, Volume 1, November 1876, p. 678.
7   *Crime and Punishment*, trans. Oliver Ready, p. 164.
8   *The Karamazov Brothers*, trans. Pevear and Volokhonsky, p. 4.
9   Letter to Mikhail, 22 December 1849.
10 'About F. M. Dostoevsky' by Orest Miller, in *The Dostoevsky Archive* by Peter Sekirin (McFarland & Co., 1997), p. 94.
11 *Lectures on Dostoevsky*, p. 52.
12 Letter to Mikhail, 22 December 1849.
13 *The Idiot*, p. 53.
14 Letter to Mikhail, 22 December 1849.
15 *The Idiot*, p. 54.
16 *The Idiot*, p. 57.
17 *The Brothers Karamazov*, trans. Garnett, p. 806.
18 *The Idiot*, p. 57.
19 Letter to Mikhail, 22 December 1849.
20 *The Insulted and Injured*, p. 11.

21 *Netochka Nezvanova*, p. 30.

22 *The Adolescent*, p. 71.

23 *Netochka Nezvanova*, p. 130.

24 Similarly, in *Devils*, Stepan Trofimovich remembers of his son: 'When he said his prayers going to bed he used to bow down to the ground, and make the sign of the cross on his pillow that he might not die in the night.' (*Devils*, p. 90)

25 *Poor Folk*, p. 125.

26 'The Peasant Marey', quoted in *Notes from the Underground and Other Stories*, trans. Garnett, pp. 638–40.

27 'The Peasant Marey', p. 640.

28 *A Writer's Diary*, Volume 1, April 1876, p. 438.

29 *The Brothers Karamazov*, trans. Garnett, p. 569.

30 *Poor Folk*, p. 29.

31 *Netochka Nezvanova*, p. 34.

32 *Poor Folk*, p. 29.

33 *Poor Folk*, p. 29.

34 *Netochka Nezvanova*, p. 158.

35 *The Insulted and the Injured*, p. 307.

36 *The Adolescent*, p. 219.

37 This line from the 1792 poem 'Epitaph' later appears in *The Idiot*, and also in a macabre short story, published in *A Writer's Diary*, of decaying bodies chatting to each other in a waterlogged cemetery.

38 *The Adolescent*, p. 219.

39 *Netochka Nezvanova*, p. 144.

40 *A Writer's Diary*, Volume One, *1873–1876*, trans. Kenneth Lantz, pp. 326–9.

41 *A Writer's Diary*, Volume One, pp. 326–9.

42 22 April 1847, *Dostoevsky's Occasional Writings*, ed. and trans. David Magarshack, 1963, p. 11.

43 *Notes from the Underground*, from *Notes from the Underground and Other Stories*, p. 458.

44 11 May 1847, *Dostoevsky's Occasional Writings*, ed. and trans. David Magarshack, 1963, pp. 24–5.

45 *Poor Folk*, 28 July and 5 August.

46 Frank, p. 47.

47 *Netochka Nezvanova*, p. 8.

48 These scant details compare unfavourably with the unusual arrangement between Totsky and the child Nastasya in *The Idiot*, pp. 36–9: 'Totsky, like all gentlemen who have lived freely in their day, felt contemptuously how cheaply he had obtained this virginal soul.'

49 *Netochka Nezvanova*, p. 10.

50 'Petersburg Visions in Verse and Prose', trans. Michael R. Katz, *New England Review*, 24:4 (2003), p. 101.

51 'Petersburg Visions in Verse and Prose', p. 101.

52 *Notes from the Underground*, pp. 483–4.

53 'Petersburg Visions in Verse and Prose', p. 102.

54 Letter to Mikhail, 30 September 1844.

55 Letter to Mikhail, 24 March 1845.

56 'Petersburg Visions in Verse and Prose', p. 103.

57 Letter to Mikhail, 30 September 1844.

58 *The Insulted and Injured*, p. 21.

59 Letter to Mikhail, 4 May 1845.

60 *A Writer's Diary*, Volume 2, January 1877, pp. 840ff.

61 *A Writer's Diary*, Volume 2, January 1877.

62 *A Writer's Diary*, Volume 2, January 1877.

63 *The Adolescent*, p. 53.

64 Grossman, p. 64.

65 *A Writer's Diary*, Volume 2, January 1877.

66 *A Writer's Diary*, Volume 2, January 1877.

67 Letter to Mikhail, 16 November 1845.

68 The work Turgenev read from was 'A Novel in Nine Letters'. In letter six, one slighted character writes, 'From the very beginning of our acquaintance you captivated me by your clever manners, by the subtlety of your behaviour, your knowledge of affairs and the advantages to be gained by association with you. I imagined I had found a true friend and well-wisher. Now I recognise clearly that there are many people who under a flattering and brilliant exterior hide venom in their hearts.' In letter seven, the indignant reply contains a passing reference to *Don Quixote*. For Dostoevsky, life would often follow art.

69 Letter to Mikhail, 16 November 1845.

70 22 April 1847, *Dostoevsky's Occasional Writings*, ed. and trans. David Magarshack, 1963, pp. 13–14.

71 *The Idiot*, p. 224. They seem to have been sending up Cervantes' *Don Quixote* via Pushkin's poem 'The Poor Knight'. Dostoevsky would spend a lifetime trying to turn this comparison to his advantage.

72 My version. For an alternative, full translation, see Marullo, p. 267.

73 *Netochka Nezvanova*, p. 21.

74 Frank, pp. 131–2.

75 *The Insulted and Injured*, pp. 46–7.

76 15 June 1847, *Dostoevsky's Occasional Writings*, p. 33.

77 'White Nights', p. 239.

78 Grossman, p. 105.

79 *Devils*, p. 33.

80 *Devils*, p. 22.

81 *Devils*, pp. 41–2.

82 *Crime and Punishment*, p. 562.

83 Frank, p. 149.

84 *Devils*, p. 398.

85 Frank, p. 158.

86 Frank, p. 152.

87 Robert Payne, *Dostoyevsky: A Human Portrait* (Knopf, 1961), p. 63.

88 *Crime and Punishment*, p. 527.

89 Maikov's recollection, quoted in Grossman, pp. 124–5.

90 *Crime and Punishment*, p. 456. When given a final chance to make a statement to the military court, he wrote: 'I never acted with an evil and premeditated intention against the government – what I did was done thoughtlessly and almost accidentally'. Even after his prison term, in 1856, he writes to Maikov that it was 'nothing but an accident'.

91 Frank, p. 183.

92 Sekirin, p. 108.

93 *The Brothers Karamazov*, trans. Garnett, p. 356.

94 *Memoirs from the House of the Dead*, trans. Jessie Coulson, 1956, p. 23, and *The House of the Dead*, trans. Constance Garnett, p. 22. I have used two translations for this chapter. The Russian word *zapiski* (записки) means notes or scribblings, the intention being that, like *Notes from the Underground*, these are incidental, discovered jottings by an imagined third party.

95 Frank, p. 191.

96 Frank, p. 191.

97 Garnett, p. 60, Coulson, p. 68.

98 Letter to Mikhail, 22 February 1854.

99 Garnett, p. 61, Coulson, p. 69.

100 Garnett, p. 70, Coulson, p. 78.

101 Garnett, p. 25, Coulson, p. 26.

102 Garnett, p. 14, Coulson, pp. 13–14.

103 Garnett, p. 10, Coulson, p. 9.

104 Garnett, p. 31, Coulson, p. 35.

105 Garnett, p. 34, Coulson, p. 38.

106 Garnett, p. 81, Coulson, p. 93.

107 Garnett, p. 87, Coulson, p. 99.

108 Garnett, p. 90, Coulson, p. 103.

109 Garnett, p. 92, Coulson, p. 106.

110 Garnett, pp. 94–5, Coulson, p. 109.

111 Garnett, p. 95, Coulson, p. 110.

112 Garnett, p. 23, Coulson, p. 24.

113 Garnett, p. 23, Coulson, p. 24.

114 Garnett, pp. 97–8, Coulson, pp. 112–13.

115 Garnett, p. 110, Coulson, p. 126.

116 Garnett, pp. 125–6, Coulson, p. 144.

117 Garnett, p. 126, Coulson, p. 145.

118 Garnett, p. 127, Coulson, p. 147.

119 Garnett, p. 99, Coulson, p. 113.

120 Garnett, p. 41, Coulson, p. 45.

121 Garnett, p. 45, Coulson, pp. 50–1.

122 'The Peasant Marey', quoted in *Notes from the Underground and Other Stories*, trans. Garnett, pp. 638–40.

123 'The Peasant Marey', p. 639.

124 Garnett, pp. 32–3, Coulson, p. 36, Frank, p. 192.

125 *The Brothers Karamazov*, p. 868.

126 Garnett, p. 171, Coulson, p. 199.

127 Garnett, p. 175, Coulson, p. 204.

128 Garnett, p. 177, Coulson, p. 207.

129 Garnett, p. 200, Coulson, p. 234.

130 Garnett, p. 201, Coulson, p. 236.

131 *The Insulted and Injured*, p. 249.

132 Garnett, p. 259, Coulson, p. 303.

133 Letter to Mikhail, 22 February 1854.

134 Garnett, p. 291, Coulson, p. 343.
135 Coulson, p. 266, Garnett, p. 228.
136 Garnett, p. 303, Coulson, p. 357.
137 Garnett, p. 304, Coulson, p. 357.
138 Letter to Natalia Fonvizina, 20 February 1854.
139 Garnett, p. 307, Coulson, p. 361.
140 Garnett, p. 307, Coulson, p. 361.
141 Quoted in *Crime and Punishment*, p. 393.
142 Letter to Mikhail, 22 February 1854.
143 Letter to Mikhail, 22 February 1854.
144 *The Insulted and Injured*, p. 1.
145 Letter to Natalia Fonvizina, 20 February 1854.
146 'Several Lost Letters of Dostoevsky', in Sekirin, p. 115.
147 Letter to Mikhail, 13 January 1856.
148 Letter to Mikhail, 13 January 1856.
149 Letter to Natalia Fonvizina, 20 February 1854.
150 Letter to Mikhail, 13 January 1856.
151 *Crime and Punishment*, trans. Ready, p. 31.
152 Letter to Maria, 4 June 1855.
153 Grossman, p. 195, Sekirin, p. 125.
154 *Crime and Punishment*, p. 317.
155 Letter to Maria, 4 June 1855.
156 Letter to Maria, 4 June 1855.
157 Letter to Maikov, 18 January 1856.
158 Letter to Wrangel, 23 March 1856.
159 Letter to Wrangel, 23 March 1856.
160 *Notes from the Underground*, p. 459.
161 *The Insulted and Injured*, p. 30.
162 Letter to Wrangel, 14 July 1856.
163 Letter to Wrangel, 14 July 1856.
164 Letter to Wrangel, 14 July 1856.
165 Letter to Wrangel, 14 July 1856.
166 *The Insulted and Injured*, p. 39.
167 Letter to Wrangel, 14 July 1856.
168 Letter to Wrangel, 9 November 1856.
169 *Crime and Punishment*, trans. Ready, pp. 31–2.
170 *The Idiot*, pp. 203–4.
171 *Devils*, p. 610.

172 *The Idiot*, pp. 204. I have used a little poetic licence here: Strakhov describes this exact fit, with its feeling of exaltation, as occurring on Easter Eve 1863. (Catteau, p. 114)

173 Letter to Mikhail, 9 March 1857.

174 Letter to Mikhail, 9 March 1857.

175 *Crime and Punishment*, trans. Ready, pp. 22, 30–1.

176 *A Writer's Diary*, Volume 2, September 1877, pp. 1,130.

177 Letter to Varvara Konstant, 30 November 1857.

178 Interestingly, in his *Writer's Diary* of 1881, one of the last articles that he wrote, he repurposes his Columbus analogy to argue for Russia to turn away from Europe and towards Asia: 'When we turn to Asia [it will be akin to] what happened to Europe when they discovered America. It's true – Asia is our America, which we still haven't discovered.'

179 *The Insulted and Injured*, p. 74.

180 *The Insulted and Injured*, p. 75.

181 *The Insulted and Injured*, p. 11.

182 Letter to Mikhail, 9 May 1859.

183 Letter to Artemy Geybovich, 23 October 1859.

184 Letter to Wrangel, 22 September 1859.

185 Sekirin, p. 143.

186 *Devils*, p. 106.

187 *Crime and Punishment*, trans. Ready, pp. 138–9.

188 *Crime and Punishment*, trans. Ready, pp. 139–40.

189 Letter to Alexandra Shubert, 3 May 1860.

190 *Time* editorial, quoted in Grossman, p. 223.

191 *The Idiot*, p. 184.

192 Letter to Miliukov, 10 September 1860.

193 *The Insulted and Injured*, p. 284.

194 *The Insulted and Injured*, p. 311.

195 'Why was Dostoevsky not Published in the Prestigious Journals?' by P. M. Kovalevsky, quoted in Sekirin, pp. 147–8.

196 *Crime and Punishment*, p. 311.

197 *Devils*, p. 307.

198 *The Brothers Karamazov*, p. 160.

199 *Devils*, p. 496.

200 *Devils*, p. 511.

201 *Devils*, p. 535.

202 *A Writer's Diary*, Volume 1, p. 148.

203 *A Writer's Diary*, Volume 1, p. 149.

204 *Winter Notes on Summer Impressions*, p. 30.

205 Frank, p. 348.

206 Walter G. Moss, *Russia in the Age of Alexander II, Tolstoy and Dostoevsky*, Anthem, 2002, p. 79.

207 Letter to Strakhov, 26 June (8 July) 1862.

208 Letter to Yakov Polonsky, 31 July 1861.

209 Letter to Strakhov, 26 June (8 July) 1862.

210 *Winter Notes on Summer Impressions*, p. 52.

211 *Winter Notes on Summer Impressions*, p. 54.

212 *Winter Notes on Summer Impressions*, p. 55.

213 Letter to Nikolai Dostoevsky, 16 (28) August 1863.

214 Polina's diary, from *The Gambler*, trans. Victor Terras, pp. 205–6.

215 *The Idiot*, p. 386.

216 Polina's diary, from *The Gambler*, p. 202.

217 Letter to Varvara Constant, 20 August (1 September) 1863.

218 Polina's diary, from *The Gambler*, p. 211.

219 Grossman, pp. 285ff.

220 *The Gambler*, trans. Garnett, p. 8.

221 *The Gambler*, trans. Garnett, p. 48.

222 Polina's diary, from *The Gambler*, p. 214.

223 *The Gambler,* trans. Terras, p. 23, trans. Garnett, p. 326.

224 Letter to Mikhail, 8 (20) September 1863.

225 Letter to Varvara Constant, 20 August (1 September) 1863.

226 *The Idiot*, p. 330.

227 Polina's diary, from *The Gambler*, p. 217.

228 Frank, p. 394.

229 *The Gambler*, trans. Terras, pp. 142–3, trans. Garnett, p. 413.

230 Polina's diary, from *The Gambler*, p. 219.

231 Polina's diary, from *The Gambler*, pp. 219–20.

232 *The Gambler*, trans. Terras p. 14, trans. Garnett, p. 319.

233 Letter to Strakhov, 18 (30) September 1863.

234 *Crime and Punishment*, p. 343.

235 *Notes from the Underground*, p. 468.

236 *Notes from the Underground*, p. 472.

237 *Notes from the Underground*, p. 475.

238 *Notes from the Underground*, passim.

239 Letter to Mikhail, 26 March 1864.

240 *The Idiot*, p. 65.

241 Letter to Mikhail, 26 March 1864.

242 *Crime and Punishment*, trans. Ready, p. 519.

243 *Crime and Punishment*, trans. Ready, p. 506.

244 *Crime and Punishment*, trans. Ready, p. 521.

245 Letter to Wrangel, 31 March 1865.

246 Letter to Andrei Dostoevsky, 29 July 1864.

247 Letter to Wrangel, 9 March 1865 (continued 9 April, 14 April).

248 *The Idiot*, p. 112.

249 Letter to Wrangel, 9 March 1865 (continued 9 April, 14 April).

250 *Crime and Punishment*, trans. Ready, p. 530.

251 *Crime and Punishment*, trans. Ready, p. 530.

252 *Notes from the Underground*, p. 515.

253 *Crime and Punishment*, trans. Ready, p. 346.

254 We see a tantalising hint of Martha in *The Idiot*, when Nastasya says to Myshkin, 'Nobody ever spoke to me like that before. They bought and sold me, but no decent man ever wooed me.'

255 *Crime and Punishment*, trans. Ready, p. 403.

256 Frank, p. 450.

257 'How Dostoevsky proposed to Anna Korvin-Krukovskaya' by Sofia Kovalevskaya, in Sekirin, pp. 176–7.

258 Letter to Nadezhda Suslova, 19 April 1865.

259 Letter to Wrangel, 9 March 1865 (continued 9 April, 14 April).

260 Letter to Katkov, September 1865.

261 *Crime and Punishment*, trans. Ready, p. 547.

262 *Crime and Punishment*, trans. Ready, p. 501.

263 *The Idiot*, p. 410.

264 *Notebooks for Crime and Punishment*, trans. Edward Wasiolek (1967), p. 64. The metaphor had been on his mind since the drafting of *Notes from the Underground* – see p. 513, in which the Underground Man punches his driver in the back of the head. He had also recently read a new poem by Nekrasov in *The Contemporary*, 'About the Weather', in which a weak horse is mercilessly beaten by its owner.

265 Letter to Anna Korvin-Krukovskaya, 17 June 1866.

266 *The Adolescent*, p. 158.

267 *The Adolescent*, p. 158.

268 Letter to Polina, 12 (24) August 1865.

269 Letter to Wrangel, 16 (28) September 1865.

270 Letter to Katkov, 25 April 1866.

271 Letter to Anna Korvin-Krukovskaya, April–May 1866.

272 Letter to Alexander Miliukov, 10–15 July 1866.

273 This insult would be used by fictional children 12 years later to humiliate Captain Snegiryov in *The Brothers Karamazov*.

274 *Crime and Punishment*, p. 615.

275 Letter to Anna Korvin-Krukovskaya, 17 June 1866.

276 Letter to Miliukov, 10–15 July 1866.

277 Miliukov's recollection, quoted in Grossman, pp. 391ff.

278 *Notes from the Underground*, p. 540.

279 *Dostoevsky Portrayed by His Wife*, ed. and trans. S. S. Koteliansky, p. 9.

280 *Dostoevsky Portrayed by His Wife*, pp. 12–13.

281 *The Eternal Husband*, in *Three Short Novels of Dostoevsky*, p. 298.

282 *Dostoevsky Portrayed by His Wife*, p. 22.

283 *Dostoevsky Portrayed by His Wife*, p. 23.

284 Frank, p. 514.

285 *Dostoevsky Portrayed by His Wife*, p. 24.

286 *Dostoevsky Portrayed by His Wife*, p. 31.

287 *Crime and Punishment*, trans. Ready, p. 570.

288 *Dostoevsky Portrayed by his Wife*, pp. 42–4.

289 *Crime and Punishment*, p. 571.

290 *Dostoevsky: Reminiscences*, p. 65.

291 *Notes from the Underground*, p. 463.

292 Letter to Polina, 23 April (5 May) 1867.

293 Letter to Polina, 23 April (5 May) 1867.

294 Letter to Maikov, 16 (28) August 1867.

295 *Winter Notes on Summer Impressions*, p. 69.

296 Letter to Anna, 12 (24) May 1867.

297 *Devils*, p. 25. It is interesting to see how the *Sistine Madonna* evolves as a symbol up to the final novel, when Dmitri Karamazov laments: 'I can't endure the thought that man starts with the ideal of the Madonna and ends with the ideal of Sodom. What's worse is that the man with Sodom in his soul doesn't renounce the ideal of the Madonna, and his heart may be on fire with that ideal, genuinely on fire, just as in his days of youth and innocence.' (*The Brothers Karamazov*, p. 114)

298 Anna became quite fascinated with a young invalid girl who was accompanied everywhere by a handsome young man she seemed to adore, not unlike the characters of Stavrogin and Maria in *Devils*.

299 *Notes from the Underground*, p. 522.

300 Letter to Maikov, 16 (28) August 1867.

301 *The Adolescent*, p. 183.

302 *The Adolescent*, p. 200.

303 *The Idiot*, p. 281.

304 *The Unpublished Dostoevsky*, Volume 2, p. 72.

305 *Devils*, p. 331.

306 *Devils*, p. 358.

307 *Devils*, p. 357.

308 Letter to Maikov, 16 (28) August 1867. Anna recounts a version of the conversation in her diary, pp. 238–9.

309 'Memoirs about Turgenev and Dostoevsky' by E. M. Garshin, quoted in Sekirin, p. 243.

310 Letter to Maikov, 16 (28) August 1867.

311 *The Adolescent*, p. 182.

312 *The Adolescent*, p. 7.

313 *Devils*, pp. 424–5 (from Stavrogin's unpublished confession).

314 *The Diary of Dostoyevsky's Wife*, p. 266.

315 *The Diary of Dostoyevsky's Wife*, p. 298.

316 *The Idiot*, p. 309.

317 Letter to Maikov, 16 (28) August 1867.

318 Letter to Stepan Yanovsky, 21–22 February (4–5 March) 1868.

319 Letter to Maikov, 16 (28) August 1867.

320 Letter to Sofia Ivanova, 29 September (11 October) 1867.

321 Letter to Sofia Ivanova, 29 September (11 October) 1867.

322 Letter to Maikov, 31 December 1867 (12 January 1868).

323 Letter to Maikov, 31 December 1867 (12 January 1868).

324 *The Idiot*, p. 485.

325 Letter to Maikov, 18 February (1 March) 1868.

326 *The Idiot*, p. 181.

327 Letter to Maikov, 18 February (1 March) 1868. He reprises the theme in his letter to Maikov on 21–22 March (2–3 April).

328 *The Idiot*, p. 343.

329 *The Idiot*, p. 338.

330 *The Idiot*, p. 339.

331 *The Idiot*, p. 411.

332 Letter to Pasha, 19 February (2 March) 1868.

333 *Devils*, p. 611. Shatov is the figure most closely aligned with Dostoevsky in the book.

334 Letter to Stepan Yanovsky, 21–22 February (4–5 March) 1868.

335 *Devils*, p. 611.

336 *Devils*, p. 612.

337 Letter to Maikov, 21–22 March (2–3 April) 1868.

338 *The Idiot*, p. 199.

339 *The Idiot*, p. 365.

340 Letter to Anna, 23 March (4 April) 1868.

341 Letter to Maikov, 18 (30) May 1868.

342 *The Adolescent*, p. 62.

343 *The Adolescent*, p. 62.

344 *The Adolescent*, p. 62.

345 Letter to Maikov, 18 (30) May 1868.

346 *Reminiscences*, ed. S. V. Belov and V. A. Tunimanov, p. 148.

347 *The Idiot*, p. 383.

348 *The Idiot*, pp. 278–9.

349 It is interesting to compare Pasha's behaviour, as described in the letter to Katkov, 3 March 1868, with the attitude of Arkady Dolgoruky in the first part of *The Adolescent*.

350 Letter to Maikov, 18 (30) May 1868.

351 'The Dream of a Ridiculous Man', from *Notes from the Underground and Other Stories*, p. 648.

352 Letter to Maikov, 22 June (4 July) 1868.

353 *The Idiot*, p. 345.

354 Letter to Maikov, 26 October (7 November) 1868.

355 According to research presented by Valentina Supino at the XVII Symposium of the International Dostoevsky Society (2019).

356 Letter to Strakhov, 14 (26) August 1869.

357 Letter to Strakhov, 26 February (10 March) 1869.

358 Letter to Sofia Ivanovna, 29 August (10 September) 1869.

359 Anna sees in it a fictional mirror of his 1866 holiday in Liublino, with Alexander Lobov an idealised version of Pasha, and Velchaninov sharing some characteristics with Dostoevsky.

360 Letter to Maikov, 12 (24) February 1870.

361 *The Idiot*, p. 232.

362 *Devils*, p. 346.
363 Letter to Strakhov, 26 February (10 March) 1869.
364 *The Unpublished Dostoevsky*, Volume 3, p. 139.
365 Frank, p. 604.
366 Letter to Maikov, 9 (21) October 1870.
367 Letter to Sofia Ivanova, 9 (21) October 1870.
368 Letter to Katkov, 8 (20) October 1870.
369 Letter to Sofia Ivanova, 17 (29) August 1870.
370 Letter to Strakhov, 18 (30) May 1871.
371 *The Adolescent*, pp. 180–1.
372 Letter to Anna, 16 (28) April 1871.
373 Letter to Maikov, 30 December 1870 (11 January 1871).
374 Grossman (p. 49). *The Dostoevsky Encyclopedia* (p. 200) attributes the quotation to something he wrote in the album of an acquaintance in 1873, which would imply either that he didn't know his real age, or that he didn't want to give it. This is corroborated by a letter dated 9 April 1876, when, at 54, he claims to be 53.
375 Letter to Strakhov, 2 (14) December 1870.
376 *Devils*, p. 567.
377 'Bobok', from *A Writer's Diary*, Volume 1, p. 171.
378 'Bobok', from *A Writer's Diary*, Volume 1, p. 170.
379 *Reminiscences*, p. 204.
380 *The Adolescent*, p. 111.
381 Letter to Strakhov, 23 April (5 May) 1871.
382 'Bobok', in *Notes from the Underground and Other Stories*, p. 580.
383 'The Heavenly Christmas Tree', in *Notes from the Underground and Other Stories*, p. 596.
384 Letter to Meshchersky, 12 November 1873. The last sentence was inked out in the original.
385 *The Adolescent*, p. 351.
386 Frank, p. 673.
387 Letter to Strakhov, 18 (30) May 1871.
388 *The Adolescent*, p. 364.
389 *Reminiscences*, p. 229.
390 *The Adolescent*, p. 94.
391 Letter to Anna, 6 February 1875.
392 Vsevolod Soloviev's recollection, in Sekirin, pp. 209–10.
393 Letter to Anna, 7 February 1875.

394   Letter to Anna, 10 (22) June 1875.

395   Letter to Anna, 13 (25) June 1875. An intriguing counterfactual would be to consider whether anything might have changed if Tolstoy's novel had been published in *Notes of the Fatherland* and Dostoevsky's in *The Russian Herald*. Of his five long novels, *The Adolescent* is the least well known and also the only one that didn't benefit from the circulation of *The Russian Herald* and the influence of Katkov as a patron. How much did his reputation suffer from alienating the readership he had been cultivating for the past ten years?

396   *A Writer's Diary*, Volume 2, July and August 1877, recalling the spring of 1876.

397   *Devils*, pp. 124–5.

398   *Devils*, pp. 124–5. His *Writer's Diary* was wildly popular at the time, though he is now more respected as a novelist and philosopher than as a political commentator. One of his more bizarre military ideas was for Russia to build a huge, slow, flat-bottomed ship – a sitting duck, effectively – to send to Europe as a sign that it wanted peace rather than war. Funnily enough, Russia did unintentionally construct a similar warship around this time, known as the Popovka, a slow, circular, flat-bottomed ship that spun off course whenever one of its cannon was fired: *Popovki too are essential.* (*The Unpublished Dostoevsky*, Volume 3, p. 79)

399   Letter to Pyotr Bykov, 15 April 1876. *I will observe in parenthesis that a true autobiography is almost impossible, and that man is bound to lie about himself* (*Notes from the Underground*, p. 481). At this time, he may have been reluctant: as Arkady says at the opening of *The Adolescent*, 'I shall never sit down to write my autobiography even if I live to be a hundred. One must be too disgustingly in love with the self to write without shame about oneself.' (*The Adolescent*, p. 3) Nevertheless, he later warmed to the idea.

400   *Reminiscences*, pp. 262–4.

401   Letter to Anna, 6 (18) August 1876 Many of the bluest passages in the letters are inked out by Anna, but some of Fyodor's allusions to feet are saved – see also his letter of 16 (28) August 1879: 'I am dying to kiss every toe on your foot . . . If I weren't put out by what you say about postal censorship, God only knows what I'd write to you.'

He shares this fixation with the character of Rakitin in *The Brothers Karamazov*, who writes a poem about Madame Hokhlakov's 'captivating little foot', a pastiche of Pushkin, who wrote about the love of women's feet in *Eugene Onegin*.

402 Letter to Anna, 17 July 1877.

403 She is embodied in the character of Stinking Lizaveta in *The Brothers Karamazov*.

404 *A Writer's Diary*, Volume 2, December 1877.

405 *Reminiscences*, p. 288.

406 *A Writer's Diary*, Volume 2, December 1877.

407 Letter to Stephan Yanovsky, 17 December 1877.

408 *The Idiot*, p. 13.

409 *The Idiot*, p. 60.

410 *The Idiot*, p. 212.

411 Letter to Nikolai Dostoevsky, 16 May 1878.

412 *The Brothers Karamazov*, pp. 49–50.

413 *The Brothers Karamazov*, p. 50. Joseph Frank points to these words as 'those that Father Ambrose told Dostoevsky to convey to his wife'. Frank, *Dostoevsky: The Mantle of the Prophet, 1871–1881*, Volume 5 (2002), p. 385.

414 *The Brothers Karamazov*, pp. 266–8.

415 Letter to Pobedonostsev, 9 (21) August 1879.

416 'Dostoevsky's meeting with the Anti-Christ' by I. I. Iasinsky, from Sekirin, pp. 226–7.

417 Sekirin, pp. 227–8.

418 *The Adolescent*, p. 15.

419 *Devils*, p. 499.

420 *Crime and Punishment*, p. 483.

421 *Devils*, p. 505.

422 Quotes are as printed in *A Writer's Diary*, Volume 2, August 1880.

423 He had been developing this argument since *The Adolescent*, pp. 302ff. Towards the end of his life, Dostoevsky is often accused of foam-flecked nationalism, but his excesses deserve to be set in context. Even the cosmopolitan Turgenev wrote in an 1860 letter, 'I cannot tell you how deeply I hate everything French and especially Parisian.' (Figes, *The Europeans*, p. 259) This is, after all, the era of Italian and German unification, and the grand unifying

theory that Dostoevsky posits in his Pushkin speech is not so very different from Victor Hugo's idea of a federated Europe with Paris as its capital.

424 *The Brothers Karamazov*, p. 837.

425 *The Brothers Karamazov*, p. 841.

426 Letter to Anna, 8 June 1880.

427 Letter to Anna, 8 June 1880.

428 Sekirin, p. 253.

429 Sekirin, p. 253.

430 Letter to Pelageya Egorovna Guseva, 15 October 1880.

431 *Crime and Punishment*, pp. 538–9.

432 *The Idiot*, pp. 36–7.

433 Frank, *Dostoevsky: The Mantle of the Prophet, 1871–1881*, Volume 5 (2002), p. 561.

434 Letter to Nikolai Lyubimov, 8 November 1880.

435 *The Adolescent*, p. 338.

436 *Crime and Punishment*, p. 529.

437 *Crime and Punishment*, p. 347.

438 *The Adolescent*, p. 140.

439 *Notebook for A Raw Youth*, p. 464.

440 *The Adolescent*, p. 50.

441 *The Adolescent*, pp. 305–6.

442 *Reminiscences*, p. 346.

443 'The Dream of a Ridiculous Man', from *Notes from the Underground and Other Stories*, pp. 651ff.

444 After Dostoevsky's death, Maikov recalled: '"Oh, if only people could understand, then there would be paradise on earth," he used to say.' (Sekirin, p. 285)

445 Raskolnikov kisses the earth in repentance at the end of *Crime and Punishment*; Shatov urges Stavrogin to kiss the earth in *Devils*, but Stavrogin's confession was never published and redemption eludes him (in contrast to his wife Maria, who kisses the earth when she prays); at the exact midpoint of *The Brothers Karamazov* Alyosha kisses the earth in holy rapture. *It was as if threads from all those innumerable worlds all came together in his soul, and it was trembling all over, touching other worlds.* (*The Brothers Karamazov*, p. 404)

446 *Devils*, p. 209.
447 *Imperial Russia: A Source Book*, ed. Basil Dmytryshyn (Holt, Rinehart
     & Winston, 1967), p. 314.
448 *The Village of Stepanchikovo*, p. xxi.
449 *Dostoevsky Portrayed by his Wife*, p. xi.
450 *Dostoevsky Portrayed by his Wife*, p. xvi.
451 *The Adolescent*, p. 232.
452 *Notes from the Underground*, p. 545.

SELECT BIBLIOGRAPHY
(with a note on the translation wars)

I am not a translator but Dostoevsky's writing had to end up in English one way or another. Over the last hundred years, there have been heated debates about the translation of Dostoevsky's work into English (and critiques of the debates, making the whole discussion a fractal nightmare). In the past couple of decades some have claimed that Richard Pevear and Larissa Volokhonsky have produced the most authoritative modern translations, notably David Remnick in his *New Yorker* essay, 'The Translation Wars'. Gary Saul Morson, a literary critic and Slavist at Northwestern University, vehemently disagreed in an article on 'The Pevearsion [sic] of Russian Literature', where he argued that they 'take glorious works and reduce them to awkward and unsightly muddles'. By contrast, he thought Constance Garnett's translations 'magnificent'.

Undoubtedly Garnett has the dubious privilege, as Dostoevsky's first popular translator,* of fighting off each new challenger. Ernest Hemingway loved her translations, but Vladimir Nabokov hated them.† Penguin translator David Magarshack felt that Garnett had failed to capture Dostoevsky's humour (according to academic

---

*With apologies to Fred Whishaw.

† Although it's worth pointing out that Nabokov also hated Dostoevsky himself with a passion that can only be described as Oedipal, calling him 'a claptrap journalist and a slapdash comedian' and claiming that 'his sensitive murderers and soulful prostitutes are not to be endured'. Funny, then, that he borrowed so liberally: Nabokov's best-known protagonist, Humbert Humbert, is a direct descendant of Stavrogin and Svidrigailov; his Hermann Karlovich, in *Despair*, an explicit descendant of Golyadkin and Raskolnikov.

Cathy McAteer, his own translations restored Dostoevsky's famed polyphony, but 'some of Magarshack's decisions irritated readers'). Joseph Frank uses Garnett's translations because 'she takes fewer liberties with the literal meaning than more recent translators', but Pevear and Volokhonsky weren't translating when he began his monumental project. Boris Jakim's translations are well regarded but do not cover all of Dostoevsky's works. Victor Terras, in his *Reading Dostoevsky*, is judicious: 'Pevear's translation serves the scholarly reader better, as it brings him or her closer to Dostoevsky's craftsmanship. Garnett's somewhat old-fashioned English has great charm and is close to the ethos of Dostoevsky's Victorian narrator. It is not quite Dostoevsky, falling short of the prodigious energy of his dialogue, but the general reader may find it preferable to Pevear's.' She translated most of Dostoevsky's fiction, allowing for a relatively consistent voice, but most importantly, I like her style (my dream that Oliver Ready will take a twenty-year sabbatical to translate the complete works is yet to be realised).

Garnett is sometimes accused of sanding down Dostoevsky's tone and register, of smoothing and filtering him so that he might be poured out of bone china. The *Paris Review*, in its 'Art of Translation' series, takes issue with her 'Victorian elision', which is very unfair because most of her translations were Edwardian. Where I felt that Garnett might be making Dostoevsky appear uncharacteristically diplomatic or toothless, as in *Notes from the House of the Dead*, the translations I present were informed by others.

Below, I have given the print editions that are most widely available, though the lesser works are more easily accessible in ebook. The Garnett translations were first published in a 12-volume octavo edition produced by William Heinemann between 1913 and 1920. The most authoritative edition of Dostoevsky's work in Russian is the 30-volume complete collected works published by the Institute of Russian Literature (Leningrad, 1972–90), which contains his correspondence. Translations of the latter are available from Ardis (complete, albeit out of print and hard to get) and from Routledge (selected) – in addition to these, I am grateful for the translation advice of Ilona Chavasse, who helped ensure the translations and paraphrases I used remained faithful to the sense of the original. There are also thorough resources available online at fedordostoevsky.ru and dostoevsky-lit.ru.

Beer, Daniel, *The House of the Dead* (Allen Lane, 2016)

Carr, Edward Hallett, *Dostoevsky: A New Biography* (George Allen & Unwin, 1931)

Catteau, Jacques, *Dostoyevsky and the Process of Literary Creation* (Cambridge University Press, 1989)

Dostoevsky, Andrey, *Vospominaniia* (Izdatel'stvo pisateleĭ v Leningrade, 1930)*

Dostoevsky,† Anna, *The Diary of Dostoyevsky's Wife*, ed. René Fülöp-Miller and Friedrich Echstein, trans. Madge Pemberton (Gollancz, 1928)

Dostoevsky, Anna, *Dostoevsky Portrayed by his Wife*, ed. and trans. S. S. Koteliansky (Routledge, 1926)

Dostoevsky, Anna, *Dostoevsky: Reminiscences*, ed. S. V. Belov and V. A. Tunimanov (W. W. Norton, 1975)

Dostoevsky, Fyodor, *Complete Letters*, Volume One, *1832–1859*, ed. and trans. David Lowe and Ronald Meyer (Ardis, 1988)

Dostoevsky, Fyodor, *Complete Letters*, Volume Two, *1860–1867*, ed. and trans. David Lowe and Ronald Meyer (Ardis, 1988)

Dostoevsky, Fyodor, *Complete Letters*, Volume Three, *1868–1871*, ed. and trans. David Lowe and Ronald Meyer (Ardis, 1988)

Dostoevsky, Fyodor, *Complete Letters*, Volume Four, *1872–1877*, ed. and trans. David Lowe and Ronald Meyer (Ardis, 1988)

Dostoevsky, Fyodor, *Complete Letters*, Volume Five, *1878–1881*, ed. and trans. David Lowe and Ronald Meyer (Ardis, 1988)

Dostoevsky, Fyodor, *Crime and Punishment*, trans. Constance Garnett (Wordsworth Editions, 2000)

*This is one of the few primary sources not translated into English in its entirety, which is sad because it contains such a wealth of detail on Dostoevsky's early life. Portions are available in the works of Joseph Frank, Thomas Marullo, Peter Sekirin and a few others.

† Her surname in Russian is Dostoevskaya.

Dostoevsky, Fyodor, *Devils*, trans. Constance Garnett (Wordsworth Editions, 2005)*

Dostoevsky, Fyodor, *Dostoevsky: Letters and Reminiscences*, trans. S. S. Koteliansky and J. Middleton Murray (Chatto & Windus 1923)

Dostoevsky, Fyodor, *Dostoevsky's Occasional Writings*, ed. and trans. David Magarshack (Random House, 1963)

Dostoevsky, Fyodor, *The Friend of the Family; or, Stepantchikovo and its Inhabitants*,† trans. Constance Garnett (William Heinemann, 1920)

Dostoevsky, Fyodor, *The Gambler & Other Stories* [containing *Poor Folk*], trans. Constance Garnett (Macmillan, 1917)

Dostoevsky, Fyodor, *The Gambler with the Diary of Polina Suslova*, trans. Victor Terras, ed. Edward Wasiolek (University of Chicago Press, 1972)

Dostoevsky, Fyodor, *The House of the Dead & The Gambler*, trans. Constance Garnett (Wordsworth Editions, 2010)‡

Dostoevsky, Fyodor, *The Idiot*, trans. Constance Garnett (Wordsworth Editions, 2010)

Dostoevsky, Fyodor, *The Insulted and Injured*,§ trans. Constance Garnett (William Heinemann, 1947)

Dostoevsky, Fyodor, *The Karamazov Brothers*,¶ trans. Constance Garnett (Wordsworth Editions, 2007)

Dostoevsky, Fyodor, *Memoirs from the House of the Dead*, trans. Jessie Coulson (Oxford, 1983)

* The title has been variously translated as *Devils*, *Demons* and *The Possessed*. The Russian title, Бесы or *besy*, is a house devil from folk tradition, but in the relevant passage of the novel it is an extended metaphor taken from the Biblical story of the devils being exorcised and cast into the swine. In this metaphor, Russia is the sick man, and so the revolutionaries are not 'the possessed' but the devils that must be cast out.
† Now better known as *The Village of Stepanchikovo*.
‡ Strictly speaking it should be *Notes from the House of the Dead*. The Russian word Записки or *zapiski* points to a Russian genre that means notes or scribblings, the intention being that, like *Notes from the Underground*, these are the incidental papers of an imagined third party.
§ The interminable versions of this title include *Humiliated and Insulted*, *Insulted and Humiliated* and *Injury and Insult*. This is probably the title that could most easily stand as a spoof title for any of his other books and the phrase crops up throughout his fiction, as early as *Netochka Nezvanova* (p. 28).
¶ More commonly styled *The Brothers Karamazov*.

Dostoevsky, Fyodor, *The Notebooks for The Brothers Karamazov*, ed. and trans. Edward Wasiolek (University of Chicago Press, 1971)

Dostoevsky, Fyodor, *The Notebooks for Crime and Punishment*, ed. and trans. Edward Wasiolek (University of Chicago Press, 1967)

Dostoevsky, Fyodor, *The Notebooks for The Idiot*, ed. Edward Wasiolek, trans. Katharine Strelsky (University of Chicago Press, 1967)

Dostoevsky, Fyodor, *The Notebooks for A Raw Youth*, ed. Edward Wasiolek, trans. Victor Terras (University of Chicago Press, 1969)

Dostoevsky, Fyodor, *The Notebooks for The Possessed*, ed. Edward Wasiolek, trans. Victor Terras (University of Chicago Press, 1968)

Dostoevsky, Fyodor, *Notes from the Underground & Other Stories*, trans. Constance Garnett (Wordsworth Editions, 2015)*

Dostoevsky, Fyodor, *Poor People*, trans. Hugh Aplin (Alma, 2002)

Dostoevsky, Fyodor, *Three Short Novels of Dostoevsky* [from which I quote *The Eternal Husband*], trans. Constance Garnett (International Collectors Library, 1960)†

Dostoevsky, Fyodor, *The Unpublished Dostoevsky*, Volume 1, ed. Carl R. Proffer (Ardis, 1973)

Dostoevsky, Fyodor, *The Unpublished Dostoevsky*, Volume 2, ed. Carl R. Proffer (Ardis, 1975)

Dostoevsky, Fyodor, *The Unpublished Dostoevsky*, Volume 3, ed. Carl R. Proffer (Ardis, 1976)

Dostoevsky, Fyodor, *Winter Notes on Summer Impressions*, trans. Kyril Fitzlyon (Oneworld Classics, 2008)

Dostoevsky, Fyodor, *A Writer's Diary*, Volume 1, trans. Kenneth Lantz (Northwestern University Press, 1993)

Dostoevsky, Fyodor, *A Writer's Diary*, Volume 2, trans. Kenneth Lantz (Northwestern University Press, 1994)

Dostoyevsky, Fyodor, *Crime and Punishment*, trans. Oliver Ready (Penguin, 2015)

---

* Literally, *Notes from Under the Floorboards*. Under the floorboards is where you might look for evil spirits in Russia, whereas English monsters seem to prefer living under the bed. C. J. Hogarth translated it as *Letters from the Underworld*, which is so bad the average reader could have done better with a Russian–French dictionary.

† Whishaw translates *The Eternal Husband* as the rather more flatfooted *The Permanent Husband*.

Dostoyevsky, Fyodor, *A Raw Youth (The Adolescent)*, trans. Constance Garnett (Digireads, 2009)*

Dostoyevsky, Fyodor, *Selected Letters of Fyodor Dostoyevsky*, ed. Joseph Frank and David I. Goldstein, trans. Andrew MacAndrew (Rutgers University Press, 1989)

Dostoyevsky, Fyodor, *The Village of Stepanchikovo*, trans. Ignat Avsey (Angel, 1983)

Figes, Orlando, *The Europeans* (Allen Lane, 2019)

Frank, Joseph, *Dostoevsky* (Princeton University Press, 2010)†

Frank, Joseph, *Lectures on Dostoevsky*, ed. Marina Brodskaya and Marguerite Frank (Princeton University Press, 2020)

Grossman, Leonid, *Dostoevsky*, trans. Mary Mackler (Allen Lane, 1974)

Jones, John, *Dostoevsky* (Oxford University Press, 1985)

Kelly, Laurence, *St Petersburg* (Constable, 1981)

Kjetsaa, Geir, *Fyodor Dostoevsky: A Writer's Life* (Macmillan, 1988)

Lantz, Kenneth, *The Dostoevsky Encyclopedia* (Greenwood, 2004)

Marullo, Thomas Gaiton, *Fyodor Dostoevsky: In the Beginning, 1821–1845* (Northern Illinois University Press, 2016)

Miles, Jonathan, *St Petersburg* (Windmill, 2018)

Sekirin, Peter, *The Dostoevsky Archive* (McFarland & Co., 1997)

Slonim, Marc, *Three Loves of Dostoevsky* (Alvin Redman, 1957)

Terras, Victor, *Reading Dostoevsky* (University of Wisconsin Press, 1998)

Troyat, Henri, *Firebrand*, trans. Norbert Guterman (Roy, 1946)

Turgenev, Ivan, *Letters*, Volume One, ed. and trans. David Lowe (Ardis, 1983)

Turgenev, Ivan, *Letters*, Volume Two, ed. and trans. David Lowe (Ardis, 1983)

Hadn't I better end my notes here?[452]

* Garnett's first translation of the book is titled *A Raw Youth*, but the Russian title, *Podrostok* (Подросток), literally means 'adolescent'. Richard Freeborn's translation goes with *An Accidental Family*, taking up the theme of unconventional families that Dostoevsky develops towards the end of the novel. Dostoevsky argued, in a separate 1877 essay, that Tolstoy's families were all alike, whereas Dostoevsky's families were all unhappy in their own way.

† Except where I have made reference to a specific volume, I have cited the single-volume edition, which brilliantly captures the detail and sweep of Dostoevsky's life without getting too bogged down in the socio-political ferment of nineteenth-century Russia.

ACKNOWLEDGEMENTS

I owe a huge debt of gratitude to those who helped to make this book possible. First and foremost, to my editor, Jamie Birkett, for trusting me to apply a creative method to a serious biography, and to my agent, Jonny Pegg, and his counterpart Doug Stewart, for helping a novelist sneak onto the non-fiction shelves. A huge thanks also to Richard Mason, Jude Drake, Rosie Parnham, and everyone else who has worked on the book at Bloomsbury.

I'm grateful to my academic readers for their invaluable feedback on early drafts of the manuscript. I am a storyteller, not a specialist, and recognise that a scholar might have balked at the idea of writing this book in this way. Any remaining errors are of course my own. To Professor Konstantin Barsht at the Institute of Russian Literature (Pushkin House), for entertaining my suggestion of using spectrophotometry on the portions of Dostoevsky's letters that had been inked out by Anna, though they remain a tantalising mystery for now. To Ilona Chavasse for helping me capture the nuances of the correspondence, and for our fascinating conversations about untranslatable Russian words.

Thanks to Louis Brooke, Alex Lawrence-Archer and Rosa Rankin-Gee for letting me hole up elsewhere when I needed to write uninterrupted, and to Samira Shackle and Cal Flyn for moral support when fatigue set in. To Anthony Rowland for accompanying me as I retraced Fyodor's footsteps through St Petersburg (though I'm still recovering from the Russian policy that drinking vodka without beer is throwing money to the wind). To my family, Chris, Jan, Antony, Mel, Olympia, Adam, Kirsty and Thea. And to Bernadette, who hadn't asked to live with Dostoevsky, and who was almost as patient as Anna.

A NOTE ON THE TYPE

The text of this book is set in Adobe Caslon, named after the English punch-cutter and type-founder William Caslon I (1692–1766). Caslon's rather old-fashioned types were modelled on seventeenth-century Dutch designs, but found wide acceptance throughout the English-speaking world for much of the eighteenth century until replaced by newer types towards the end of the century. Used in 1776 to print the Declaration of Independence, they were revived in the nineteenth century and have been popular ever since, particularly amongst fine printers. There are several digital versions, of which Carol Twombly's Adobe Caslon is one.

Alex Christofi is the author of two novels, *Let Us Be True* and *Glass*, which was longlisted for the Desmond Elliott Prize and won the Society of Authors' Betty Trask Prize. He is also Editorial Director at Transworld Publishers. His essays and reviews have been published in the *Guardian, New Humanist, Prospect, The White Review* and *The Brixton Review of Books*. He lives in south London.